T0199690

The GDPR Challenge

Privacy, Technology, and Compliance in an Age of Accelerating Change

Editor

Amie Taal
CEO and Founder
Stratagem Tech Solutions Limited

CRC Press
Taylor & Francis Group
Boca Raton London New York

CRC Press is an imprint of the
Taylor & Francis Group, an **informa** business
A SCIENCE PUBLISHERS BOOK

First edition published 2022
by CRC Press
6000 Broken Sound Parkway NW, Suite 300, Boca Raton, FL 33487-2742

and by CRC Press
2 Park Square, Milton Park, Abingdon, Oxon, OX14 4RN

© 2022 Taylor & Francis Group, LLC

CRC Press is an imprint of Taylor & Francis Group, LLC

Library of Congress Cataloging-in-Publication Data

Names: Taal, Amie, 1967- editor.
Title: The GDPR challenge : privacy, technology, and compliance in an age
   of accelerating change / editor Amie Taal, CEO and Founder Stratagem
   Tech Solutions Limited.
Description: First edition. | Boca Raton, FL : CRC Press, an imprint of
   Taylor & Francis Group, LLC, 2021. | Includes bibliographical references
   and index. | Summary: "The GDPR Challenge: Privacy, Technology, and
   Compliance in an Age of Accelerating Change is brimming with meaningful
   professional experiences and research from the trenches, a great book
   providing useful advice on navigating GDPR by authors working in various
   industries, Law (EU and US); Academia; Banks; Cyber Security; Digital
   Forensics; eDiscovery; investigations; and Cyber Insurance. Technology
   innovations are here to stay and this book will show you a path to data
   privacy compliance"-- Provided by publisher.
Identifiers: LCCN 2020055571 | ISBN 9780367257262 (hardcover)
Subjects: LCSH: European Parliament. General Data Protection Regulation. |
   Data protection--Law and legislation--European Union countries. |
   Privacy, Right of--European Union countries. | Right to be
   forgotten--European Union countries.
Classification: LCC KJE1626.A432016 G363 2021 | DDC 342.2408/58--dc23
LC record available at https://lccn.loc.gov/2020055571

ISBN: 978-0-367-25726-2 (hbk)
ISBN: 978-0-367-75708-3 (pbk)
ISBN: 978-0-429-32593-9 (ebk)

DOI: 10.1201/9780429325939

Typeset in Palatino Roman
by Innovative Processors

Foreword

When the General Data Protection Regulation (GDPR) came into force on May 25, 2018, the idea of privacy as a regulation – binding and applicable to EU member states, as opposed to the 1995 Data Privacy Directive – seemed to hit both sides of the Atlantic with interest, some trepidation, and a modicum of excitement. Since then, plenty of ink has been spilled regarding the reality of the GDPR's application as well as what's still to come, including just how much the GDPR has influenced not only those parties within the EU directly affected by it but also aspirational governments around the world.

This book, *The GDPR Challenge - Privacy, Technology and Compliance in an Age of Accelerating Change*, seizes on many of the themes that have emerged since 2018 and tells the story of a regulation applied across a variety of legal and related disciplines. Beginning with the titular Chapter 1, the authors explain how this regulation, focused on a proposed fundamental right of individual privacy, is (and must be) embedded in considerations of privacy in the pursuit of compliance even when the technological sands beneath our feet shift seemingly daily.

The book ties the triad of privacy, technology, and compliance together with the human element in Chapter 12, where it discusses the importance and reality of human culture and behavioral factors when making decisions regarding the application of the GDPR. As examined in the book, the behavioral economist view is a critical one when addressing the GDPR's risk-based approach to data protection. There are no perfect solutions here, and pursuit of the adequate is the realistic takeaway from this author's presentation.

The risk-based approach is certainly front and center in Chapter 2, which addresses the use of algorithms in the C-suite. This chapter presents and examines lessons learned in and applied to information governance best practices and considers how one might achieve greater post-GDPR algorithmic accountability as provided for within the GDPR. An examination of the C-suite and board and executive considerations for client practices and business opportunities continues in Chapter 8, which examines business opportunities in light of the GDPR while also considering business opportunities inherent **in** the GDPR, while Chapter 3 looks to the protection of the C-suite's interests through the use of cyber insurance and related technological innovation and approaches.

Chapter 5 presents a "selfie" from social media and its examination under the GDPR, where technology advances careen toward changing social mores and have to contend with the GDPR's articulation of fundamental privacy rights, even when individuals seem intent on trading away those rights for additional likes. Chapter 10 continues in the same vein and considers where privacy challenges are emerging in the areas of biometric and other advanced technologies. And in response to those new data sets that are growing within corporate servers and the cloud, Chapter 4 considers and presents a proposal for a multiple learning framework application to protect data access rights for those individuals protected by the GDPR.

While the GDPR has brought additional, warranted focus to those fundamental privacy rights it seeks to support and protect, it has also brought additional scrutiny to suspect practices and concerns organizations correctly have regarding their employees, systems, and approaches. Chapter 9 considers that scrutiny when discussing processes related to streamlined and cost-effective investigations across disparate data sources and pairs nicely with Chapter 11's discussion of the intersection of the GDPR, U.S. discovery and technology when applied to financial crime.

Discovery of those issues, the subjects of the investigations and the crimes uncovered lead quite naturally to the remaining chapters presented in the book. Chapter 6 takes the discussion of financial crime discovery and broadens it to consider U.S. litigation practices more generally when presenting strategic, legal and technical considerations for the inclusion of EU data within the course of U.S. discovery. Chapter 7 then presents general principles in response to implications for information governance, eDiscovery and the privacy by design embedded in the GDPR. Finally, Chapter 13 presents a practical application of new technologies and innovation directed toward portable solutions and their use case for eDiscovery performed according to the reality of the GDPR.

The book's chapters, written by expert practitioners deeply versed in and experienced with the GDPR and their respective subject matter, may be read singly or by theme. Regardless, *The GDPR Challenge - Privacy, Technology and Compliance in an Age of Accelerating Change* presents an opportunity for the reader to enjoy grounded, knowledgeable and accurate stories from the front line of GDPR compliance – not just academic descriptions of how the GDPR **should** operate, but the reality of what current and proposed practice **is**.

James A. Sherer
July 31, 2020

Contents

List of Contributors

Amie Taal is an internationally regarded expert in Forensic Investigations, Cyber Security, eDiscovery, Data Analytics and Artificial Intelligence. A former Vice President at Deutsche Bank, Amie has built a career in Europe, Africa, Middle East, Asia and United States helping companies identify and respond to technology incidents, litigation matters, information risk, data privacy issues and dealing with civil and criminal investigations within the public and private sector including the Big 4, financial services and non-financial organisations.

Amie is also a specialist in data privacy and provides internal and external training on GDPR practice and procedures, legal and regulations rules and evidence handling procedures.

In addition to the above, Amie is a public speaker and a university lecturer in the postgraduate space teaching IT and Internet Law, evidence handle procedures, data privacy, AI and Cyber Security. She has also published many papers and contributed to many books in this space as a subject matter expect.

Al-Karim Makhani, Esq. is Vice President of Consulting & Information Governance at TransPerfect Legal Solutions and leads the EMEA and APAC practice groups. Al advises on a spectrum of legal technology issues including preservation/collection of data, analytics/AI workflows, disclosure rules, court applications, cross border transfers and data privacy concerns. More holistically, he advises GCs on innovation, strategy and cost efficiency through tech. Prior to TLS, Al was a senior litigator in the London and Hong Kong offices of a top tier disputes practice. He litigated commercial issues including fraud, joint ventures, investigations and a landmark decision on legal professional privilege. Al read Law at the University of London, followed by distinction in the Legal Practice Course from Nottingham Law School. He is a member of various professional bodies through which he regularly speaks and writes on legal technology issues.

Ami Rodrigues is an as Assistant General Counsel - Privacy at Chipotle Mexican Grill, Inc., Ami leads establishing and running a global privacy program. Ami additionally oversees legal compliance for AI/ML partnerships, IoT integrations, and partners with Chipotle's cybersecurity team to provide proper legal support. Prior to CMG, Ami was privacy counsel advising Fortune 100 companies, start-ups, and government agencies, where she worked on setting up privacy programs, participated in privacy audits, worked with regulators, and defended against privacy-related litigation. She holds a CIPP/US, CIPP/E, CIP, and FIP certifications from the International Association of Privacy Professionals and a Privacy Law Specialist designation. Ami holds a JD from Emory University School of Law and a bachelor's degree from The George Washington University.

Andrew Neal is a practitioner and consultant in the information security community. As the President of TransPerfect's Information Security and Compliance Services division he executes security, governance and investigatory projects for corporations and law firms around the globe. He has an extensive background in technology and security, and advises clients across a wide range of industries on business issues related to information security, data privacy and regulatory compliance. Andrew frequently shares his experience as a speaker, adviser, board member and mentor, and is active in several international security-related professional organizations.

Ben Quarmby is a partner with the litigation boutique of MoloLamken LLP. His practice focuses on business disputes and intellectual property litigation. He has represented clients as lead counsel in federal and state trial courts, the International Trade Commission, federal courts of appeals, the United States Patent & Trademark Office, and in arbitration.

Mr. Quarmby represents both plaintiffs and defendants in cases around the US. His clients include US corporations, individuals, and family offices, as well as many French and Japanese companies.

Mr. Quarmby frequently publishes on topics including patent, trademark and trade secret law, the General Data Protection Regulation (GDPR), shareholder appraisal rights, artificial intelligence, social media, and privacy. He is also a frequent speaker on issues such as third-party litigation funding, developments in patent, trademark and copyright law, and international arbitration.

Prior to joining MoloLamken LLP, Mr. Quarmby practiced business and IP litigation with the law firm of Quinn Emanuel Urquhart & Sullivan. He also clerked for the Honorable Garrett E. Brown, Jr., Chief Judge for the District of New Jersey.

Camille C. Bent is a Partner in BakerHostetler's Bankruptcy and Restructuring practice group, concentrating in the areas of corporate bankruptcy, restructuring and commercial litigation. She specializes in disputes and transactions arising out of corporate insolvencies, including asset sale, fraudulent transfer, negligent misrepresentation, and wrongful redemption cases. Camille has represented debtors, creditors, trustees, committees, and other interested parties, and her practice is industry agnostic. She currently represents Irving H. Picard, Securities Investor Protection Act Trustee for the liquidation of Bernard L. Madoff Investment Securities, LLC, and litigates multimillion-dollar avoidance and recovery actions against foreign and domestic entities.

Camille is a member of the Bankruptcy & Restructuring Committee at the New York City Bar Association, and she is Co-Chair of BakerHostetler's New York Diversity Committee. Camille earned her J.D./M.B.A. from Emory University, and a B.A. in International Relations from Johns Hopkins University. Following law school, she clerked for the Honorable Pamela Pepper in the Eastern District of Wisconsin.

Claudia T. Morgan is eDiscovery Counsel in Wachtell, Lipton, Rosen & Katz's Litigation Department. She focuses her practice on electronic discovery and information management, both domestically and abroad. She has significant experience in responding to and advising on litigation in federal and state courts, regulatory requests for information, and internal investigations.

Ms. Morgan has managed all aspects of discovery, including coordinating with clients' litigation departments, directing and consulting with vendors, and hiring and managing teams of contract attorneys and paralegals. Ms. Morgan counsels clients on a range of information risk management issues, including eDiscovery and Records and Information Management (RIM) best practices and litigation preparation. She has worked with clients in overhauling their corporate RIM policies and procedures.

Ms. Morgan received a B.S.F.S. from Georgetown University in 1992 and completed her J.D., with honors, from George Mason University School of Law in 1998. She is a member of the American Bar Association, the New York State Bar Association, and The Sedona Conference Working Groups 1 (Electronic Document Retention and Production), 6 (International Electronic Information Management, Discovery and Disclosure), and 11 (Data Security and Privacy Liability).

Daniel S. Meyers, Esq. is the President of TransPerfect Legal Solutions' Consulting & Information Governance division. Dan advises clients on e-discovery best practices and motion practice, litigation readiness plans, defensible data disposition programs, and data privacy concerns, with a particular emphasis on cross-border data transfers. His clients range from financial institutions and multinational corporations to start-ups and small-to-medium businesses. Dan is certified as an E-Discovery Specialist (ACEDS) and an Information Privacy Professional (CIPP/E/US). Prior to joining TLS, Dan was a Commercial Litigation Partner at an Am Law 100 law firm in New York City and the Founder and Chair of the firm's E-Discovery & Information Governance practice group.

Debbie Reynolds is the Founder, CEO, and Chief Data Privacy Officer of Debbie Reynolds Consulting LLC. Debbie Reynolds, "The Data Diva," is a world-renowned technologist, thought-leader, and advisor to Multinational Corporations for handling global Data Privacy, Cyber Data Breach response, and complex cross-functional data-driven projects. Ms. Reynolds is an internationally published author, highly sought speaker, and top media presence about global Data Privacy, Data Protection, and Emerging Technology issues. Ms. Reynolds has also been recognized as a worldwide leader in the Data Privacy industry, a Technology Visionary, and named to the Global Top 20 CyberRisk Communicators by The European Risk Policy Institute, 2020.

Ms. Reynolds is the author of works in books, The GDPR Challenge: Privacy, Technology, and Compliance In An Age of Accelerating Change, and eDiscovery for Corporate Counsel; She is the author of works in publications like The International Journal for the Data Protection Officer, Privacy Officer, and Privacy Counsel, Bloomberg Law, Thomson Reuters West, Westlaw Journal, Today's General Counsel Magazine (TGC), Law360 and the International Legal Technology Association (ILTA); She has been interviewed and quoted in media outlets, Tycoon, Authority Magazine, Medium, Lifewitre, CMSWire, Bloomberg Big Law Business, Public Broadcasting Service (PBS), Digiday, LegalTech News, Law.com, Law360, The Recorder, High Performance Counsel (HPC), Legal Business World, Toyo Keizai Japan, and American Lawyer.

Ms. Reynolds is the Global Data Privacy Officer for Women In Identity, Expert Evaluator - AR VR XR Spatial Computing Privacy Framework Evaluation Committee for XRSI, Technology & Cybersecurity Committee Member of the New York State Bar Association (NYSBA), Founding Executive Member of Digital Directors Network (DDN) – Board members for Data Privacy & Cybersecurity, Advisory Board Member Enterprise Management 360 (EM360) (UK),

Global Data Privacy Advisory Board Member for EDRM (Electronic Discovery Reference Model), Advisory Board Member and Faculty for Advisory Board Member & Contributor, International Journal for the Data Protection Officer, Privacy Officer, and Privacy Counsel, The Data Litigator, High Performance Counsel #Think Tank, The Masters Conference, and The Cleveland Marshall College of Law - eDiscovery Technology Professional Certificate Program. Ms. Reynolds is also a board member and advisor to technology companies and has also been an Adjunct Professor at Georgetown University and Cleveland Marshall College of Law.

Emily Fedeles is a Chief Data Privacy Counsel at Colgate-Palmolive Company, Emily Fedeles is responsible for the establishment and maintenance of a comprehensive global data privacy compliance program. She also oversees Colgate's cyber security efforts in coordination with Colgate's IT risk management team. Emily provides legal support for Colgate's digital initiatives including its connected devices, digital marketing, and social media activities, in connection with the negotiation of information technology and digital transactions. Prior to her time at Colgate, Emily was an eDiscovery, privacy, and litigation associate at law firms in New York City; Geneva, Switzerland; and Tampa, Florida, where she worked on issues ranging from discovery management processes, records and information governance, data privacy and security, artificial intelligence, and products liability litigation. She holds CIPP/E data privacy professional credentials and is a member of The Sedona Conference® Working Groups One, Six, and Eleven. Emily has a JD from Emory University School of Law and a bachelor's degree from Emory University.

Gail Gottehrer is the Founder of the Law Office of Gail Gottehrer LLC in Stamford, CT. Her practice focuses on emerging technologies, including autonomous vehicles, AI, biometrics, robots and facial recognition technology, and the privacy and security laws and ethical issues associated with the data collected and used by these technologies. She is one of the few defense lawyers to have been involved in the trial of a class action to verdict before a jury. Gail teaches Law for Knowledge Innovation at Columbia University, and is a member of the Advisory Board for Rutgers University's Leading Disruptive Innovation Program, and a Fellow at the Center for Legal Innovation at Vermont Law School.

Gail is a member of the New York State Bar Association's Task Force on Autonomous Vehicles and the Law and the State of Connecticut's Task Force to Study Fully Autonomous Vehicles. Gail also serves as Co-Chair of the New York State Bar Association's Technology and the Legal Profession Committee, a member of the New York State Bar Association's Transportation Law Committee, and as Chair-Elect of the ABA TIPS Automobile Litigation Committee. She is the New York Regional Co-Chair for the ABA's Judicial Intern Opportunity Program, Co-Chair of the Programming Committee of the ABA's Woman Advocate Committee, Co-Chair of the National Association of Women Lawyers' IP & Technology Affinity Group, Editor of the ABA's Pretrial Practice and Discovery Newsletter, and a member of the Sedona Conference Working Group 1.

Gail was selected as one the Profiles in Diversity Journal's 2017 Women Worth Watching in STEM and one of the Connecticut Technology Council's 2016 Women of Innovation. She is a graduate of the University of Pennsylvania Law School, and served as a law clerk to the Honorable Murray C. Goldman, in the Philadelphia County Court of Common Pleas. Gail is admitted to practice in New York, New Jersey, Connecticut, and Pennsylvania.

Gregory R. Baden is the General Counsel of Aras Corporation, a leading provider of enterprise product lifecycle management software. Prior to his role at Aras, he practiced at the litigation boutique MoloLamken, the intellectual property and technology practice at Davis Polk & Wardwell in New York, and the corporate practice at Cravath, Swaine & Moore in New York and London. Before practicing law, Mr. Baden developed and implemented enterprise software systems, with a focus on engineering, product development, and supply chain solutions. Mr. Baden received a bachelor's degree in mechanical engineering from Texas A&M University, a master's degree in software engineering from the University of Maryland – University College, and a juris doctorate from the University of Texas at Austin.

Jason R. Baron holds the position of Professor of the Practice at the University of Maryland's College of Information Studies. Previously, he served as Of Counsel in the Information Governance and eDiscovery group at Faegre Drinker LLP. Mr. Baron was appointed as the first Director of Litigation at the U.S. National Archives and Records Administration, after serving as trial attorney and senior counsel at the U.S. Department of Justice. He has been an adjunct faculty member at the American University Washington College of Law. He holds a B.A., magna cum laude with honors, from Wesleyan University, and a J.D. from Boston University School of Law.

Joseph Pochron is the former President of TransPerfect's Forensic Technology and Consulting division. He provides advisory services for clients around the world, developing strategy and executing projects related to digital forensics. Based in San Francisco, Joe led a global network of forensic labs and technical specialists in the U.S., Europe, and Asia. Prior to joining TransPerfect, Joseph spent many years in law enforcement. He was a detective for the Upper Saucon Twp, PA Police Department where he was assigned to the Pennsylvania State Police Computer Crimes and Internet Crimes Against Children Task Forces, respectively. In 2011 Joseph served as the Commanding Officer of the Lehigh County District Attorney's Office Computer Crimes Task Force & Digital Forensic Laboratory. Additionally, he has taught at the university level for various institutions and is a frequent speaker at technical or legal conferences. Active in the professional community, he holds multiple certifications as well as a BA and MA in Criminal Justice.

Judy Selby brings 25 years of insurance coverage litigation experience to her insurance consulting work. She has a particular expertise in cyber insurance and coverage under various policy forms for today's emerging risks. Judy provides coverage evaluation, policy negotiation, and gap analysis to companies across multiple industries. She also provides expert witness services, insurance due diligence, and regulatory compliance consulting. Judy also authored the eBooks "Demystifying Cyber Insurance" and "Big Data for Business Leaders."

In addition to her law degree, Judy has completed courses in Finance with Harvard Business School HBX, Big Data, Crisis Management/ Business Continuity, Cyber Security & the Internet of Things (IoT) with the Massachusetts Institute of Technology Professional Education, Cloud Computing with IEEE, and EU GDPR Data Protection Officer with Advisera.

Katherine E. Armstrong, CIPP-US, serves as Deputy Director of the National Advertising Division in the Better Business Bureau, National Programs. Previously, she served as Counsel at Faegre Drinker LLP, where she co-led the firm's Information, Privacy, Security and Governance Initiative. In that role, Ms. Armstrong assisted clients with compliance matters relating to privacy and data security laws, including the General Data Protection Regulation. She previously served for over 30 years at the U.S. Federal Trade Commission, including as an attorney to a former Chairman and a former Commissioner. She holds a B.A. from Pitzer College, and a J.D. from Lewis & Clark Law School.

Kenneth N. Rashbaum, a partner in the New York office of Barton LLP, advises multinational corporations, financial services organizations and life sciences organizations in the areas of privacy, cybersecurity, e-discovery for litigation and regulatory proceedings and information management. He counsels these entities on information governance and its compliance with federal, state, and non-U.S. laws and the interface of e-commerce and legal and regulatory liabilities in areas such as cybersecurity and breach response. Ken has vast experience in preparation and negotiation of technology contracts, including service level agreements and license agreements relating to compliance with data protection and privacy laws in the U.S. and other countries. He also leads information security and data breach response assessments, investigations and remediation initiatives; prepares policies for social media legal and regulatory compliance; and represents technology and life sciences organizations in federal and state investigations, audits, litigation.

Ken was appointed to the faculty of the Federal Judicial Center for its September 2010 session and the Georgetown Advanced E-Discovery Institute (November 2009 and December 2012 sessions) to lead sessions on international e-discovery issues and challenges. From 2018-2019, he served as a special consultant to the New Jersey Assembly assisting in the preparation of a bill that, if passed, would become New Jersey's first comprehensive privacy and cybersecurity law. Ken testified regarding the bill as a cybersecurity and privacy expert before the New Jersey Assembly Homeland Security and State Preparedness Committee. He is an Adjunct Professor of Law at Fordham University School of Law and had been a member of the Adjunct Faculty at the Maurice A. Deane School of Law at Hofstra University from 2013 – 2015. Prior to joining Barton, Ken was a senior litigation partner in the New York office of Sedgwick LLP (formerly Sedgwick, Detert, Moran & Arnold) where he was the Founding Co-Chair of the E-Discovery, Compliance and Data Management and HIPAA Practice Groups.

Kerri Ann Bent is a New York licensed attorney currently working at UBS. She works in the Financial Crime Prevention group focusing on Economic Sanctions, Anti-Money Laundering, and Anti-Bribery and Corruption. As the Head of the Americas Sanctions team, she provides transactional guidance relating to the regulatory regimes in place against Russia, Iran, Cuba, Sudan, Syria, Venezuela and North Korea, with emphasis on regulations administered by the United States Department of the Treasury's Office of Foreign Assets Control (OFAC). Ms. Bent also serves as a mentor to start-up Fin Tech Companies. As an American Bar Association Fellow, she plays a key role in advancing principles of the legal progression and expansion of justice to underdeveloped communities. Ms. Bent received her B.A. in Political Science and Finance from Rutgers University and a J.D. from Seton Hall Law School. During law school she spent time studying at the American University in Cairo, Egypt focusing on Admiralty Law, Islamic Law and Oil and Gas transactions and she is currently an active member of the American Bar Association International Law, Economic Sanctions and Export Controls Committee. Ms. Bent is a frequent guest speaker and writer on topics relating to ethics, compliance and the practice of law.

Mari Martin is a Corporate Counsel and Data Protection Manager for Software AG, Mari is responsible for providing ongoing legal counsel on a broad range of issues related to data protection, intellectual property, commercial, and regulatory matters. She advises on implementing and maintaining an integrated global approach to privacy and data protection, focusing on coordinating compliance with legal obligations in Europe and the Americas. Prior to her time at Software AG, Mari worked as an associate in the Munich, Germany office of DLA Piper and the Washington, DC office of Baker Hostetler, where she advised U.S., German, and multinational clients across diverse technology-driven industries (IT, telecoms, defense, life sciences, IoT), focusing on data protection, commercial, and trade compliance issues. Mari is a graduate of Vanderbilt University and the Emory University School of Law.

Odunayo Fadahunsi is a technology risk management professional highly regarded for his expertise in technology risk management, cybersecurity, data analytics and machine learning. He is currently a VP at Deutsche Bank. Odunayo's experience spans across the 3 lines of defence at different capacities, including leadership roles across Europe and Africa including Big 4 within Information Technology (IT) Risk Management, Governance, Control, Assurance and Cloud Risk Management. Odunayo's research interests include Petri nets, Network and Data Science as applied in the context of decision making in Economics, Accounting, Finance and Risk Management domains. He has co-authored and had previous works presented in international journals and conferences.

Owen Burns is the President of Access Limits and has spent 20 years helping organizations engage technology solutions to meet their business needs while exceeding legal and regulatory standards. He has spoken on the challenges of information governance and published articles on the challenge of managing big data with ever-expanding on-line data volumes. Passionate about protecting one's privacy, Owen is also a proponent of using social media and maintaining an online profile. He believes privacy is an inherent individual right. As such, it is the moral and ethical duty for every business to act with integrity while treating each person with dignity and respect. His quest is to develop and promote technology solutions which will embolden the individual with the systems and process to live freely with complete privacy protection.

Rachael N. Clark is an attorney, and Certified Information Privacy Professional (CIPP/US) based in New York, NY. She capitalizes on her multidisciplinary background to offer innovative, culturally sound solutions for clients facing the challenge of keeping pace with the increasingly complex data privacy and cybersecurity landscape. She leads teams in the execution of projects with a wide variety of companies trying to achieve compliance with GDPR and US regulations.

She was a Manager in PwC's Cybersecurity and Privacy Solutions practice, prior to which she was in-house counsel for a consulting organization offering business solutions to companies in the healthcare space, and she started her career as a litigator specializing in insurance defense. Prior to earning her law degree at the Indiana University Maurer School of Law in Bloomington, she worked in Moscow, Russia at an English-language newspaper and as a communications coordinator at

Deloitte. She speaks Russian and French, and received her undergraduate degree in Religion from Colgate University.

An active member of the professional community, Rachael volunteers with the International Association of Privacy Professionals, is a Director on the Board of the Association of Corporate Counsel, New York City Chapter and is Co-chair of the In House Subcommittee of the New York City Bar Association's Women in the Legal Profession Committee.

Scott Tees is a former police officer for 24 years in front line operational and community policing and specialises in cyber security, focusing on human behaviour online. For the last 7 years, he was the Police Scotland National Lead for Cybercrime Prevention, providing specialist support and advice to the public and private sector.

Scott recently moved to the private sector and he is now the Managing Director of Decode Cyber Solutions Ltd, an innovative organisation which seeks to improve and enhance cyber security through positively influencing organisational culture and online behaviour. He works with large and small companies to build resilience, to online threat and risk proactively influence the organisation's online culture and best practices.

In addition to the above, Scott is a trained Hostage and Crisis Negotiator, he also served within HM Forces for 10 years with the Royal Military Police prior to joining the Police Forces.

Shaun Werbelow is an associate at Wachtell, Lipton, Rosen & Katz. Prior to joining Wachtell Lipton, Mr. Werbelow served as a law clerk to the Honorable Harry T. Edwards of the United States Court of Appeals for the District of Columbia Circuit and as a law clerk to the Honorable Katherine B. Forrest of the United States District Court for the Southern District of New York.

Mr. Werbelow received a B.S. with Honors in Industrial and Labor Relations from Cornell University in 2011 and earned his J.D. magna cum laude from the New York University School of Law in 2014, where he was a Butler Scholar, Order of the Coif, and served as an Articles Editor for the New York University Law Review.

Susie Wakefield is a Partner and Head of Commercial Insurance at Shoosmiths, LLP, a leading UK national law firm. She has 22 years' of experience in domestic and international commercial litigation and arbitration focusing on insurance and reinsurance. She is also tri-qualified having qualified and practiced for many years in New York and Bermuda as well as the U.K.

Susie advises Bermuda, U.S. and London market insurers and reinsurers as well as other market players in litigation in federal and state courts in New York, the Supreme Court of Bermuda, as well as in the High Court in London and in arbitration. She has represented clients in complex, multimillion-dollar disputes, including cases with substantive international and multijurisdictional aspects. Her work spans many lines of business including IT, media, IP and cyber risks. She also advises on insurance regulatory issues including those arising out of insurtech, and tech-enabled products.

Susie co-authored the "Lloyd's and London Market" chapter of volume seven of the New Appleman on Insurance Law Library Edition, 2012. Legal 500 has recognised Susie as "an 'outstanding leader' who has significant experience of litigation across England, New York and Bermuda". Chambers describes her as "exceptionally good".

Introduction

Amie Taal[1]

> *"Accountability is at the centre of all of this: of getting it right today, getting it right in May 2018 and getting it right beyond that."*

> Elizabeth Denham
> Information Commissioner, UK

Introduction

The General Data Protection Regulation ("GDPR") is no doubt a step up from what had existed in the past to protect EU data subject rights. It has changed the way data is handled in all industries from a process-driven activity to a risk-based approach. Still, the most significant impact is the far reach of this regulation, and adherence is not just specific to the European Union ("EU"). Since 2016, it has become the baseline for data privacy laws around the globe making it a landmark in the evolution of data privacy as a global phenomenon.

The two-year grace period from 2016–2018 prior to enforcement of the regulation in 2018 came with a foray of discontent, uncertainty and in some instances confusion. What was very clear is that no particular jurisdiction especially in the EU was 100% compliant. From an individual standpoint, data privacy was almost a distant memory or a forgotten right.

Outside the EU, the regulation sent shockwaves especially after the decision of Maximillian Schrems—v-Data Protection Commissioner, joint party Digital Right Ireland Ltd; which rendered the Safe Harbour agreement null and void on October 6, 2015, thanks to the fact that Facebook Ireland Ltd ('Facebook Ireland') transferred and stored their

---

[1] Amie Taal is the CEO and Founder of Stratagem Tech Solutions Limited — amie@stratagemtechsolutions.com

EU users' personal identifiable information ("PII") in the United States of America ("USA"), which was a blatant breach of the Safe Harbour agreement. In the wake of impactful international data breaches like Cambridge Analytica, Equifax and TalkTalk, many non-EU citizens now have increased awareness and heightened concerns about the use and security of their personal identifiable information.

The conception of this book came about from the panic and uncertainty GDPR brought following the announcement in 2016 of the imminent regulation and importantly the enforcement date of 25th May 2018. The focus of this edited volume is specific in highlighting the impact of GDPR on heavily technology-reliant fields, including investigations, application development, eDiscovery and new technology innovations such as Artificial Intelligence, Machine Learning and Blockchain; and to provide take-on workable solutions that have always been employed in the data privacy space. So many people working in various fields of technology and in non-technological roles have dealt with data privacy requirements and issues for many years and have become fully learned on the application of regulatory requirements. To have an opportunity to gather a group of professionals who are truly respected in their field, showcase their skills and experiences coupled with simultaneously sharing some great techniques and methodologies, was too enticing to ignore.

It was an absolute pleasure working with so many talented and knowledgeable professionals on this book. The reader will be far from disappointed on the knowledge and experiences exhibited in the following chapters and the rich array of guidance and usable examples from practitioners and academia alike.

The book starts by diving straight into the core of technology and data privacy; and Information Governance best practices. Chapter 2 confronts questions of accountability and transparency concerning corporate algorithmic decision-making with examples of strategies grounded both in the experience of the US Federal Trade Commission, in dealing with fairness issues arising out of traditional credit scoring, as well as best practices in the emerging field of information governance. This is then followed by Chapter 3 "Cyber Insurance and Technology Innovation", a hot topic and very timely. The threat of penalties and fines from cyber security incidents and now coupled with GDPR breaches is enough to make any organization panic, and the good news is that the cyber insurance market is growing with a predicted growth of 26.3% by 2020.[1] Plans at board level for all global corporations now include the acquisition of cyber insurance, and the insured are well-positioned to negotiate for broader coverage regarding GDPR exposure.

Chapter 4 looks at the application of Multiple Instance Learning Framework to protect data access rights and academic research exploring machine learning to evidence GDPR compliance. Chapter 5 focuses on

Social Media and sheds some light on the real business model behind social media, defining key privacy issues, and making a case for how the GDPR will help provide security when sharing users' data. Chapters 6 and 7 explore eDiscovery from different angles including Legal, Technical, Privacy by Design, Information Governance and Data Portability.

Chapter 8 discusses ongoing challenges with Big Data and presents opportunities for cost savings through efficiencies required to meet its mandates, and increased business by adherence to contractual requirements to ensure that the organization meets their customers' needs for GDPR compliance. This is a must-read for all eDiscovery practitioners and litigators.

Taking the theme of Big Data further, Chapter 9 explores tools and techniques to manage a streamlined and effective investigation process across disparate data sources, a nightmare for investigators on both civil and criminal matters. The chapter goes further in providing ways in which companies can access, search and manage their enterprise data in an efficient, defensible, compliant manner by utilizing new and innovative technologies like knowledge integration platforms, artificial intelligence and machine learning.

The usefulness of technology to enable GDPR compliance is explored further in Chapter 10, "Existing and Emerging Biometric Data Technologies". The chapter examines the use of biometric data from its ancient historical context to its present-day use in state-of-the-art technology, where it became a semi-automated and then an automated classification system with great examples of how this type of data and technology is regulated. Chapter 11 explores the challenges financial crime investigators and litigators alike must face to successfully access, process and transfer data under GDPR, as well as the opportunities and limitations presented by available technology.

The penultimate chapter explores and discusses the human behavioural aspect of GDPR, a vital factor of GDPR compliance yet often forgotten or given little importance in this area. Chapter 12 looks at the correlation between human behaviour and organizational culture that has the potential to undermine GDPR compliance and lead to cyber security and data privacy breaches. Finally, Chapter 13 continues with the eDiscovery theme. It takes a deep dive on portable eDiscovery solutions currently on the market, solutions that take discovery efforts and capabilities to the source of the data.

How we use technology and at the same time adhere to data privacy regulations and legislation around the world, is a crucial factor and the focus of this book. We wanted to cover topics which were relevant and kept people in industry awake at night simultaneously. By reading this book from cover-to-cover or dipping in and out of it as a reference guide, it will provide the knowledge and practical examples for both academia and industry alike.

GDPR Background

One cannot discuss or work in the data privacy space without having an understanding of what personal Identifiable Information means or its definition as set out in the GDPR.

As detailed in the regulation, *"personal data" shall mean any information relating to an identified or identifiable natural person ('Data subject'); an identifiable person is one who can be identified, directly or indirectly, by reference in particular to an identification number or to one or more factors specific to his physical, physiological, mental, economic, cultural or social identity"* (GDPR, Article 4*)*.

The EU Data Protection Directive 95/46/EC was regarded by many as law and this caused some confusion, and in addition to this each EU jurisdiction had the right to pass a privacy law to protect their citizens or incorporate their citizens' privacy rights in existing law(s). The impact was that no standardised way of dealing with data privacy breaches across the EU, and some countries were seen as being soft on the way privacy rights were enforced.

A short timeline of privacy laws in the UK since the 1995 EU Directive:

- EU Data Protection Directive 95/46/EC
- Data Protection Act 1998
- Human Right 1998
- Safe Harbor Agreement 2000
- Freedom of Information Act 2000
- EU–US Privacy Shield 2016
- General Data Protection Regulation (GDPR) 2018
- Data Protection Act 2018

As early as 2001 prior to the first anniversary of the Safe Harbour Agreement 2000, there were companies which could self-certify that they adhered to the seven directive data privacy principles, and complied with both the EU Data Protection Directive and Swiss requirements. This was heavily abused and caused discontent with and criticism of the agreement that it was not adequately policed; there was no means of redress for breach; and Edward Snowden voiced great concerns over state supervisions (USA PATRIOT). For the US court, cross-border data privacy requirements caused issues and the biggest being that eDiscovery information required for US litigation was not exempt from EU data privacy requirements.

In 1996 the Article 29 Working Party was established *"the Working Party on the Protection of Individuals with regard to the Processing of*

Personal Data", an advisory body made up of a representative from the data protection authority of each EU Member State, the European Data Protection Supervisor and the European Commission. In 2011 the work on GDPR commenced, and in 2015 an agreement on GDPR between the European Parliament, the Council and the Commission was reached on and on February 2, 2016, an action plan for implementation of GDPR was issued. GDPR was passed on April 14, 2016, the enforcement date was May 25, 2018 and it replaced the data protection directive of 1995. The regulation does not prevent jurisdictions from having their own privacy laws, and in 2018 a lot of new privacy legislations were seen in the EU to ensure GDPR adherence.

What are the new changes from the 1995 Directive?

- Scope of Personal Data
- Consent (Articles 6–8)
- Privacy By Design (PbD) and Privacy By Default (Article 25)
- Data Protection Impact Assessments (DPIAs) (Article 35)
- Accountability: Data controller, data processor and appointment of a Data Protection Officer (DPO)
- Breach notification – 72 hr rule (Articles 33–34)
- One Data Protection Authority or DPA as lead
- Judicial Redress and Compensation for data subjects (Articles 77–84)
- Data Portability (Article 20)
- International Transfers (Articles 44–50)
  o *The Commission's adequacy decisions will be re-examined periodically (once every four years)*
  o *The Commission will identify* jurisdictions offering adequate data protection
- Safeguards for transfers to inadequate jurisdictions
  o *Standard contractual clauses or Approved industry codes of conduct*

Accountability is a crucial aspect of GDPR, if one does not understand the role they play especially with regard to data privacy in their organization, the consequence is that they will not be GDPR compliant. The roles and responsibilities are clearly defined in the regulation, such as the Supervisory Authority (Articles 51–59), Data Protection Officer (Articles 37–39).

Under Article 4 (Definitions) in the regulation, the role and responsibility of a Controller and Processor is stated as "… *'controller' means the natural or legal person, public authority, agency or other body which, alone or jointly with others, determines the purpose and means of processing personal data; where the purpose and means of such processing are determined by a Union or Member State law, the controller or the specific criteria for its nomination may be provided for by the Union or Member State law; and 'processor' means a natural or legal person, public authority, agency or other body which processes personal data on behalf of the controller.* (GDPR, 2018). The diagram below shows the data protection model under GDPR.

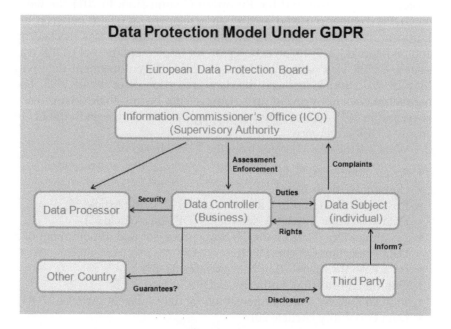

Fig. 1.1. Data Protection Model under GDPR (ICO)

To comply with Article 51 each EU member state has nominated a Supervisory Authority. In the UK, it is the Information Commissioner's Office (ICO); in Germany - Die Bundesbeauftragte für den Datenschutz und die Informationsfreiheit; Belgium - Commission de la protection de la vie privée; France - Commission Nationale de l'Informatique et des Libertés (CNIL); and Ireland - Data Protection Commissioner, to name but a few. There are now 27 EU member states[2] and the UK complied, prior to their withdrawal from the EU and there are no plans to change that.

The most significant concerns on Data subject rights (Articles 12–23) prior to GDPR enforcement day in May 2018 were consent (Data Subject Access Right requests – DSARs), withdrawal, privacy by design and right to be forgotten, not just on the data subjects' information residing in the EU but globally and this resulted in the implementation of the EU–US Privacy Shield or commonly referred to as "Safe Harbour 2.0".

The importance of Cross-border data transfers (Articles 44–50) and the requirements in the GDPR can never be underrated. For this and many other challenges and impacts from the loss of PII data, many jurisdictions around the world are passing privacy laws to protect their citizens, including some states in the USA such as The California Consumer Privacy

Act of 2018 and Virginia Personal Information Privacy Act 2020 with the Washington Privacy Act pending. To date, 80 countries around the world have enacted privacy laws,[3] closely modelled after the EU Directive 1995 and GDPR 2018.

GDPR Challenges

The biggest uncertainty following the decision on the Schrem's case in late 2015 was the cross-border data transfers for eDiscovery, multi-jurisdiction investigations and new/advanced technology such as Artificial Intelligence ("AI") and Blockchain. There is also the issue of companies being reluctant to purge PII data they have collected or accumulated for many years and in some instances, decades. Before GDPR, the 1995 EU Directive and earlier data privacy laws detailed clearly that data must be "Processed only for specified and lawful purposes" and "Kept for no longer than necessary" but unfortunately, for the sake of marketing and the chase for repeat business this was ignored which then led to the big hunt for GDPR loopholes.

Most organizations did not have defensible deletion processes to maintain compliance, and even now, almost three years after enforcement many still do not have a data minimisation programme. In the end, the focus for many was to be seen as being in the process of being compliant, rather than fully compliant by May 25, 2018. For eDiscovery, data you do not have is not discoverable in litigation.

Cross-border Data Transfers

It is recognised that cross-border data transfers of EU data subject's information to other countries is a necessity for commercial and legal purposes. This requirement is amplified in the litigation space to satisfy disclosure orders. To enable US companies to have access to EU PII data the EU–US Privacy Shield was put in place, a politically driven agreement.

In 2016, the Article 29 Data Protection Working Parties stated that this agreement was an improvement but many would disagree, as it was not seen as a step up from its predecessor Safe Harbour agreement and the process of certification especially. There is no guarantee that there would be the same level of adequate protection of data in accordance with GDPR, such as:

- Inform individuals about data processing activities
- Provide free and accessible dispute resolutions
- Cooperate with the US Department of Commerce
- Maintain data integrity and purpose limitation
- Ensure accountability for data transfer to third parties

- Maintain transparency related to enforcement action
- Ensure commitments are kept as long as data is held.

It is important to note that this agreement was not and has never been a GDPR compliance requirement; it was put in place as a mechanism for the USA to meet the GDPR requirements for third-party data transfer. As of July 16, 2020, the EU-US Privacy Shield is no longer valid, and the guidelines of the European Court of Justice's decision on Schrems II(C-3111/18) are as under :

- Inform individuals about data processing activities
- Provide free and accessible dispute resolutions
- Cooperate with the dept of Commerce
- Maintain data integrity and purpose limitation
- Ensure accountability for data transfer to third parties
- Maintain transparency related to enforcement action
- Ensure commitments are kept as long as data is held.

Technology

Cyber security and data privacy have always been an afterthought in the technology space and at times, the responsibilities in the event of a breach were transferred or left to their customers. GDPR fosters a risk-based approach, and with the Right-to-be-forgotten and Privacy-by-Design requirements of the regulations, there was a big panic in the two years leading up to enforcement by some technology innovating companies, from application developers to autonomous vehicle manufacturers, believing that GDPR will stifle innovation.

To comply with "Privacy by Design and by Default", organizations now had to assess whether their technology systems had been updated to allow for the protection, amendment or deletion of personal data. As a result, issues with existing technology functionalities not designed to meet GDPR requirements were identified, coupled with organizations reluctant to spend or increase their IT budgets to refresh and revamp existing technology. At the same time, it was recognised that the reason for big data is technology and only technology can assist an organization in complying with GDPR. This does not by any means minimise the need for governance and the human element.

Artificial Intelligence, Machine Learning, Blockchain, automation and cross-discipline technology and techniques are all being used to promote GDPR compliance.

Brexit

The UK government recently announced a proposal to overturn part of the Brexit Withdrawal Agreement *"Agreement on the withdrawal of the*

United Kingdom of Great Britain and Northern Ireland from the European Union and the European Atomic Energy Community" signed on January 24, 2020. This has caused an uproar within the core of British politics, and it is summed up better with the joint letter by John Major and Tony Blair, on September 13, 2020 urging MPs to reject the proposed Internal Market Bill, *"It raises questions that go far beyond the impact on Ireland, the peace process and negotiations for a trade deal – crucial though they are. It questions the very integrity of our nation."*

It is virtually impossible for global organizations to segregate data subjects' PII by region or country, so many have responded with new privacy policies that apply GDPR standards across the board, to *all* data for *all* 'data subjects' irrespective of their citizenship, residency or data location. The GDPR has therefore effectively established a new *international* standard for data privacy protection and understanding the data subject's rights. Articles 12–23; and Accountability (Controller and Processor role), Articles 24–43 are a great start to being GDPR compliant.

We also saw some other challenges and unknown difficulties as early as 2016 during the two-year preparation period prior to GDPR enforcement and thereafter, which were not on anyone's radar.

Information Assurance (IA) and Information Governance (IG)

Data is generated every second, including PII data and with this comes responsibilities for the information to be stored securely to protect the Confidentiality, Integrity and Authentication (CIA) of data.

Information Assurance is defined as 'managing the risks associated with an information system's storage, processing, and data transmission'.[4] To comply with GDPR, having an Information Assurance programme is mandatory and such programmes are found in any organization. Still, the question of whether it is robust enough to understand the risks faced in the organization is another matter.

Policies, processes, procedures and guideline offer a roadmap for daily operational activities and assist with ensuring compliance with GDPR and other Laws and Regulations. This falls under Information Governance, a subset of corporate governance.[5] They provide standardised details on how the organization will deal with the management of information and records including PII related to business operations.[6]

Digital transformation and rapidly changing technology imply that there has been a shift in approaching projects, new technology and managing risk.[7] On this basis, it is essential to have an Information Governance policy that addresses the requirements of the GDPR and local data privacy legislation, an example being the UK Data Protection Act 2018.

Implementing information assurance and cyber risk management programmes are not one-off projects, and these programmes need to be continuously reviewed and tested to ensure that they are fit for purpose and provide the correct level of assurances and risk management as required by GDPR. Having a good programme is the key to avoiding a €20 million fine.

Cyber Security Threats

"I am convinced that there are only two types of companies: those that have been hacked and those that will be. And even they are converging into one category: those that have been hacked and will be hacked again".[8]

In 2020 alone, the top cyber attacks were Phishing (which saw a considerable increase during the pandemic), Ransomware, Cryptojacking, IoT attacks, state-sponsored attacks and compromised Smart Medical Devices and Electronic Medical Records (EMRs). The prize to the threat actor for the majority of these attacks is PII which holds excellent monetary value or otherwise and the impact of a breach to any organization is damaging. The whole idea of GDPR is to ensure that one looks at data privacy from a risk standpoint and proactively implements adequate controls to reduce cyber security risks and minimise the impact in the event of an attack. These threats are the reason for passing and the enforcement of data protection laws in the last three years in non-EU jurisdictions.

Vendor Risk

Third parties such as vendors and contractors pose a massive risk to organizations and a majority of organizations do not have secure systems or a dedicated team in place to manage their vendor management risk. This was brought to the forefront in 2016 during the preparations for GDPR.

As cyber criminals become increasingly sophisticated and cyber security threats continue to rise, organizations are becoming more and more aware of the potential danger posed by third parties.

Vendor management risk must be included in Data Protection Impact Assessment (DPIA) and adequate agreements between the vendor (processor) and organization (controller) are in place to ensure the processing of data as defined by the controllers and in line with GDPR. The desire to use the very latest and advanced technology has pushed the need to work collaboratively in partnership with vendors, and this does blur the boundaries. Focusing on a risk-based approach, with clear directions and contractual agreements is a winning position in adhering to GDPR.

Covid-19 Pandemic

No one anticipated that life as we know it would come to a standstill, and the most basic ways of working would change. We are now in a period commonly referred to as the "New Normal" and this brings a lot of changes even with GDPR. It would be a great mistake for us to think or believe that GDPR requirements have been relaxed because of the pandemic, the lockdown and other impacts we are witnessing at present in every single industry. This is far from the truth, the Corona virus track, trace and research data shared on infected subjects are exceptions and not the rule. This must not be seen as an acceptable action for organizations to lapse on their GDPR responsibilities towards data subject owners, especially in the EU.

In addition to this, working from home has become the norm and organizations must ensure that with the changes in working environments even more caution and controls are put in place, to ensure that customer and employee's private, sensitive and confidential data is still maintained. The integrity of data and usability as required by cyber security, cyber risk management and Information assurance to comply with GDPR and local privacy legislations, must be maintained.

It is going to be difficult moving forward when one has to comply with data privacy and all the issues that come with the new normal, we now find ourselves living in. We know that with the pandemic and the impact it is having on businesses in all industries and the continuous uncertainty with Covid-19, there is very little trust from a global viewpoint. Past research has shown that pandemics have profound economic effects, and we are witnessing this now. Today, the question on everyone's mind, globally is: What are the long term impacts on the economy, trade, laws and regulations such as GDPR.

Now more than ever, we must ensure that the right decisions are made with data subjects' privacy. The Information Commissioner Office (ICO) in the UK continuously and actively monitors and enforces GDPR and a case in point, is the increase and types of data privacy issues they are currently dealing with.

At the start of enforcement, it was believed that the low hanging fruit (small companies and government departments) would be impacted the most as they were easier and cheaper to deal with. In the UK this was further reinforced by the first enforcement of GDPR in December 2019, in the form of a fine of £275,000 imposed on Doorstep Dispensaree Ltd., a company running a pharmacy based in Edgware in London.[9]

It can now be said that the enforcers' focus has expanded due to some maturity on enforcement plans, as shown in March 2020 (UK), when Cathay Pacific Airways Limited was fined £500,000 for failing to protect the security of its customers' data. Between October 2014 and May 2018, Cathay Pacific's computer systems lacked appropriate security measures which led to customers' personal details being exposed.[10] In 2019, Google was fined \$57 million by the French data protection watchdog, its first GDPR fine.

We have not got to the point, where we have some good precedent to explore the implementation of GDPR fully. It is now three years since the enforcement of GDPR, and we should start seeing some really good cases coming through, to show the importance of adherence and severe impacts of a breach.

Conclusion and Future

GDPR as it stands is not perfect, as it has not been thoroughly tested, and we are yet to see legal precedents set in the courts.

The need for data privacy has been magnified because of cyber attacks and the magnitude of losses for both organizations and individuals. The loss for an organization is financial as well as a damaged reputation and other regulatory impacts, not to mention the €20 million GDPR fine, which in my humble opinion is just the tip of the iceberg.

The contributions in this book provide a cross-disciplinary overview of forefront implementation of GDPR. Data Privacy is a right to some, an expectation to others and in the cyber security space, a must to protect the public from threat factors. Further work in the future will showcase the maturity of GDPR and clarity on enforcement by EU supervisory authorities, and those responsible for jurisdictional data privacy protection around the world.

The GDPR Challenge: Privacy, Technology, and Compliance in an Age of Accelerating Change is brimming with meaningful professional experiences and research from the trenches. This is a great book providing useful advice on navigating GDPR, by the authors of various chapters with an experience of having worked in a number of industries in the EU and USA. Technology innovation is here to stay, and this book will show you a path to data privacy compliance.

"Running an organisation without keeping an eye on new regulations is like driving a car without checking the tyres – at some point you're going to crash...or get caught"

– Gydeline Ltd

References

1. GlobeNewswire (2020). *Cyber Insurance Market to Grow with 26.3% CAGR between 2020 and 2030: P&S Intelligence*. Retrieved from https://www.globenewswire.com/news-release/2020/06/25/2053157/0/en/Cyber-Insurance-Market-to-Grow-with-26-3-CAGR-Between-2020-and-2030-P-S-Intelligence.html

2. Worldometer (2020). *Countries in the EU by population (2020)*. Retrieved from https://www.worldometers.info/population/countries-in-the-eu-by-population/
3. Privacy Policy Blog (2019). *What's Data Privacy Law In Your Country?* Retrieved from https://www.privacypolicies.com/blog/privacy-law-by-country/
4. Dryden, R.K. (2019). *Transferring Risk Through Contractual Deterrents to Cloud Service Providers: A Phenomenological Study with Information*. Capella University: ProQuest.
5. Short, J. and Gerrard, M. (2009). *IT Governance Must Be Driven by Corporate Governance*. Gartner-Research, ID (G00172463).
6. Smallwood, R. (2019). *Information Governance: Concepts, Strategies and Best Practices*. Second Edition. USA: John Wiley & Sons.
7. Hodson, C. (2019). *Cyber Risk Management: Prioritize Threats, Identify Vulnerabilities and Apply Controls*. First Edition. London: Kogan Page Limited.
8. Mueller, R.S. (2012). *Director Federal Bureau of Investigation's Speech at RSA Cyber Security Conference San Francisco, CA*. Retrieved from https://archives.fbi.gov/archives/news/speeches/combating-threats-in-the-cyber-world-outsmarting-terrorists-hackers-and-spies
9. ICO Enforcement Action (2019–2020). *Enforcement Action*. Retrieved from https://ico.org.uk/action-weve-taken/enforcement/
10. ICO (2020). *Cathy Pacific Ltd*. Retrieved from https://ico.org.uk/action-weve-taken/enforcement/cathay-pacific/

The Algorithm in the C-Suite: Applying Lessons Learned and Information Governance Best Practices to Achieve Greater Post-GDPR Algorithmic Accountability

Jason R. Baron* and Katherine E. Armstrong

Introduction

With each passing day, we increasingly live in an algorithmic universe, due to the easy accumulation of big data in online networks, as well as from an ever-increasing variety of sources (e.g., the Internet of Things). Questions of corporate responsibility inevitably arise in a 24/7 world of "filter bubbles" – where Facebook has the ability to customize how liberal or conservative one's newsfeed is based on prior postings, Google personalizes ads popping up on Gmail based on the content of our conversations, and merchants like Amazon feed us personalized recommendations based on our prior purchases and everything we click on. Much of this is not per se nefarious in its intent – it is simply more and more a fact of life.

Frank Pasquale refers to this environment as our "black box society," where "authority is increasingly expressed algorithmically," and "[d]ecisions that used to be based on human reflection are now made automatically."[1] But, in the words of one computer scientist, "The irony is that the more we design artificial intelligence technology that successfully mimics humans, the more that A.I. is learning in a way that we do, with

*Corresponding author: jrbaron@umd.edu

all of our biases and limitations."[2] Or as a group of leading thinkers have put it in a recent "Social Impact Statement" on algorithmic accountability:

> Algorithms and the data that drive them are designed and created by people – There is always a human ultimately responsible for decisions made or informed by an algorithm. 'The algorithm did it' is not an acceptable excuse if algorithmic systems make mistakes or have undesired consequences, including from machine-learning processes.[3]

While (at least in theory) we remain free in our personal lives to make certain choices to volunteer information that flows into the stream of big data, increasingly often what we are exposed to in our working lives is the result of subtle, unexplained bias in software. For example, in workplace hiring decisions, facially neutral algorithms sometimes reveal a hidden bias based on how features are selected and weighted, or where certain variables used in the algorithm essentially function as "proxies" for real world racial or ethnic differences. A software feature using the variable "commuting distance from work" as a factor in deciding which candidates to hire may, depending on local geography, discriminate based on race. As Gideon Mann and Cathy O'Neill have written, "When humans build algorithmic screening software, they may unintentionally determine which applicants will be selected or rejected based on outdated information—going back to a time when there were fewer women in the workforce, for example—leading to a legally and morally unacceptable result."[4]

Once on the job, employees may experience a very different kind of filter bias through software targeting the risk of internal threats to the company.[5] The more advanced programs entering the market use sentiment analysis (e.g., algorithms looking at language used in emails) to predict whether certain individuals are more likely to display anger or other inappropriate behavior in the workplace. This capacity can be combined with external sources of data on individuals obtained online, including credit report updates, crime reports, and certain types of medical information, to essentially triage the employee population into "high-risk" and lower risk categories, so as to target the keystrokes made by a few. In this respect, we are truly in a pre-crime, *Minority Report*, world.

As consumers, part of the new algorithmic universe also involves our more or less willing participation in being part of a "scored" society of individuals, who are evaluated on various types of social measures. A 2016 episode of the television series *Black Mirror*, entitled "Nosedive," involved a woman caught up in a near-dystopian future where individuals are rated by everyone around them, and receive premium goods and services based on those ratings (which increasingly loom large in their lives, for good or ill).[6] The plot elements of "Nosedive" have eerily become the stuff of present reality in China, where the government is in the process of instituting a social credit system based in part on the scoring of individuals by individuals.[7] These new forms of scoring and the accountability issues they raise suggest if not fairly compel revisiting our collective experience especially with well-known aspects of credit reporting, where there are lessons learned that can be applied to the coming wider world of algorithms and algorithmic scoring more generally.

As the prospect of big data being used for varied corporate purposes has loomed ever larger over the past half-decade there also has emerged the discipline of "information governance" (IG), defined as "the activities and technologies that organizations employ to maximize the value of their information while minimizing risks and costs."[8] IG calls for the C-suite paying greater attention to information flows within corporate institutions, including monitoring a variety of privacy, security, compliance and other risks and benefits involved in the retention of records and data. A working consensus has come into fashion on what management structures should be considered in an attempt to tame (or at least get a handle on) wild, unregulated, exponential data growth.

The enactment of the General Data Protection Regulation (GDPR), which became effective on May 25, 2018, has in turn acted as a catalyst for accelerated attention to data issues being paid by companies both in and outside of the EU, who through their global footprint control or otherwise process data on EU citizens. The GDPR requires, among other things, that covered entities put into place new forms of notice to their employees, customers and constituents reflecting various privacy-related requirements. Receiving somewhat less attention – except in scholarly circles – has been a set of GDPR provisions aimed at placing some kind of controls on the use of algorithms in the corporate environment. How institutions further respond to the GDPR's requirements on algorithmic accountability and transparency will be bound to have profound implications for the black box society in which we all live.

Article 22 of the GDPR states that a "data subject shall have the right not to be subject to a decision based solely on automated processing, including profiling, which produces legal effects concerning him or her or similarly significantly affects him or her." In accompanying Recital 71, the GDPR's relevant provisions on automated processing are interpreted as providing a data subject with the right to "specific information . . . and the right to obtain human intervention, to express his or her point of view, *to obtain an explanation of the decision reached* after such assessment and to challenge the decision" (emphasis added).

Together, these two specific GDPR provisions generated a great deal of academic scholarship in the run up to GDPR's effective date, with respect to both (i) the circumstances under which the GDPR precludes the use of algorithms for decision-making purposes, and (ii) what constitutes a "meaningful" explanation of an algorithmic process, assuming one is necessary in a given case.[9] Without wading too deep into the ongoing scholarly exegesis of the GDPR's wording, there is nevertheless an obvious and immediate need for more practical advice as to what reasonable steps should be taken by private and public sector institutions to come into compliance with GDPR mandates. Certainly, the presence of potentially massive fines to the tune of up to 4% of global revenue tends to seize the C-suite's attention with respect to what can be done to show reasonable compliance, including with respect to algorithmic accountability.

In Part I, we provide a brief overview of the key provisions in the GDPR that will frame our discussion regarding the use of algorithms and the right to an explanation in the context of information governance. To highlight the challenge institutions face in an increasingly algorithmic-driven world, and to simplify the discussion, we focus on Article 22 and related GDPR provisions applicable to decisions based *solely* on automated processing, where we are choosing to interpret (or limit) the term "automated" to be synonymous with "algorithmic." A more general discussion of the ramifications of partially automated decision-making, or the larger world of profiling as carried out by people and software, is beyond our scope.

In Part II, we revisit the U.S. experience with algorithmic scoring of a specific type, namely, policymaking by the Federal Trade Commission around the subject of credit scores. In our view, the fairly comprehensive template laid out by the FTC on how to handle accountability and transparency issues in connection with implementation of the Fair Credit Reporting Act (FCRA) anticipates in significant respects the discussion about algorithmic accountability under the newer GDPR framework, and should therefore be cited to and discussed in connection with implementation issues which will arise under Article 22 and its related GDPR provisions.

In Part III, we argue that the emerging discipline of information governance provides an appropriate framework to achieve what might be considered "best practices" regarding algorithmic accountability in a post-GDPR world. As provided in greater detail below, institutions may use a governance framework to anticipate and/or escalate the types of algorithmic processing issues that may be arising in the corporate near-term future. We go on to propose a set of concrete, non-mutually exclusive, strategies for corporate institutions to consider adoption of, including (i) expressly considering algorithmic accountability as part of an IG portfolio; (ii) incorporation of an ethical review board into the IG function; and (iii) establishing algorithmic expertise at the board of director level.

I. Algorithmic Accountability under the GDPR

Broadly speaking, the GDPR constitutes a regulatory regime providing EU citizens with basic rights with respect to their personal data. The GDPR requires private and public sector institutions to adopt a "checklist" of concrete actions to ensure that EU citizens are kept informed of their rights when their data is subject to "processing" or otherwise under a "data controller's" authority.[10] Personal data is defined broadly as including any information relating to an identified or identifiable natural person.[11]

Four provisions of the GDPR expressly inform citizens of their rights with respect to automated processes. As alluded to above, Article 22 provides that data subjects have the right not to be subject to a decision based solely on automated processing, including profiling; the article further provides that significant automated processing can be used if it is necessary to enter into, or to perform, a contract between a data subject and a controller; authorized by Union or Member state law; or is based on the individual's "explicit consent."

Three additional provisions expressly reference Article 22. Article 13, which provides for rights of data subjects in cases where personal data has been collected, states that controllers must provide data subjects with certain "information necessary to ensure fair and transparent processing," including for our purposes here, "the existence of automated processing, including profiling" and "meaningful information about the logic involved, as well as the significance and the envisaged consequences" of such automated processing. Article 14 repeats the same rights formulation for data subjects whose information may have been collected by third parties, and Article 15 again repeats the above phrases as a right of access data subjects have that can be invoked at "reasonable intervals." These rights are subject to only limited exceptions, for example, for certain intellectual property rights held by the controller.[12]

The provisions of the GDPR include *Recitals,* which "cast light on the interpretation to be given to a legal rule" but "cannot in itself constitute such a rule."[13] Recital 71, quoted above for the proposition that data subjects have the right to an explanation of algorithmic decisions, goes on to provide a laundry list of "technical and organizational" measures to mitigate the possibility of algorithmic bias or discrimination, "to ensure, in particular, that factors which result in inaccuracies in personal data are corrected and the risk of errors is minimized," and also "to prevent . . . discriminatory effects on natural persons on the basis of racial or ethnic origin, political opinion, religion or beliefs, trade union membership, genetic or health status or sexual orientation, or processing that results in measures having such an effect."

In addition to interpretative guidance contained in Recitals, the Article 29 Data Protection Working Party issued "Guidelines on Automated individual decision-making and Profiling for the purposes of Regulation 2016/679" ("WP29 Guidelines" or "Guidelines"), in a final revised version dated 6 February 2018.[14] The WP29 was an advisory body made up of representatives from various EU data protection authorities, which upon enactment of the GDPR was replaced by a new "European Data Protection Board." As Margot Kaminski points out, the WP29 guidelines "do not have the direct force of law. They are, however, strongly indicative of how the law will be interpreted by its enforcers."[15]

The WP29 Guidelines state that "[g]iven the core principle of transparency underpinning the GDPR, controllers must ensure they explain clearly and simply to individuals how the . . . automated decision-making process works."[16] The Guidelines go on to state that "[t]he GDPR recognizes that automated decision-making . . . can have serious consequences for individuals," but that Article 22, limited to solely automated decisions that have "legal effects" or "similarly significantly affect[] him or her," should be seen as covering within its scope only those solely automated decisions that cause "serious impactful effects."[17] Such effects might include cancellation of a contract; entitlement to or denial of a particular social benefit granted by law; refused admission to a country or denial of citizenship; automatic refusal of an online credit application; or e-recruiting practices without any human intervention.[18] The Guidelines speculate that the following types of decisions "could" fall into the Article 22 category, including:

- decisions that affect someone's financial circumstances, such as their eligibility to credit;
- decisions that affect someone's access to health services;
- decisions to deny someone an employment opportunity or put them at a serious disadvantage;
- decisions that affect someone's access to education, for example university admissions.

The WP29 Guidelines establish that an institution cannot escape the prohibition in Article 22 by "fabricating human involvement"; hence, the involvement of a human must be meaningful. In Kaminski's words, the "GDPR will thus have the effect of requiring companies to think about how they structure their 'human in the loop' of algorithmic decision-making, so as to escape Article 22's prohibition or forego its safeguard requirements."[19]

Notwithstanding the broad sweep of Article 22, its related provisions, and the interpretative guidance found in Recital 71, it has been pointed out by a range of computer scientists and scholars that "meaningful consent" to the "logic" of algorithmic processes within the black box remains, at least in part, aspirational.[20] Simply put, "[I]t is nearly impossible to explain the logic behind an algorithm making a decision."[21]

The WP29 Guidelines, as revised in 2018 in partial response to the academic debate over what meaningful information about the logic involved in a particular decision might mean, went on to state:

> The growth and complexity of machine-learning can make it challenging to understand how an automated decision-making process . . . works. * * * The controller should find simple ways to tell the data subject about the rationale behind, or the criteria relied on in reaching the decision. The GDPR requires the controller to provide meaningful information about the logic involved, not necessarily a complex explanation of the algorithms used or disclosure of the full algorithm. The information provided should, however, be sufficiently comprehensive for the data subject to understand the reasons for the decision.[22]

The Guidelines provide a helpful example on the subject of credit scoring, where in compliance with Article 22

> [a] controller explains that this process helps them provide fair and responsible lending decisions . . . [and] provides details of the main characteristics considered in reaching the decision, the source of this information and the relevance. These may include, for example: the information provided by the data subject on the application form; information about previous account conduct, including any payment arrears; and official public records information such as fraud record information and insolvency records. The controller also includes information to advise the data subject that the credit scoring methods used are regularly tested to ensure they remain fair, effective and unbiased. . . .[23]

Assuming, as do the WP29 Guidelines, that the GDPR requires at least *some* baseline right to an explanation of the logic behind algorithmic decision-making, we turn to lessons learned from US regulatory experience, as well as best practices in the IG space, for a roadmap to algorithmic accountability on the part of private and public sector institutions.

II. Lessons Learned on Algorithmic Accountability: The Federal Trade Commission's Enforcement of the Fair Credit Reporting Act

Before addressing relevant guidance and insight from the Federal Trade Commission (FTC), it is important to understand the vastly different regulatory approaches of the US and EU when it comes to consumer data and privacy. While the EU's GDPR has taken a comprehensive approach to regulating privacy, and to some extent data security, the US has taken a sectoral approach. With respect to processing (collecting, using, sharing, protecting) personal information, the general rule in the US is that such processing is allowed, except where specifically prohibited. Nevertheless, there are a variety of federal laws such as the FCRA, the Gramm Leach Bliley Act (GLBA), the Health Insurance Portability and Accountability Act (HIPAA) and others, that touch on privacy. In addition, there is overlapping jurisdiction among a range of federal agencies that share enforcement authority over these laws as well as ever-increasing legislative activity at the state level. There are now 50 separate state breach notification laws, as well as specific statutes such as the recently enacted California Consumer Privacy Act of 2018 (CCPA), with an effective date of January 1, 2020,[24] and the New York State Cyber Regulations.[25]

Despite the fact that there is no overarching privacy law at the federal level, the FTC has taken a leadership role in the area of consumer data and privacy. By way of background, the FTC was created in 1914 to prevent unfair methods of competition in commerce as part of the battle to "bust the trusts," and over the years Congress has passed additional laws that give the FTC greater authority which includes the FTC's section 5 authority that prohibits the use of "unfair and deceptive acts or practices." The FTC has used its section 5 authority to challenge certain privacy and data security lapses in over 100 matters, and enforces a broad variety of other consumer protection laws, including the FCRA.[26] In addition to its law enforcement efforts, the FTC recently has hosted a variety of workshops and written reports on a variety of topics related to privacy, data brokers, and big data.

The FTC's principal tool is to bring enforcement actions to stop law violations and require companies to take affirmative steps to remediate the unlawful behavior. This includes, when appropriate, the implementation of comprehensive privacy and security programs and, when authorized by statute, monetary relief. In addition, most settlements also provide robust transparency and choice mechanisms for consumers. Through all of these efforts, the FTC has been engaged as a leader with respect to the development of policy and best practices in the area of consumer privacy and data security.

The FTC does not, however, have specific statutory authority to engage in rulemaking. In order to provide guidance to business and consumer education, the Commission has hosted numerous workshops and other public forums that include stakeholders from a variety of disciplines and industry sectors. Often, at the conclusion of a workshop and with the aid of public comments, the FTC staff will prepare a report or summary for the Commission.

FTC Reports

Three reports, discussed below, are of particular relevance to the discussion of big data, privacy, algorithms and consumer choice. These reports each make specific recommendations relating to what the FTC considers to be best practices with respect to consumer choice and privacy.

The first report is the 2012 *Protecting Consumer Privacy in an Era of Rapid Change: Recommendations for Businesses and Policymakers.*[27] This report represents the culmination of a number of workshops and the review of hundreds of comments.

The report called on companies handling consumer data to implement:

- Privacy by Design – companies should build in privacy protection for consumers at every stage in developing their products. These include reasonable security for consumer data, limited collection and retention of such data, and reasonable procedures to promote data accuracy.
- Simplified choice of businesses and consumers – companies should give consumers the option to decide what information is shared about them, and with whom. This should include a Do-Not-Track mechanism that would provide a simple, easy way for consumers to control the tracking of their online activities.
- Greater transparency – companies should disclose details about their collection and use of consumers' information and provide consumers access to the data collected about them.

The second report is the FTC's 2014 Data Broker Report, *Data Brokers: A Call for Transparency and Accountability.*[28] For this report, the FTC conducted a study of nine data brokers representing a cross-section of the industry. The goal was to shed light on the data broker industry. Data brokers, a term that is not statutorily defined, obtain and share vast amounts of consumer information, often without consumers' knowledge. "Consumer reporting agencies" (CRAs), a type of data broker, are subject to regulation by the FCRA (see below); other types of data brokers are not regulated at the federal level, although some states are beginning to enact their own laws.[29]

The Data Broker Report found, among other things, that:

- Data brokers collect consumer data from extensive online and offline sources, largely without consumers' knowledge, ranging from consumer purchase data, social media activity, warranty registrations, magazine subscriptions, religious and political affiliations, and other details of consumers' everyday lives.
- Consumer data often passes through multiple layers of data brokers sharing data with each other.
- Data brokers combine online and offline data to market to consumers online.

- Data brokers combine and analyze data about consumers to make inferences about them, including potentially sensitive inferences such as those related to ethnicity, income, religion, political leanings, age, and health conditions.
- Many of the purposes for which data brokers collect and use data pose risks to consumers, such as unanticipated uses of the data. For example, a category like "Biker Enthusiasts" could be used to offer discounts on motorcycles to a consumer, but could also be used by an insurance provider as a sign of risky behavior.
- To the extent data brokers currently offer consumers choices about their data, the choices are largely invisible and incomplete.

Finally, the FTC's *Big Data: A Tool for Inclusion or Exclusion? Understanding the Issues*[30] draws on a 2014 workshop and extensive public comments. The report highlights a number of innovative uses of big data that provide benefits to underserved populations, but also looks at possible risks that could result from biases or inaccuracies about the data. The workshop participants, academics, and others addressed the ways big data analytics could affect low-income, underserved populations, and protected groups noting that research indicates that there is a potential for incorporating errors and biases at every stage – from choosing the data set used to make predictions, to defining the problem to be addressed through analytics, to making decisions based on the data.

The Big Data Report encouraged companies to consider the following questions raised by research in this area:

- How representative is the data set? Consider whether the data sets are missing information about certain populations and take steps to address issues of underrepresentation and overrepresentation. For example, if a company targets services to consumers who communicate through an application or social media, they may be neglecting populations that are not as tech-savvy.
- Does the data model account for biases? Consider whether biases are being incorporated at both the collection and analytics stages of big data's life cycle, and develop strategies to overcome them. For example, an algorithm that only considers applicants from "top tier" colleges to help them make hiring decisions, may be incorporating previous biases in college admission decisions.
- How accurate are the predictions based on big data? Although big data is good at detecting correlations, it does not explain which correlations are meaningful.
- Does reliance on big data raise ethical or fairness concerns? It is important to assess the factors that go into an analytics model and balance the predictive value of the model with fairness considerations.

The report outlines some of the various laws that apply to the uses of big data especially in regards to possible issues of discrimination or exclusion, including the FCRA, equal opportunity laws, and section 5 of the FTC Act, the latter of which unlike the FCRA or equal opportunity laws is not confined to market sectors.

The FCRA was enacted in 1970 in part to provide transparency with respect to the use of information collected about consumers and used in the credit granting process. Prior to its enactment, there was very little visibility in the credit granting process, so one of the original congressional purposes in passing the FCRA was to make consumer credit reporting data accessible, understandable and correctable. Accordingly, the guiding principles of the FCRA include privacy, fairness, and accuracy.

Specifically, the FCRA regulates consumer report information and CRAs. CRAs assemble and evaluate consumer report information and provide such data to third parties who use such information to make eligibility determinations for credit, employment, insurance, housing, or other similar decisions about consumers' eligibility for certain benefits and transactions. CRAs can only provide consumer reports to those entities that will use the reports for certain specified permissible purposes, such as for credit, employment, insurance, or housing eligibility determinations.[31] In addition, CRAs are required to implement reasonable procedures to ensure maximum possible accuracy of consumer report information,[32] and to provide consumers with access to their own information, along with the ability to correct any inaccurate negative information.[33]

The FCRA includes a number of provisions that encourage transparency and fairness with respect to the consumer reporting process. For example, there is a built in obsolescence provision that prohibits the reporting of "old" information.[34] In addition, consumers have an opportunity to dispute inaccurate information about them which is usually triggered when they receive an adverse action notice from a creditor after they have been denied credit.[35] The adverse action notice describes the dispute process. Finally, the FCRA was amended in 2003 to provide consumers with the opportunity to obtain annual free reports from the three major consumer reporting agencies.[36]

Lessons from the U.S. Experience with Credit Scoring

Over the years, credit scores have been developed as a way to predict certain credit related behavior. A credit score is a number compiled from a consumer's credit report using a proprietary algorithm that scores some or all of the factors considered in the underwriting process. Credit scores are used to predict the probability that consumers with a certain score will engage in a particular behavior, e.g. delinquency, default, etc.

The FCRA defines credit score as:

[A] numerical value or a categorization derived from a statistical tool or modeling system used by a person who makes or arranges a loan to predict the likelihood of certain credit behaviors, including default (and the numerical value or the categorization derived from such analysis may be referred to as a "risk predictor" or "risk score").[37]

Regulation B[38] of the Equal Credit Opportunity Act (ECOA)[39] requires that a credit scoring system satisfy four criteria:

- The data used to develop the system must constitute either the entire applicant file or an appropriate sample of it;
- The system must have the purpose of predicting applicants' creditworthiness with respect to "legitimate business interests" of the creditor using it;
- The system must be "developed and validated using accepted statistical principles and methodology"; and
- The system should be periodically reviewed and re-validated as to its predictive ability and adjusted accordingly.

Historically, most credit scoring systems were custom models built for a particular lender or users. There are also more generic scores which are developed for generalized use. In addition, there are specialty scores for things like automobile finance or other financial products. Some scores are designed to predict a specific event such as bankruptcy, while others are used for things such as prescreened credit card offers and predict whether a consumer is a good prospect for accepting an offer. Credit scores are increasingly used to determine eligibility and rate for automobile and homeowner's insurance.

Because credit scores are based on consumer report information, they will change as consumer credit reports are updated and reflect recent payments or late payments. The FCRA requires that creditors, when providing an adverse action or risk-based notice, include in the notice the actual credit score used in making the decision.[40] Further, when consumers are denied credit based on a credit score, they are provided with some information about their credit score,[41] but are not provided with information about the algorithm. The information that is required to be in the notice is intended to provide context to the consumer about what their credit score means.

Other Scoring Models

While credit scores were among the first scoring models and as noted above are covered by the FCRA, there are a variety of other scoring models that have been developed and are used for marketing and advertising, insurance, and other purposes. These scoring models are largely unregulated.

In 2014, the World Privacy Forum published a report: *The Scoring of America: How Secret Consumer Scores Threaten Your Privacy and Your Future.*[42] The report highlights the unexpected problems that can arise from predictive consumer scoring which is largely unregulated by the FCRA or the ECOA. In particular, the report describes how thousands of pieces of information about consumers' pasts are used to predict how they will behave in the future, and expresses concern about issues of secrecy and fairness in the use of such scores. While identifying a number of regulatory gaps and specific scoring categories, such as identity and authentication scores, fraud scores, and household segmentation scores, it concludes by suggesting that the FCRA model with respect to credit scores be expanded to include all consumer scoring.

III. Applying IG Best Practices to Achieve Greater Algorithmic Accountability

IG Strategies in General

Advocates of IG argue that corporations with an interest in maturing an IG program put in place a mechanism to escalate data-related issues to an IG standing committee, consisting of either C-suite representatives or their delegates. In a growing number of corporate models, an individual with some kind of IG designation in their title will, as leader of the committee, be given authority to call together ad hoc groups to resolve specific data policy issues.

In particular, some have championed the idea of creating the position of Chief Information Governance Officer (CIGO) within corporations, where that individual is charged with owning and coordinating the solutions to complex and overlapping information challenges. In many cases, no one "owns" specific information problems as they arise – certainly not in the same way as a chief information security officer (CISO) owns information security. So too, in most organizations a vast amount of data accumulates but is inaccessible or unknown to senior management. The three primary gaps within the corporate space that a CIGO (or similarly titled individual) would aim to fill include: (i) information-focused leadership; (ii) organization-wide information coordination; and (iii) being a balancer of information value and risk. Such an individual may also function as a designated "data protection officer"[43] for purposes of GDPR compliance.

The process for getting a better handle on both the risk and the value of a company's information assets starts with the question: what constitute the company's information assets, and which are the most valuable? Which consist of intellectual property? Which are informational assets relating to a customer or consumer base? Where does the data reside physically (controlled by an in-house IT staff or in a third-party data center including in the Cloud)? How is the company protecting personally identifiable information (PII) in consumer and employee data, and what are the company's policies (algorithmic or otherwise) with respect to monetizing consumer data, including in interactions with third-party data brokers? How does the company purport to measure Return on Investment (ROI) for its IG projects and activities? These questions collectively fall under the concept of establishing a data map or engaging in asset classification – a valuable exercise not only for informing what needs to go into a cyber-incident response protocol, but also simply to become more informed on information risk and information value for any would-be IG project, including those involving algorithmic processes.

The above questions are by no means intended to be comprehensive – they represent only suitable entry points to a more robust conversation among senior officials about issues including use of algorithmic processes. But drilling down in asking a CIGO or other agency senior official these types of questions quickly establishes the extent to which the company "knows what it knows" (or whether it doesn't have a clue). Establishing a baseline as to senior officials' IG strategies is simply a form of IG due diligence, as well as proper management of risk.

Application to Algorithmic Processes

As Kaminski envisions, "most companies deploying algorithmic decision-making must themselves set up internal accountability and disclosure regimes, both in the process of performing a data protection impact assessment, and in response to an internal but independent data protection officer who also has, at least on paper, deep information-forcing abilities."[44] Three overarching strategies suggest themselves as being useful in achieving algorithmic accountability.

Audits

One could well imagine a chief information governance officer convening an ad hoc task force of the IG council, including a C-suite representative of the corporate human relations (HR) department, along with the person who approved or manages the data analytics software used by HR and a senior counsel, to perform an "audit" of what algorithms are used in hiring practices. This would presumably include a thorough assessment of the "logic" involved in the algorithm, including inputs and proxy variables used in the modelling.

Similarly, an ad hoc task force including the chief information security officer, senior HR office personnel, and other IT representatives and senior counsel could be asked to review how well internal monitoring of employees is working and how much transparency or notice should be given to staff on such monitoring.

On the subject of audits, serious consideration should be given to putting into place auditing processes that themselves involve the use of "examination" algorithms, i.e., algorithms that act as substitutes for attempting human eyes-on review when the logic is "inscrutable."[45] The WP29 Guidelines listed as an appropriate safeguard the suggestion that controllers consider when making automated decisions the use of "algorithmic auditing – testing the algorithms used and developed by machine learning systems to prove that they are actually performing, as intended, and not producing discriminator, erroneous, or unjustified results."[46] A growing body of technical literature exists on "fairness-aware" data mining techniques.[47]

In adapting additional recommendations contained in the WG29 Guidelines Annex 1, the IG function within organizations could monitor and suggest best practices in particular algorithmic instances, including:

- regular quality assurance checks of any systems using algorithmic processes;
- independent "third party" auditing (including academic researchers), including providing the auditor with all necessary information about how the algorithm or machine learning system works;[48]
- obtaining contractual assurances for third party algorithms that auditing and testing has been carried out and the algorithm is compliant with agreed standards; and
- crafting a code of conduct for auditing processes involving machine learning.[49]

Organizations may also wish to develop policies that allow individuals subject to an algorithmic process the right to express their point of view and to contest or appeal the decision, and may consider enhancing their IG process to include designating one or more individuals who would be expected to be responsible including for:

- Assessing the social impact of the algorithm, and for monitoring the algorithm for unintended consequences.
- Making provision for a "sunset plan" to manage an algorithm once the software is not being actively developed.
- Providing for how decisions will be explained to subjects of those decisions, including where appropriate developing an automated explanation for each decision.
- Allowing for individuals to have visibility into the data stored about them and access to a process in order to make modifications to that data.
- Disclosing the sources of any data used and as much as possible about the specific attributes of the data.
- Assessing the potential for errors in a system and the resulting potential for harm to users.

- Undertaking a sensitivity analysis to assess how uncertainty in the output of the algorithm relates to uncertainty in the inputs.
- Performing a validity check by randomly sampling a portion of your data (e.g., input and/or training data) and manually checking its correctness.[50]

There is no shortage of potential "tasks" or "action items" to be assigned to members of an IG function in the service of enhancing corporate algorithmic accountability.

Ethical Review Board

Along these lines, organizations might consider tasking a group of individuals—under the auspices either of the IG structure or as a freestanding committee—to perform a similar function to a present-day institutional review board (IRB), whose task would be to obtain greater insight as to the biases embedded within corporate algorithms. For example, such an "ethical review board" or "algorithm review board" would be charged with providing approval and/or oversight of any use of analytics in the workplace aimed at targeting present employees or prospective hires, so as to serve as a check against possible hidden bias or a lack of notice where appropriate. Indeed, the idea is endorsed in Annex 1 to the WP29 Guidelines, which contain a good practice recommendation under a subsection titled "Appropriate safeguards" that states: "Controllers can also explore options such as . . . ethical review boards to assess the potential harms and benefits to society of particular applications of profiling."[51]

Some corporations, including Microsoft and Facebook, have taken initial steps to implement, at least on a selected basis and at widely varying levels of transparency, some form of ethics review committee.[52] However, the practice remains rare across all industry verticals, notwithstanding the growing power of analytics in all aspects of daily life. This could well change due to the need to confront Article 22 and other GDPR requirements.

Boards of Directors with Algorithmic Expertise

In the governance space we recently have seen emerge a variety of calls for boards of directors to be asking questions of their CEOs, CIOs, and CISOs about how companies are preparing for breaches, and how they will deal with their aftermath through agreed-upon protocols.[53] No question exists that factoring in cyber risk is an increasingly necessary part of the corporate world. Arguably, however, there is also a need for board expertise that embraces a greater range of issues falling under an overall information governance strategy or framework for decision-making across an enterprise. Such expertise could well include knowledge and consideration of algorithmic processes.

As an overarching matter, we maintain that board members should be asking their CEO at the outset of any conversation about corporate IG practice:

- Has our company put into place an IG Steering Committee, comprised of senior officials from the C-suite (or their delegates), to perform a coordinating function for the formulation of policies and practices across the many various facets of IG? And, if not, why not?
- Does our company have a designated official, either with the title of Chief Information Governance Officer, or something similar, who performs either an executive secretariat function for IG issues, and/or takes a leadership role for the IG Steering Committee if there is one? And if not, why not?
- How is the corporation using algorithmic processes, e.g., in hiring and other work-related decisions? And how is consumer data being made subject to profiling and other forms of algorithmic process, and what impact does doing so have in targeting a customer base?

These questions will necessarily shed light on the present state of attention C-suite members are paying to IG best practices, the maturity of the IG program itself, and how much attention should be given to algorithmic accountability. Where a company has a mature IG program with a designated "go to" individual responsible for facets of IG, and where a cross-functional IG steering committee of some sort exists, board members and their CEO have a known place to start any inquiries they have. Board members should, of course, feel free to jump-start a conversation about IG, irrespective of parallel lines of inquiry being undertaken by members of the C-suite.

One important caveat to emphasize is that the call for a designation of a CIGO or equivalent IG senior-level position is not intended in any way to limit the ability of board members (or the CEO) to obtain feedback from any and all senior management officials of their choice, regarding specific problems or challenges that have arisen with respect to corporate use of algorithms. To the contrary, a CIGO may act as an appropriate conduit for facilitating board questioning of individuals with specific algorithmic subject matter expertise.

Especially with the advent of Sarbanes-Oxley (SOX) legislation in the US,[54] it has become increasingly apparent that boards of directors directly benefit from one or more individuals having a special expertise, which in the specific case of SOX means understanding financial statements. For covered entities, SOX expressly requires that an audit committee be set up on boards of directors, and that the committee "be directly responsible for the appointment, compensation and oversight of the work of any registered public accounting firm employed by [the] issuer."[55] This, in turn, has led to the appointment of one or more board directors with expertise in auditing and financial affairs.

More recently, in some instances boards have indeed set up a cyber risk subcommittee, charged with the responsibility of making recommendations to the full board on ways to mitigate cyber risk.[56] Following in the footsteps of this model, boards could elect to have a standing information governance subcommittee, which may elect to include issues surrounding algorithmic accountability within its scope. The ideal board member(s) overseeing this function would feel comfortable in pursuing issues at the intersection of information technology, law, privacy, big data analytics, and ethics.

Regardless of whether the chosen structure includes an IG designation or subcommittee, boards should consider engaging in requesting periodic updates from senior staff with regard to the maturity of the company's IG profile, including hearing reports on algorithmic uses. The accelerating pace of change in technology demands vigilant, continuing attention. Board members should fairly demand that a CIGO or equivalent officer of IG steering committee have a well-established escalation process, which encourages business executives to bring forth newly emerging risk issues across all relevant policy areas, including with respect to algorithmic accountability.

Conclusion

Article 22 and the accompanying GDPR provisions represent an attempt at moving towards a greater "algorithm-in-the-sunshine" regulatory approach, where EU citizens achieve greater understanding of the impact of algorithmic processes on their lives. Unquestionably, Article 22 is destined to have a worldwide impact as corporate entities everywhere consider how they need to modify existing governance frameworks to account for a new algorithmic accountability paradigm. That said, the accelerating pace of artificial intelligence in the 21st century constitutes an ever-greater challenge to the noble goals embodied in the GDPR.

Nearly 50 years ago when the FCRA was enacted, the U.S. Congress identified the importance of accuracy and fairness with respect to credit reporting. Specifically, the Congressional findings to the FCRA provide in part: "[C]onsumer reporting agencies [shall] adopt reasonable procedures … in a manner which is fair and equitable to the consumer, with regard to the confidentiality, accuracy, relevancy, and proper utilization of such information in accordance with the requirements of this title."[57]

As has been the case with lessons learned from the FTC experience, progress can be made in achieving greater insight into algorithms by means of requiring explanations, audits, and, as suggested above, using sophisticated technology (e.g., examination algorithms) to root out subtle bias and discriminatory features. As argued here, there are well-known practical strategies that can be carried out to do this by C-suite champions of information governance.

As algorithms continue to be developed and implemented in ways that impact decisions made about individuals (including both consumers and employees), it will continue to be important when considering issues regarding accountability, transparency and fairness, that institutions engage in pro-actively assessing whether their model accounts for bias, testing the accuracy of predictions, and identifying whether particular algorithmic applications have unintended consequences that could be discriminatory. With Article 22 and Recital 71 acting as drivers toward algorithmic accountability, institutions hold the keys to the kingdom in their hands through successful implementation of a robust, mature IG program that anticipates having an inside corporate dialogue on these issues, as part of a well-thought approach to the brave new world of AI and big data we all are facing.

Note: This chapter represents a greatly expanded reworking of an article by Mr. Baron in Legal tech News, under the heading "Hidden Bias in the Black Box: Information Governance as a Key Check to Algorithmic Bias," published on June 15, 2017.

References

1. Frank Pasquale (2015). The Black Box Society: The Secret Algorithms That Control Money and Information.
2. University of Utah (2015, Aug. 14). Programming and prejudice: Computer scientists discover how to find bias in algorithms. https://phys.org/news/2015-08-prejudice-scientists-bias-algorithms.html.
3. FAT/ML, Principles for Accountable Algorithms and a Social Impact Statement for Algorithms. (Social Impact Statement), https://www.fatml.org/resources/principles-for-accountable-algorithms. The principles of algorithmic accountability set out in the Social Impact Statement include (1) responsibility; (2) explainability; (3) accuracy; (4) auditability; and (5) fairness. See also IEEE Ethically Aligned Design, First Edition: A Vision for Prioritizing Human Well-being with Autonomous and Intelligent Systems (2019), https://ethicsinaction.ieee.org; Organization for Economic Co-operation and Development (OECD) AI Principles, Recommendation of the Council on Artificial Intelligence, OECD/Legal/0449 (adopted 21 May 2019), https://www.oecd.org/going-digital/ai/principles/; Data & Society, "Algorithmic Accountability: A Primer" (April 2018), https://datasociety.net/wpcontent/uploads/2018/04/

Data_Society_Algorithmic_Accountability_Primer_FINAL-4.pdf;   Nikolas Diakopoulos, "Algorithmic Accountability Reporting: On the Investigation of Black Boxes," https://academiccommons.columbia.edu/catalog/ac:2ngf1vhhn4.

4. Hiring Algorithms Are Not Neutral. *Harvard Business Review.* (2016, 9 Dec.), https://hbr.org/2016/12/hiring-algorithms-are-not-neutral.

5. Aimee O'Driscoll (2017, 13 Oct.). A Guide to employee monitoring and workplace privacy. VPN & Privacy. https://www.comparitech.com/blog/vpn-privacy/a-guide-to-employee-monitoring-and-workplace-privacy/

6. *Black Mirror*, Series 3, Episode 1 (21 Oct. 2016), see http://en.m.wikipedia.org/nosedive.

7. Gabrielle Bruney (2018, 17 March). A 'Black Mirror' Episode is Coming to Life in China. *Esquire*, https://www.esquire.com/news-politics/a19467976/black-mirror-social-credit-china/.

8. Information Governance Initiative Annual Report 2014: Information Governance Goes To Work. https://www.viewpointe.com/uploadedfiles/viewpointe/pdfs/2014-igi-annual-report-viewpointe.pdf.   See   generally, www.iginitiative.com.

9. See Margot E. Kaminski (2018, 15 June). The Right to an Explanation, Explained. U of Colorado Law Legal Studies Research Paper No. 18-24 (collecting scholarly authorities). Available at SSRN: https://ssrn.com/abstract=3196985 or http://dx.doi.org/10.2139/ssrn.3196985.

10. See GDPR, https://eur-lex.europa.eu/legal-content/EN/TXT/HTML/?uri=CELEX:02016R0679-20160504&from=EN.

11. Id., § 4; see https://ec.europa.eu/info/law/law-topic/data-protection/reform/what-personal-data_en.

12. See GDPR Recital 63, http://www.privacy-regulation.eu/en/recital-63-GDPR.htm.

13. Case 215/88 Casa Fleischhandels [1989] European Court of Justice ECR 2789, cited in Kaminski, The Right to an Explanation, supra n.9, at 8 n.40.

14. See   https://ec.europa.eu/newsroom/article29/item-detail.cfm?item_id=612053

15. Kaminski, The Right to Explanation, supra n.9, at 8.

16. WP29 Guidelines, supra n.14, at 16.

17. Id., at 21.

18. Id.

19. Kaminski, The Right to Explanation, supra n.9, at 11.

20. See Andrew D. Selbst and Julia Prowles (2017). Meaningful Information and the Right to Explanation, 7(4) International Data Privacy Law 233; Kaminski, The Right to Explanation, supra n.9, at 20-22; Lillian Edwards and Michael Veale (2017). Slave to the Algorithm? Why a 'Right to an Explanation' Is Probably Not The Remedy You Are Looking For. 16 Duke Law & Tech. Review 18.

21. Maja Brkan (22 Feb. 2018). Do Algorithms Rule the World? Algorithmic Decision-Making in the Framework of the GDPR and Beyond. Paper submitted at Technology Policy Institute conference, Washington, D.C. https://www.researchgate.net/publication/323981467_Do_Algorithms_Rule_the_World_Algorithmic_Decision-Making_in_the_Framework_of_the_GDPR_and_Beyond.

22. WP29 Guidelines, *supra* n.14, at 25 (internal footnote omitted); *see also id.*, Annex 1 – Good Practice recommendations (first listed recommendation discussing providing "clear and comprehensive ways to deliver" information to data subjects, including categories of data that have been or will be used and why these categories are considered pertinent).
23. *Id.* at 26 (internal bullets omitted).
24. Title 1.81.5 (commencing with Section 1798.100), as added to Part 4 of Division 3 of the California Civil Code. The CCPA has been amended by a ballot initiative titled the California Privacy Rights Act, effective 1 January 2023. See https://vig.cdn.sos.ca.gov/2020/general/pdf/topl-prop24.pdf.
25. See https://www.dfs.ny.gov/legal/regulations/adoptions/dfsrf500txt.pdf.
26. 15 U.S.C. § 1681-1681x.
27. See https://www.ftc.gov/sites/default/files/documents/reports/federal-trade-commission-report-protecting-consumer-privacy-era-rapid-change-re commendations/120326privacyreport.pdf.
28. See https://www.ftc.gov/reports/data-brokers-call-transparency-accountability-report-federal-trade-commission-may-2014.
29. For example, in 2018 Vermont passed a first-of-its kind data broker law that defines data broker as: "a business, or unit or units of a business, separately or together, that knowingly collects and sells or licenses to third parties the brokered personal information of a consumer with whom the business does not have a direct relationship." 9 V.S.A. § 2430(4)(A). In addition, a number of states have introduced comprehensive privacy legislation that may give consumers greater rights against data brokers. See, e.g., CCPA, *supra* n.24.
30. See https://www.ftc.gov/reports/big-data-tool-inclusion-or-exclusion-understanding-issues-ftc-report.
31. 15 U.S.C. § 1681b(a).
32. *Id.* § 1681e(b).
33. *Id.* § 1681f-1681j.
34. *Id.* § 1681c(a).
35. *Id.* § 1681m.
36. 16 CFR Part 610.
37. 15 U.S.C. § 1681g(f)(2)(A)(ii).
38. Reg. B, 12 C.F.R. § 102.2(p)(1).
39. 15 U.S.C. §§ 1691-1691f.
40. 15 U.S.C. §§ 1681m(a)(2), 1681m(h)(5)(E).
41. *Id.* § 1681g(f)(1).
42. http://www.worldprivacyforum.org/wp-content/uploads/2014/04/WPF_Scoring_of_America_April2014_fs.pdf.
43. GDPR, Art. 37, http://www.privacy-regulation.eu/en/article-37-designation-of-the-data-protection-officer-GDPR.htm.
44. Kaminski, The Right to Explanation, *supra* n.9, at 23.
45. See Andrew Selbst and Solon Barocas, Regulating Inscrutable Systems, http://www.werobot2017.com/wp-content/uploads/2017/03/Selbst-and-Barocas-Regulating-Inscrutable-Systems-1.pdf.
46. WP29 Guidelines, *supra* n.14 at 32, https://iapp.org/media/pdf/resource_center/W29-auto-decision_profiling_02-2018.pdf
47. See Toshihiro Kamishima (2012). Considerations on Fairness Aware Data Mining. 2012 IEEE 12th International Conference on Data Mining Workshops,

http://www.kamishima.net/archive/2012-ws-icdm-print.pdf; see also FAT/ML Resource list, https://www.fatml.org/resources.
48. See, e.g., Margot E. Kaminski (2019). Binary Governance: Lessons from the GDPR's Approach to Algorithmic Accountability. 92 So. Cal. L. Rev. No. 6, U of Colorado Law Legal Studies Research Paper No. 19-9 (9 April 2019). Available at: https://papers.ssrn.com/sol3/papers.cfm?abstract_id=3351404##.
49. *Id.* See also Council of European Study (2017). Algorithms and Human Rights: Study on the human rights dimensions of automated data processing techniques and possible regulatory implications. DGI, 12, https://slidelegend.com/queue/algorithms-and-human-rights-web-authentication-system-council-_5afb6bd08ead0eb5108b4579.html.
50. These examples paraphrase or re-state relevant bullet points appearing in the Social Impact Statement, referenced *supra*, n.3.
51. WP29 Guidelines, *supra* n.14, Annex 1 at 32, https://iapp.org/media/pdf/resource_center/W29-auto-decision_profiling_02-2018.pdf/
52. Jordan Novet (2018, 3 May). Facebook forms a special ethics team to prevent bias in its A.I. software. CNBC, https://www.cnbc.com/2018/05/03/facebook-ethics-team-prevents-bias-in-ai-software.html; Deepmind Ethics and Society Team, https://deepmind.com/blog/why-we-launched-deepmind-ethics-society/; Axon AI and Policing Technology Ethics Board, https://www.axon.com/info/ai-ethics; Microsoft Fairness Accountability Transparency and Ethics Group, https://www.microsoft.com/en-us/research/group/fate/; but cf. Kelsey Piper(4 April 2019). Exclusive: Google cancels AI ethics board in response to outcry. Vox, https://www.vox.com/future-perfect/2019/4/4/18295933/google-cancels-ai-ethics-board; Sam Shead (2018, 27 April). Google's Mysterious AI Ethics Board Should Be As Transparent As Axon's. Forbes, https://www.forbes.com/sites/samshead/2018/04/27/googles-mysterious-ai-ethics-board-should-be-as-transparent-as-axons/#17918fe419d1
53. See, e.g., Sam Curry (2017, 16 Nov.). Boards Should Take Responsibility for Cybersecurity. Here's How To Do It. Harvard Business Review, https://hbr.org/2017/11/boards-should-take-responsibility-for-cybersecurity-heres-how-to-do-it; Nick Price (2018, 24 Jan.). Why Cybersecurity Requirements Are Growing For Board Members. Board Effect, https://www.boardeffect.com/blog/cybersecurity-requirements-board-members/
54. Sarbanes-Oxley Act of 2002, Pub. L. 107-204, 116 Stat. 745.
55. 15 U.S.C. § 78f(m)(2), added by Sarbanes-Oxley Act of 2002, Title III, § 301.
56. See, e.g., PriceWaterhouseCoopers (Dec. 2017). How Your Board Can Be Effective in Overseeing Cyber Risk. https://www.pwc.dk/da/publikationer/2018/pwc-how-your-board-can-be-effective-in-overseeing-cyber-risk.pdf; NACD Director's Handbook on CyberRisk Oversight (12 Jan. 2017), https://www.nacdonline.org/insights/publications.cfm?ItemNumber=10687.
57. 15 U.S.C. § 1681(b).

Cyber Insurance and Technology Innovation

Judy Selby* and Susannah J. Wakefield

Introduction

The long awaited General Data Protection Regulation (GDPR) (EU) 2016/679 came into effect on 25 May 2018. As companies continue to grapple with the legal and operational impacts of the regulation, many are realizing that despite their best efforts, the odds of achieving and perpetually remaining in 100% compliance are slim to none.

As with any massive compliance undertaking, mistakes and missteps related to GDPR requirements are inevitable, especially in a world where data volumes, connectivity, mobility, risks, and threats continue to increase. Given this reality, companies should think long and hard about transferring some of their GDPR-related risks through insurance.

It's critical to note, though, that finding comprehensive coverage for GDPR exposures requires careful analysis. That undertaking should include a review of the various mandates contained in the GDPR, as well as the company's practices around protected data, its insurance policies, and the law governing interpretation of those policies. Importantly, even companies that currently have cyber insurance coverage may not have optimal GDPR coverage in place.

Overview of Cyber Insurance

Cyber insurance can provide much-needed tactical and financial support for companies confronted with a cyber incident. Generally speaking, cyber

Judy Selby is a partner at Hinshaw & Culbertson LLP – jselby@hinshawlaw.com and Susie Wakefield is a partner at Shoosmiths LLP – susie.wakefield@shoosmiths. co.uk .
*Corresponding author: jselby@hinshawlaw.com

insurance policies provide coverage for both first-party and third-party risks. First-party coverage applies to costs incurred by the insured when responding to a covered cyber event, while third-party coverage responds to claims and demands by third parties against the insured arising from a covered incident.

First-Party Coverage

First-party coverage can be triggered by a variety of events, including the theft or disclosure of protected information, malicious destruction of data, accidental damage to data, network downtime, cyber extortion, viruses and malware. First-party coverage typically includes comprehensive breach response services, including the retention of an attorney, a so-called breach coach, to coordinate the insured's response to a cyber incident, as well as forensic specialists, notification providers, public relations firms, and credit monitoring services.

Third-Party Coverage

Third-party or liability coverage can be implicated in a variety of ways, by claims for breach of privacy including, following the disclosure or theft of protected information, Payment Card Industry Data Security Standard (PCI-DSS) liabilities, regulatory investigations and penalties, defamation/ slander, or the transmission of malicious content. Coverage is available for legal defense costs, legal damages, settlements, and electronic media liability, including infringement of copyright, domain name, and trade names on an Internet site, as well as defamation libel, slander, and disparagement.

Newer Cyber Coverage

Just as cyber risks have continuously evolved, so has cyber insurance coverage. The more recent iterations of cyber policies go far beyond data breach coverage and offer protection against a wide range of the most vexing cyber threats affecting companies in every business sector. Some of the key cyber exposures for which coverage may be available are:

- Cyber Extortion – Coverage is generally available for ransomware payments, as well as for other types of cyber extortion, such as threats to publicly disclose protected information or to interrupt computer systems. Some insurers also will assist with obtaining digital currency to pay ransom demands.
- Social Engineering – Some insurers offer coverage under cyber policies that expressly applies to social engineering attacks that result in the transfer of company funds to unintended third parties. As with all other cyber coverages, care should be taken to review the scope of any

social engineering coverage carefully; some provide coverage only for impersonation of the insured's own employees. Those policies would not cover the common scenario of impersonation of the insured's vendors and other business partners.

- Coverage for Senior Executive Losses – At least one carrier insures against identity theft and theft of funds from personal bank accounts of executive officers resulting from a third-party breach of the company's network security.
- Corporate Identity Theft – Coverage may be available for losses incurred as a result of fraudulent use of the company's electronic identity, including the establishment of credit in the company's name, electronic signing of the contract, and the creation of a website designed to impersonate the company.
- Contingent Business Interruption – Some insurers offer coverage for loss of business income, forensic expenses, and extra expenses sustained as a result of the interruption of the insured's business operations caused by an unintentional and unplanned interruption of computer systems operated by a third-party business that provides necessary products or services to the insured pursuant to a written contract. This coverage can be especially valuable for companies operating in today's digital, interconnected economy.
- Telephone Hacking – Companies may be able to obtain coverage for losses resulting from the hacking of their telephone system, including reimbursement of costs for unauthorized calls and use of the company's bandwidth.
- Management Liability – Coverage may be available for senior executive officers if they are sued in connection with a covered cyber event. Care should be taken to reconcile this coverage with the company's D&O and/or other insurance coverage.
- Bricking Coverage – Some carriers offer coverage for the remediation, recreation, replacement, or restoration of devices that have been rendered useless or "bricked" by a covered event, including by a malware infection.

It's important to note that some of these coverages may not be available from all insurers, and not all insureds will qualify for all types of coverage. For example, a company may be asked about its processes around fund transfers to qualify for various levels of social engineering coverage, and companies may have to have disaster recovery processes in place in order to obtain certain business interruption coverage. In addition, some coverages may be subject to sub-limits and important conditions, such as requiring the insurance company's consent before incurring any expenses. The dramatic increase in ransomware claims and costs in 2020 is expected to drive a hardening of the cyber insurance market and an increase in premiums.

The Dynamic Cyber Insurance Market

As of 2019, 140 individual insurers wrote standalone cyber insurance policies.[1] Unlike other more traditional lines of coverage, currently there is no standard cyber insurance policy form, and there can be substantial differences in terms, definitions and exclusions from policy to policy. These differences can significantly impact the coverage provided. A policy that narrowly defines the term "security event," for instance, may provide less coverage than a policy with a broad definition of that or a functionally equivalent term. In addition, insurers frequently update and modify their own policy forms, sometimes quite significantly, in light of emerging threats and market developments. Nevertheless, depending on a variety of factors including the insured's bargaining power, some terms of a cyber insurance policy may be highly negotiable and may be tailored for an insured individual.

While selecting a cyber policy, insureds can often choose from a selection of different coverage options within an individual policy. Those coverages apply to a variety of exposures, such as third-party liability, breach response, extortion, computer fraud, regulatory defense, website media liability, and business interruption. Undoubtedly, a company that has a good grasp of its cyber risk exposures will be better able to select the coverages it needs. It should be noted, however, that certain types of coverage may not be available to all insureds, depending on factors such as the individual insured's industry grouping and its risk profile.

There also can be significant differences among cyber insurers relating to their underwriting procedures, claims handling practices, and the provision of free and/or discounted loss control services, such as security assessments and employee training, which may be quite beneficial to some insureds. In addition, some insurers prohibit the use of third party service providers – including lawyers and consultants – that are not on the carrier's approved "panel" list. This could create issues for insureds that feel strongly about working with their own preferred providers. Insureds may also want to consider the length of time the carrier has provided cyber insurance coverage, as well as its financial rating.

Today's fluid and evolving cyber insurance market can make it challenging for prospective insureds to meaningfully compare cyber offerings among different insurers. The devil is certainly in the details, and purchasing decisions based on price alone can ultimately prove to be costly. For these reasons, insureds often seek experienced advisers to help them select appropriate coverage to address their specific cyber needs. An advisor can assist in the negotiation of better coverage terms, elimination of certain exclusions, revision of onerous policy conditions and requirements, and consent to use the insured's preferred service providers in the event of a cyber incident. An advisor can also help the policyholder ensure that its cyber coverage dovetails appropriately with the other insurance policies in its portfolio in order to avoid coverage gaps, duplicative coverage and other issues that can lead to disputes with its insurers or jeopardize coverage.

Applying for Cyber Insurance

At the present time, it appears that the vast majority of cyber insurers rely on a written application process in connection with the vetting of prospective insureds. Although there is no standard market application, insurers usually ask for similar types of information from a prospective insured, including customary financial data about the company, such as assets and revenues, number of employees, and planned merger and acquisition activity. In addition, cyber applications typically seek information about the applicant's data-handling and cyber security practices, including:

- volumes and types of data (i.e., credit card data, banking records, protected health information) handled or maintained by the company;
- data collection practices, including through a website;
- business practices of selling or providing data to third parties;
- existence of written, attorney-approved and updated policies and procedures concerning the handling of information;
- compliance with security standards and regulations, and the frequency of assessments;
- existing network security programs, including the use of firewalls, antivirus software and network intrusion testing;
- employment of a chief information officer, chief technology officer or other information security professions;
- history of security incidents and breaches, including how long it took to detect any prior breach;
- prior threats to disable the company's network or website;
- awareness of any facts or circumstances that reasonably could give rise to a claim under a prospective cyber policy;
- prior cancellation of or refusal to renew a cyber policy;
- security budget;
- practices concerning data encryption, passwords, patching, and system access control;
- employee hiring and training practices, and procedures around termination;
- physical security controls (for example, use of access cards);
- audits by third-party service providers;
- technology, cloud, and other service providers;

- vendor contracts and policies;
- policies governing mobile devices and social media; and
- data backup procedures.

For larger companies, the insurer may request underwriting meetings with the company, in addition to or instead of utilizing a written application. Input from a cross section of stakeholders throughout the enterprise, including risk management, legal, human resources, and information technology, likely will be required in order to provide factually correct answers to the insurer's questions. Insurers may require the company's president, Chief Executive Officer (CEO), and/or Chief Information Officer (CIO) to sign the completed application and attest to the accuracy of the company's responses.

Regardless of the approach taken by the insurer, it is essential for prospective insureds to take great care when providing information to an insurer. Written application responses will become part of the policy if one is issued, and many policies contain provisions noting that all information provided to the insurance company in connection with procurement of the policy is considered material to the risk.

Inaccurate information provided by a company in the application process may jeopardize coverage if a claim is later tendered under the policy. For example, XYZ Inc. states in its application that it always encrypts data containing Personally Identifiable Information (PII), and an insurer issues a policy in reliance on XYZ's representations. If XYZ were to be hacked during the policy period, resulting in the theft of unencrypted PII, coverage for its claim may well be at risk. Similarly, if Company ABC represents that a qualified attorney approves all website content in advance and disparaging claims against a competitor are later posted on ABC's website by an unsupervised employee, coverage for the competitor's claim may be affected.

Some insurers also may require the prospective insured to provide updated information before a policy is issued if any responses in the submitted application are no longer accurate. This requirement is more likely to be imposed if there is a significant gap, usually more than 90 days, between the date of the completed application and policy issuance. Failure to submit the required updated information could provide a basis for the insured to later amend the issued policy, which may affect the coverage afforded to a claim. In addition, a cyber policy's "Assistance and Cooperation" condition may expressly require the insured to cooperate with the insurance company in any investigation it deems necessary concerning the application for coverage. Breach of any such policy condition could seriously jeopardize coverage.

Intersection of Technology and Cyber Insurance

Technological developments look set to play a pivotal role in the fast growing cyber insurance market. Insurers are starting to use risk analytics to better quantify and understand systematic risks across their cyber portfolio. They are also partnering with cybersecurity companies to make use of artificial intelligence in assessing the strength and vulnerabilities of an insured company's network. Applying AI machine learning technologies and predictive modelling to the underwriting process may lead to a more accurate assessment of a potential insured's cyber risk.

There is, in fact, a general move towards automated underwriting processes based on the actual security posture of the enterprise. The idea is to match a potential insured's compliance reporting requirements to the insurance policy – to allow the policy to better reflect risk across both intangible and tangible assets.

Indeed, there has been a significant growth of and investment in insurtech companies (which are playing an ever-increasing role in this market) that provide, for example, risk modelling for insurers. One provides a data listening and risk analytics solution, which combines collection of external data with risk modelling tools to support actuarial, product management, underwriting, and enterprise risk functions.

Technological developments have allowed insurers to effectively score a potential insured and, at the same time, give the necessary guidance to their insureds to conduct remediation action to increase their score. There are risk assessment vendors that analyze companies for breach risk and response preparedness and assign a security rating. These vendors are able to gather data on security breaches and use algorithms to assess a company's records management, encryption methods, and security vulnerabilities. They can then assign a security rating and provide benchmarking information to demonstrate where the company sits in the risk assessment spectrum which may in turn affect the terms offered and, in particular, premium and retention level. This may be provided as part of the underwriting process or it may be offered by insurers on behalf of their clients, periodically or as an ongoing review.

That said, and despite the availability of technology tools that would enable insurers to assess both the internal and external cyber security and privacy posture of prospective insureds, it still appears that relatively few insurers and insureds are employing those tools frequently.

This may be largely because, despite the increasing uptake of cyber insurance in certain areas, the market for cyber insurance has been under-penetrated or "soft" (albeit hardening of late of late) with an abundance of choice and available capacity. Consequently, companies are well positioned to obtain cyber coverage from carriers that do not require an in-depth review of their cyber and privacy posture. In addition, for a variety of reasons, companies may be reluctant to give an insurance company access to its internal systems.

Nevertheless, many cyber insurers do offer free or discounted technology solutions to their insureds as a matter of course after the underwriting process for loss control purposes is complete. For example, insurers may offer its insureds discounted "pre-breach" services, including risk assessments, security program design and review, virtual Chief Information and Security Officer (CISO) services, vulnerability assessments, penetration testing, and application security review.

Policyholders may also be offered access to interactive online training for employees as part of the benefits under their policy. There are other partnerships in the market which allow cyber insurers to offer discounts to joint business customers with a view to offering policyholders a more efficient and affordable way to manage cyber risks from ransomware and malware threats. However, in order to be eligible, insureds are likely to be required to use and install particular platforms and/or certain hardware. This may be a significant inconvenience to some organizations – albeit it could also present many advantages including advanced email security, endpoint protection, and malicious internet site blocking.

Coverage for GDPR Violations

Contrary to most organizations' perception, insurance coverage for GDPR violations does exist but, finding the most comprehensive coverage for GDPR exposures requires an extremely careful analysis of available insurance policy options. That analysis should include a thorough review of the various mandates contained in the GDPR, as well as the company's practices around protected data, its current insurance policy(ies), and the law governing interpretation of those policies. Importantly, even companies that currently have cyber insurance in place may not have optimal coverage for the wide variety of exposures under the GDPR.

Cover for Personal Data Breaches

The GDPR defines a personal breach as "a breach of security leading to the accidental or unlawful destruction, loss, alteration, unauthorized disclosure of, or access to, personal data." Thus, under the GDPR, there are three different types of personal data breaches:

1. a *confidentiality* breach, which involves disclosure of personal data;
2. an *availability* breach, where personal data cannot be accessed or is destroyed; and
3. an *integrity* breach, where there is an unauthorized or accidental alteration of personal data.

Coverage for a Personal Data Confidentiality Breach

Most cyber insurance policies provide excellent first-, third-party, and regulatory coverage for a confidentiality data breach. Some policies combine all three coverages in one insuring agreement, while other policies contain two or three separate insuring agreements for these coverages.

Insurers use different terms to describe the insuring agreements in their policies that provide first- and/or third-party confidentiality breach coverage. Some examples are:

1. Information Security and Privacy Liability; Privacy Breach Response Services
2. Private Data Breach
3. Privacy Coverage
4. Security Coverage
5. Security and Privacy Liability; Breach Event Costs; Notification Expenses and Breach Support and Credit Monitoring Expenses
6. Third Party Liability Coverage; First Party Coverage; Data Breach Response and Crisis Management Coverage.

To ascertain the full scope of coverage provided by the policy, it is necessary to review the insuring agreement in conjunction with the policy's definitions, terms, conditions, and exclusions.

The following are some examples of approaches taken by various insurers with regard to coverage for confidentiality data breaches.

Example 1

1. The insurer agrees to pay, on behalf of the insured, First Party Privacy Breach Exposure arising out of or resulting from any actual, alleged, or reasonably suspected Privacy Breach first discovered during the Policy Period and reported during the Policy Period or any applicable Extended Reporting Period.

   "Privacy Breach" is defined in that policy as:

   Privacy Breach means:

   a. the actual or alleged unauthorized alteration, collection, copying, disclosure, dissemination or viewing of Non-public Personal Information or Proprietary Business Information in any form, from any source, because of an Insured's failure to protect such information from unauthorized access or unauthorized use;

   b. the actual or alleged accidental release or loss of Non-public Personal Information or Proprietary Business Information;

   c. the actual or alleged wrongful collection, use or sale of Non-public Personal Information in any form;

   d. an Insured's actual or alleged failure to protect the Non-public Personal Information of a third party that is stored on the Inside

Computer System which has been affected by any of the above once notified by the affected individual or that individual's legal counsel; or

e. (i) any act, error, omission, misstatement, misleading statement, neglect, or breach of duty actually or allegedly committed or attempted by any Insured, or by someone for whom the Insured is legally responsible, or

(ii) any act of a Rogue Party that results in an actual, alleged, or reasonably suspected violation of any Breach Notification Law.

Privacy Breach includes the Named Insured's vicarious liability for the Privacy Breach, as defined in paragraphs a. through e. above, of Non-public Personal Information or Proprietary Business Information in the care, custody or control of an Information Custodian to whom the Named Insured entrusted that information.

Example 2

In the event of a "Private Data Breach" . . . we will:

1. pay on your behalf, "Claim Expenses", "Damages" and "Regulatory Assessments and Expenses", in excess of the "Retention", because of a "Claim" first made against you and reported to use during the "Policy Period" resulting from such "Private Data Breach"; and

2. pay the following amounts you incur, in excess of the "Retention", provided such "Private Data Breach" is discovered by you and reported to us during the "Policy Period":

    a. "Technical Response Costs";
    b. "Legal Services Expenses";
    c. "Notification and Credit Monitoring Costs";
    d. "Public Relations Expense"; and
    e. "PCI DSS Fines".

Private Data Breach is defined as "the acquisition, access or disclosure of "Protected Personal Information" by a person or in a manner, that is not authorized by the Named Insured or any "Subsidiary."

Example 3

A. Information Security & Privacy Liability
    To pay on behalf of the Insured:
    Damages and Claims Expenses, in excess of the Retention, which the Insured shall become legally obligated to pay because of any Claim, including a Claim for violation of a Privacy Law, first made against any Insured during the Policy Period or Optional Extension Period (if applicable) and reported in writing to the Underwriters during the Policy Period . . . for:

1. theft, loss, or Unauthorized Disclosure of Personally Identifiable Information or Third Party Information that is in the care, custody or control of the Insured Organization, or a third party for whose theft, loss or Unauthorized Disclosure of Personally Identifiable Information or Third Party Information the Insured Organization is legally liable . . . ;
2. one or more of the following acts or incidents that directly result from a failure of Computer Security to prevent a Security Breach . . . :
3. the Insured Organization's failure to timely disclose an incident described in Insuring Agreement A.1. or A.2. in violation of any Breach Notice Law . . .;

B. Privacy Breach Response Services

To provide Privacy Breach Response Services to the Insured Organization in excess of the Retention because of an incident (or reasonably suspected incident) described in Insuring Agreement A.1 or A.2 . . .

Privacy Breach Response Services means the following:
1. Computer Expert Services;
2. Legal Services;
3. Notification Services to provide notification to:
   a. individuals who are required to be notified by the Insured Organization under the applicable Breach Notice Law; or
   b. in the Underwriters' discretion, individuals affected by an incident in which their Personally Identifiable Information has been subject to theft, loss or Unauthorized Disclosure in a manner which compromises the security or privacy of such individual by posing a significant risk of financial, reputational or other harm to the individual;
4. Call Center Services;
5. Breach Resolution and Mitigation Services; and
6. Public Relations and Crisis Management Expenses.

Coverage for a Personal Data Availability Breach

Depending on the cause of the availability breach at issue, coverage typically is available for some associated costs. Insurers generally offer coverage for common causes of availability breaches, such as ransomware attacks, distributed denial of services (DDoS) attacks, and malicious code or computer viruses introduced into the insured company's computer systems.

Coverage for a ransomware attack usually includes the costs of the ransom payment as well as the retention of a forensic firm to prevent, terminate or determine the credibility of a ransomware threat. It will remain to be seen whether GDRP-imposed costs associated with notification of a ransomware availability breach, and any resulting third-party claims, will fall within the scope of coverage of most ransomware insuring agreements.

The following are some examples of ransomware insuring agreements in cyber insurance policies:

Example 1

Cyber Extortion

We will pay on your behalf cyber extortion expenses resulting from cyber extortion first discovered by you during the policy period.

Cyber extortion is defined as "any threat made by an individual or organization against you expressing the intent to . . . alter, damage, or destroy any computer program, software, or other electronic data that is stored within a computer system . . ..

Cyber extortion expense means the following reasonable and necessary costs incurred with our prior written consent:
1. money, securities, Bitcoin, or other virtual currencies paid at the direction and demand of any person committing cyber extortion and costs incurred solely in, and directly from, the process of making or attempting to make such a payment; and
2. reasonable and necessary costs, fees, and expenses to respond to a cyber extortion.

The value of cyber extortion expenses will be determined as of the date such cyber extortion expenses are paid.

Example 2

Cyber-Extortion and Ransomware

The Insurer will pay or reimburse the Insured for cyber-extortion expenses in excess of the applicable retention that the Insured incurs directly resulting from and in response to a cyber-extortion threat.

Cyber-extortion threat means a "threat made by a third party or rogue employee demanding payment in consideration for the elimination, mitigation or removal of the threat intended to . . . alter, damage, or destroy data stored on the network;

Cyber-extortion expenses means "1. Reasonable and necessary money, digital currency, property, or other consideration surrendered as payment by or on behalf of the Insured Company, to which the Insurer has consented, such consent not to be unreasonably withheld, in order to prevent, limit or respond to a cyber-extortion threat; and 2. Reasonable and necessary costs charged by: (a) breach response providers; or (b) qualified third parties with the prior consent of the Insurer, to conduct an investigation and advise the Insured on how to respond to and resolve a cyber-extortion threat.

Example 3

EXTORTION We agree to reimburse you for any ransom paid in response to an extortion demand first discovered by you during the period of the policy as a direct result of any threat to:
(a) introduce malware, or the actual introduction of malware, including Ransomware, into your computer systems;
(b) prevent access to your computer systems or data or any third party systems hosting your applications or data, including cloud computing providers;
(c) reveal your confidential information or confidential information entrusted to you; or
(d) damage your brand or reputation by posting false or misleading comments about you on social media sites.

Coverage for a Personal Data Integrity Breach

The third type of personal data breach under the GDPR involves an unauthorized or accidental alteration of data. Some carriers currently provide coverage for such breaches. For example, one cyber insurer offers coverage for a "Privacy and Security Wrongful Act," which is defined in relevant part as any "violation of any law, statute or regulation governing the *authenticity*, availability, confidentiality, storage, control, disclosure, *integrity*, or use of personally identifiable information or protected health information."

Another policy covers "Privacy Breach," which includes "the actual or alleged *unauthorized alteration*, collection, copying, disclosure, dissemination or viewing of Non-public Personal Information or Proprietary Business Information in any form, from any source, because of an Insured's failure to protect such information from unauthorized access or unauthorized use". This provision likely would be triggered by certain types of integrity breach.

Coverage for Regulatory Investigations

Cyber insurance policies generally contain coverage for certain regulatory exposures. With regard to exposures arising under the GDPR, it will be important for US companies to ensure that their regulatory coverage applies to actions by EU regulators (some US policies limit regulatory coverage to actions by US federal or state regulators pursuant to US federal or state regulations), that the incident giving rise to the regulatory action is covered by the policy (the regulatory coverage in some policies is triggered only by a confidentiality breach), and that the policy's definition of covered "information" is broad enough in scope to match up with the GDPR definition of "personal data."

The following are examples of regulatory insuring agreements which may provide only limited coverage for GDPR violations:

Example 1

Regulatory Defense and Penalties

To pay on behalf of the Insured:

Claims Expenses and Penalties . . . which the Insured shall become legally obligated to pay because of any Claim in the form of a Regulatory Proceeding . . .. For a violation of a Privacy Law **and caused by an incident in Insuring Agreement A.1. (Information Security and Privacy Liability), A.2. (Failure to prevent a Security Breach), or A.3. (Violation of Breach Notice Law)** . . ..

Example 2

The Insurer will pay, on behalf of the Insured, Damages resulting from a Regulatory Claim . . . **resulting from a Privacy Event** . . ..

The term "Privacy Event" is defined as "**actual or reasonably suspected: A. theft, loss or unauthorized public disclosure of Personally Identifiable Information or Corporate Information; and B. unauthorized access by a third party to Personally Identifiable Information or Corporate Information.**

Example 3

Regulatory Defense & Penalties

[The insurer agrees to] pay Penalties and Claims Expenses, which the Insured is legally obligated to pay because of a Regulatory Proceeding . . . **for a Data Breach or a Security Breach**.

Liability for Non-Breach GDPR Violations

Although much attention is placed on the data breach requirements in the GDPR, GDPR liability also can arise from the company's business decisions and practices around its collection, storage, use, and retention of protected information, as well as the adequacy of its policies, notices, assessments, documentation, and consents. Failure to comply with a host of additional GDPR requirements, including the following, can also lead to the imposition of liability on regulated enterprises:

- Appointment of a Representative (Article 27);
- Appointment of a Data Protection Officer (Article 37);
- Performance of a Data Protection Impact Assessment (Article 35);
- Fulfillment of Data Subject Requests (Chapter 3); and
- Inadequate Security of Processing (Article 32)

Companies should not assume that their cyber policies will respond to these exposures because, as noted, regulatory coverage often is triggered only by a confidentiality data breach or a security event. Nevertheless, the following provision from a 2018 policy form may be construed to provide broad coverage for a wide range of GDPR violations:

NETWORK SECURITY AND PRIVACY LIABILITY

Insurers agree to pay on Your behalf any Damages including Costs . . . which You become legally required to pay arising out of a Claim first made against You during the Policy Period . . . brought by:

1. A third party, resulting from an actual or alleged Breach of Network Security or Privacy . . .

"Breach of Network Security or Privacy" is defined in relevant part as "Any violation of local, state, federal or foreign law or regulation **governing the collection, storage, use, disclosure, disposal of, or transmission of Personally Identifiable Information"** . . .

The term "Claim" includes a "Regulatory Action," which is defined as a "request for information, civil investigative demand or civil regulatory proceeding brought by an applicable Regulatory Authority or PCI Authority including requests for information relating thereto."

Companies are cautioned to look past the titles of GDPR-specific policy provisions and endorsements and closely examine the scope of the coverage that is being provided. For example, one carrier has issued a "GDPR Cyber Endorsement," but a careful review of the policy language reveals that it provides coverage for violations of only a small number of GDPR articles:

In consideration of the premium charged for the Policy, it is hereby understood and agreed that the Data & Network Liability insuring agreement is amended to include:

2. Non-compliance with the following obligations under the EU General Data Protection Regulation (or legislation in the relevant jurisdiction implementing this Regulation):

(a) Article 5.1(f), also known as the Security Principle;
(b) Article 32, Security of Processing;
(c) Article 33, Communication of a Personal Data Breach to the Supervisory Authority; or
(d) Article 34, Communication of a Personal Data Breach to the Data Subject.

At least one carrier has issued a cyber policy form that appears to provide comprehensive coverage for GDPR violations. That policy states:

Regulatory Liability

We shall pay on behalf of the Insured, all Claim Expenses, Damages, including GDPR Penalties, Regulatory Penalties, and Regulatory Assessments and Expenses resulting from a Regulatory Claim first made against any Insured during the Policy Period or, if exercised, during the Extended Reporting Period, for an Information Privacy Wrongful Act.

Regulatory Claim means any Claim brought by, or on behalf of, the Federal Trade Commission, the Federal Communications Commission, any supervisory authority enforcing the General Data Protection Regulation Standard, or any state attorney general, government licensing entity, regulatory authority, or any federal, state, local, or foreign governmental entity in such entity's official capacity.

Regulatory Claim includes an investigation into a potential violation of Privacy Regulations, which may reasonably be expected to give rise to a Regulatory Claim.

Regulatory Penalties means civil fines or penalties resulting from a Regulatory Claim, including GDPR Penalties, imposed against an Insured by the Federal Trade Commission, the Federal Communications Commission, any supervisory authority enforcing the General Data Protection Regulation Standard, or any state attorney general, government licensing entity, regulatory authority, or any federal, state, local, or foreign governmental entity in such entity's official capacity.

Privacy Regulations means any local, state, federal, or foreign identity theft or privacy protection laws, statutes, legislation, or regulations which require commercial entities which collect, process, or maintain Protected Personal Information to post privacy policies, adopt specific privacy or security controls, or notify individuals in the event that Protected Personal Information has potentially or actually been compromised, accessed, or acquired without their authorization.

Privacy Regulations explicitly include, but are not limited to, the Gramm-Leach Bliley Act of 1999, Health Insurance Portability and Accountability Act of 1996, California Database Breach Act, Minnesota Plastic Card Security Act, and General Data Protection Regulation Standard, and regulations issued pursuant to such Acts or Standards, as amended if applicable.

Coverage for GDPR Fines and Penalties

Virtually every discussion about the GDPR emphasizes the massive fines that may be imposed pursuant to Article 83. Depending on the violation at issue, the GDPR provides for fines up to 20,000,000 EUR or 4% of the total worldwide annual turnover of the preceding financial year.

In many jurisdictions, issues arise concerning coverage for fines and penalties in the first instance, and even where such coverage is permitted, coverage is often precluded for punitive damages (which may be awarded in addition to compensatory damages in order to penalise the wrongdoer and deter wrongful conduct) on public policy grounds.

Although cyber insurance policies generally stipulate that they provide coverage for "regulatory fines and penalties," great care must be taken to carefully review the policy to determine the full potential scope of that coverage. For US insureds, regulatory coverage may be limited to actions by domestic regulators arising under domestic regulations. Regulatory actions arising out of the GDPR would not, therefore, trigger coverage under such policies in the US. In addition, even if the policy applies to actions by foreign regulators enforcing foreign regulations, coverage may be limited to regulatory actions arising only from a confidentiality data breach and some types of availability data breach, leaving the policyholder uninsured for all other types of GDPR liabilities.

It is, therefore, very important to carefully consider policy provisions concerning choice of law, choice of venue, and coverage for fines and penalties.

Although cyber policies rarely exclude coverage for fines and penalties, many policies provide coverage for fines and penalties only "where insurable by law." For example, one cyber policy states:

> The Underwriters will pay on behalf of an Insured the sums in excess of the retention and within the applicable Limits of Liability that such Insured becomes legally obligated to pay as a regulatory compensatory award or regulatory fines and penalties (*to the extent insurable by law*) and related defense costs resulting from a privacy regulatory proceeding instituted against the Insured because of a security breach or privacy breach . . .

Consequently, this policy's regulatory fines and penalties coverage may be rendered moot if the law applicable to the construction of the policy precludes insurance coverage.

Insurance Coverage for Fines and Penalties that are Punitive in Nature

GDPR Article 83 provides that "each supervisory authority shall ensure that the imposition of administrative fines pursuant to this Article in respect of infringements of this Regulation referred to in paragraphs 4, 5 and 6 shall in each individual case be effective, proportionate and dissuasive." Although Article 83 does not use the term "punitive," the facts surrounding the imposition of a fine may provide grounds for an insurer to argue that it is punitive, as opposed to compensatory, in nature.

In the US, this is an important distinction for insurance coverage purposes because many states, including New York and California, preclude coverage for punitive damages on public policy grounds.

In the first example below, the policy specifically designates New York as its choice of law state, provides coverage for Regulatory Penalties, but also notes:

Example 1

Penalties means:
1. any civil fine or money penalty payable to a governmental entity that was imposed in
   a Regulatory Proceeding by the Federal Trade Commission, Federal Communications Commission, or any other federal, state, local or foreign governmental entity, in such entity's regulatory or official capacity, provided, however, punitive and exemplary damages are uninsurable in the State of New York . . .

In the next example, the policy language may indicate that the insurer will adopt a flexible approach in favor of and assisting the policyholder to avoid application of a state's law that will preclude coverage for a fine that is deemed punitive in nature.

Example 2

Compensatory damages resulting from a judgment, award or settlement agreement, including pre-judgment and post-judgment interest, which the Insured becomes legally obligated to pay as a result of a claim, and punitive, exemplary, and multiple damages, if the insuring of such damages is permitted under the laws and public policy of the jurisdiction under which this Policy is construed, which the Insured becomes legally obligated to pay as a result of a claim. Enforceability of punitive, exemplary damages and multiple damages will be governed by the applicable law that most favors affirmative coverage for such damages.

But even in the case of a seemingly more favorable insurance provision like Example 2, if the insured's conduct giving rise to the fine is intentional or willful, the insurer may be inclined to dispute coverage under the policy's "intentional acts" exclusion. If the insured's liability is vicarious or indirect, however, a coverage denial may be less likely.

Successfully obtaining coverage in the UK or Europe for ICO fines is even less likely. AON's 2020 guide[2] to the insurability of GDPR fines across Europe identifies only Slovakia and Finland as European jurisdictions in which GDPR fines are insurable. From an English law perspective, there has been much talk of the "grey areas" when it comes to insurability of these types of fines. However, while uncertainties remain (and acknowledging that each case will turn on its facts and that the exact question of whether GDPR fines are recoverable from insurers has yet to be tested by the English courts), it is more likely than not that any significant GDPR fines will fall squarely within the category of statutory penalties and criminal sanctions that may not be recovered from insurers.

Under English law, the maxim of *Ex Turpi Causa*, may forbid claimants from pursuing civil remedies for damages that occurred as a result of their own wrongful or criminal acts. However, there has been some debate about the extent to which this maxim applies to quasi-criminal penalties such as regulatory or administrative breaches – as well as how, precisely, the defence should be applied.

The case of *Safeway v Twigger*[3] served to clear these muddy waters somewhat by ruling that a regulatory competition fine was sufficiently serious and involved the necessary element of "moral reprehensibility" to prevent recovery from third parties including insurers. More recently, in *Patel v Mirza*[4], the Supreme Court found that the illegality defence will only succeed if the court considers it to be in the public interest to allow the defence. Some may therefore argue that a victim of a malicious cyber-attack should not be prevented from recovery from insurers. And, depending on the facts, there may be an argument for cover in certain situations in relation to certain fines. However, if the ICO considers that the company's procedures (or lack thereof) are sufficiently serious to warrant a hefty fine, it is likely that the court will also view this conduct as reprehensible enough to prevent the company from recovering from others (including insurers) and that the victims of the cyber-attack are, in fact, the individuals whose data has been compromised.

Thus, while many policies written in the UK provide cover *"so far as insurable by law"* the reality is that the GDPR fines themselves will likely not fall for cover. There may be cover for the costs associated with complying with, defending or appealing investigations from the ICO. And insurers may, of course, elect to pay out an amount in respect of the fine (potentially leading to issues in respect of reinsurance recovery). Note also that the Bermuda legislation does not prohibit passing on liability for fines and may therefore provide some excess options worth considering.

Avoiding Pitfalls That Can Jeopardize Coverage

It's important to note that a policyholder's work is not finished once it has purchased a cyber policy. The insured needs to be cognizant of the representations it made to the insurance company in connection with procurement of the policy and understand the affirmative obligations imposed by the terms and conditions of the policy, particularly with regard to requirements concerning notice of a claim and obtaining the insurer's consent before incurring expenses and hiring lawyers and other service providers. Failure to do these things may put coverage at risk in the event of a claim.

Conclusion

For affected organizations, the GDPR creates a wide range of significant exposures that will create difficult ongoing compliance challenges. But as with other business risks, companies may look to insurance to transfer risks they cannot fully control.

Despite common misconceptions, cyber insurance is available for many, and potentially all, GDPR exposures. Coverage for any particular entity will depend on the precise wording of the policy as issue as well as the application of the law governing the interpretation of the policy. Companies are urged to carefully review any potential policy form with regard to GDPR exposures as well as to choice of law and coverage for punitive damages. Addressing these issues in advance can help companies obtain the broadest potential coverage for the gamut of potential GDPR liabilities.

References

1. Grones, G. (2019). Top 10 Cyber Insurance Companies in the US. *Insurance Business America*, viewed 13 February 2021.
2. AON & DLA Piper (2020). The Price of Data Security – A guide to the insurability of GDPR fines across Europe.
3. Safeway Stores Ltd v. Twigger (2010). EWHC 11 (Comm); EWCA Civ. 1472 [2010].
4. Patel v Mirza (2016) UKSC 42

A Proposal for Multiple Instance Learning Framework Application to Protect Data Access Rights under General Data Protection Regulation (GDPR)

Amie Taal[1]* and Odunayo Fadahunsi[2]

Introduction

Year 2021 and three years since the enforcement of GDPR in 2018, we are beginning to see court decisions on the right to be forgotten.

In *NT1 & NT2 v Google LLC* [2018][1], the High Court of Justice ruled against Google, in favour of two businessmen exercising their right to be forgotten. The two businessmen brought separate cases to court against Google following a request to remove links to searches on their names, which brought up a decade-old tax evasion and false accounting convictions. The information was out of date, irrelevant with no legitimate interest to users of Google search caused reputation damage to the individuals and had a negative impact on their businesses.

The case was initially based on the breach of Article 8 of the European Convention on Human Rights, the Data Protection Act 1998 and common law tort of misuse of private information (UK). Google's defence was that the claims were an abuse of the process. The cases also touched on the

[1] Amie Taal is the CEO and Founder of Stratagem Tech Solutions Limited.
amie@stratagemtechsolutions.com
[2] Odunayo Fadahunsi is a Vice President at Deutsche Bank
odunayf@outlook.com

*Corresponding author: amie@stratagemtechsolutions.com

data subject's right to withdraw consent and this was a consideration in the judge's decision for NT2.

Both claims were later consolidated and the decision in the High Court was: a delisting order against Google and no compensation or damages for the claimants.

In September 2019, the Court of Justice of the European Union issued judgements pertaining to the right to be forgotten on *Google v CNIL* (C-507/17),and in the same court the right to be forgotten was established in 2014 (Case C-131/12 *Google Spain and Google* EU:C:2014:317). The Court had to determine the territorial scope of the right to be forgotten among other issues and how to deal with a data subjects requests to remove (de-reference) search result links leading to PII. The options before the court were global de-referencing, European Union-wide de-referencing on the language version corresponding with the member state which made the request. The judgement on this was that the right to be forgotten has limited territorial application and this is not seen as a win in many legal arenas, but as a reduction of protection.

The case clarifies the obligations of search engines processing sensitive data (Article 9, GDPR) but it must be noted that GDPR does not provide derogation from Article 9 on the processing of sensitive data by search engines, therefore the restrictions and prohibition in this article also apply to search engine operators.

These cases highlight the enforcement uncertainty of this right and the assumption that this affords the data subject a blanket right to erasure. The right to be forgotten did exist prior to GDPR and the regulation confirms and enhances this right, an explicit right to erasure. The right is not absolute if there is a legal right for a Data Controller to continue to process the Personal Identifiable Information (PII).

There is still the concern for many on how an organisation can demonstrate compliance with the right to be forgotten especially to the data subject, regulators and the courts. The 'right-to-be-forgotten' was chosen for this case study to demonstrate how the MIL framework can be used and in particular, on email data given its ubiquity and potential to advertently or inadvertently collect personal identifiable information (PII) which may lead to privacy issues.

The chapter explores how to provide insight through the power of using multiple instance learning framework as an approach, to provide the evidence, to confirm that an organisation as a data controller or data processor has implemented a data subject's access request for deletion of PII and therefore compliant with the GDPR's 'right-to-be-forgotten' requirements.

The General Data Protection Regulation (GDPR) Overview

The General Data Protection Regulation (GDPR) is a European data protection regulation that requires both public and private companies to protect personal identifiable information (PII) of European citizens across the world and in the event of a breach, they can be liable for fines up to €20 million or 4% of their annual turnover. The importance of GDPR is not limited to the European Union (EU), and its reach is across countries' boundaries all over the world. The definition of personal data or PII in most non-EU jurisdictions is similar and in most instances, identical to Article 4 (GDPR). For example, in the United Kingdom (UK), the Information Commissioner Office (ICO) has described PII as 'any information relating to an identifiable person who can be directly or indirectly identified in particular by reference to something identifiable' which includes names, both online and manually identified.[2] The National Institute of Standards and Technology (NIST) according to McCallister, et al.[3] has a similar definition and went further, providing specific examples of PII which includes the following but are not exhaustive:

- *'Name, such as full name, maiden name, mother's maiden name, or alias*
- *Personal identification number, such as social security number (SSN), passport number, driver's license number, taxpayer identification number, or financial account or credit card number*
- *Address information, such as a street address or email address*
- *Personal characteristics, including photographic images (especially of face or other identifying characteristics), fingerprints, handwriting, or other biometric data (e.g., retina scan, voice signature, facial geometry)*
- *Information about an individual that is linked or linkable to one of the above (e.g., date of birth, place of birth, race, religion, weight, activities, geographical indicators, employment information, medical information, education information, financial information).'*

Article 4 of the GDPR (https://gdpr-info.eu/art-4-gdpr/) defines personal data and an 'identifiable natural person' as follows:

"personal data' means any information relating to an identified or identifiable natural person ('data subject'); an identifiable natural person is one who can be identified, directly or indirectly, in particular by reference to an identifier such as a name, an identification number, location data, an online identifier or to one or more factors specific to the physical, physiological, genetic, mental, economic, cultural or social identity of that natural person;"

Article 24 under GDPR details the data controller's responsibilities ('accountability') on processing data subjects' personal data (https://

gdpr-info.eu/art-5-gdpr/). As such, GDPR applies to both the entity who determines the purposes and means of processing personal data (controller) and the team responsible for 'processing personal data on behalf of a controller' (processor). These include entities within and outside the European Union (EU) with responsibilities for processing EU citizens' and residents' data through their business dealings.

Data controllers and data processors are required to monitor data flow, share data with end-users if requested and implement data subjects' right to be forgotten. This is a compliance requirement of the GDPR.[4] Data controllers and processors must be able to respond to withdrawal requests from data subjects.

To demonstrate compliance, Article 42 states that certification as an essential mechanism to demonstrate compliance with various GDPR requirements.

'The Member States, the supervisory authorities, the Board and the Commission shall encourage, the establishment of data protection certification mechanisms and its protection seals and marks, at Union level in particular for the purpose of demonstrating compliance with this Regulation of processing operations by controllers and processors.'

Examples of these requirements to demonstrate compliance are indicated in articles *(Article 25(3) for privacy by design and default (https:// gdpr-info.eu/art-25-gdpr/); Article 32(3) for appropriate technical and organisational measures to ensure data security (https://gdpr-info.eu/art-32- gdpr/); Article 46(2)(f) for support transfers of personal data to third countries or international organisations (https://gdpr-info.eu/art-46-gdpr/)).*

Email Communication and GDPR Relevance

Electronic Mail (Email) communication have become ubiquitous and information exchanged via email communications is continuously growing. Over the past few years, we have seen increasing improvement in the capabilities of data storage devices, according to Moore's law which has influenced our abilities to process and store more email data, and at times more than we need. Global organisations with email servers spread across different countries have fewer controls over the data and email content can technically be accessed and read at rest or in transit. It is challenging to segregate PII data from email communications, since email messages can be encrypted to make them secure especially in transit, not all organisations adopt this approach. An Email data repository contains PII which exposes an organisation to a lot of risks, with a potential GDPR fine of €2 million.

To comply with the "Right to be Forgotten", personal identifiable data in email exchanges will need to be filtered out before storage or archiving. This is not restricted to only personal email exchanges but also corporate email exchanges where the mode of exchange is not generalised such as having generic email addresses. There are several cases describing how potentially personal data might be exchanged via emails. The examples discussed below are not exhaustive in any case.

Emails are heavily used for marketing purposes where a corporate organisation sends out distributed emails to targeted customers, and in majority of instances, the customer had not consented to receive such email messages. Emails are also used in everyday business transactions as an efficient means of communication to exchange various types of information, such as confidential, secret, restricted and public information. Email by nature requires one to input an email address. For example, John. Smith@corporate.com – The email address as it stands constitutes personal data as it shows the name and last name (John Smith) and the company where he works ('corporate'). The nature of information contained in the emails could further complicate this. Emails are used by recruitment agencies or the human resources department of an organisation, as a means of collecting curriculum vitae and exchanging personal data such as salaries, notice periods, and other personal data about a job candidate. This clearly constitutes PII which then requires adequate protection under GDPR.

Furthermore, employees stored email addresses, home addresses and phone numbers of their friends, family and business associates in their company email accounts and this is then backed up at server level. The use of mobile devices and Bring Your Own Device (BYOD) initiatives in organisations foster the co-mingling of company data and PII even more. The additional feature of synchronising contacts to a multitude of Social Media sites offered by Google, Yahoo and Microsoft® Outlook to name a few, makes it very difficult to segregate PII from other data types, exposing an organisation to data privacy breaches.

Tracking email flow containing personal data across an organisation is a complex task. However, it is crucial to be able to identify the trail and persistence of email messages containing PII that may be a subject of a request for erasure in the future. Without knowing the trail of personal data contained in an email, it may be challenging to demonstrate to regulators that all instances of personal data have been erased for a data subject, requesting the deletion of personal data.

From an Information Governance standpoint, it is possible to implement policies and procedures around the acceptable use of emails in organisations to ensure that only relevant PII data is transmitted or stored via email messaging systems. However, it is noted that it is very difficult to monitor the contents of emails being exchanged with individuals outside the organisation to ensure that personal data is not inadvertently exchanged. Emails received from outside the organisation may contain personal data of a subject that may be the focus of a data subject access right request, for erasure in the future.

Organisations must be prepared to answer the following questions:

- How would they fulfil a subject access request to exercise the right to be forgotten and have all related PII been deleted from all data repositories in their organisation?
- How do they monitor data flows throughout the organisation in order to identify personal identifiable information?
- Do they have a process in place to map data flows to show where all PII data is stored?
- How do they demonstrate that the request from a data subject for data deletion has been executed?

If an organisation does not have clear and transparent responses to the questions above or a strategic plan in place, then compliance with the right to be forgotten is extremely difficult. In the UK, a few local councils were fined by the ICO because email files containing sensitive data of 241 individuals were inadvertently shared with the wrong National Health Service (NHS) staff. There was no way the email files could be retrieved or confirmed that it had been destroyed.[5]

Additionally, "how are personal identifiable information patterns contained in series of email communication exchanges identified?" and "how effectively are we able to detect if a particular email data contains PII or not?" "How do we demonstrate to a regulator, auditor, data subject or any other enquirer that we have stored the data subject's personal data?"

The questions enumerated above can be enhanced further by implementing supervised or unsupervised machine learning algorithms. In applying multiple instance learning algorithms to identify PII data from a set of email texts the authors also explored how the MIL framework can be enhanced through visualisation.

Multiple Instance Learning

Multiple Instance Learning (MIL) is a branch of machine learning and a variation of supervised learning, it attempts to access information from a collective (bags) based on the constituents making it up (instances). In multi-instance learning, a bag X is said to be a collection of n instances. Many authors define a bag as $X \in N^X$. As compared to single-instance learning, the property of multi-instance learning as described in the notation, allows bags to contain copies of the same instance, duplicate bags and even some bags could overlap. This is one of the higher levels of complexities that multi-instance learning algorithms can deal with.

In MIL, labels are associated mostly with bags instead of the individual objects that come together to make up their composition. MIL was first introduced by Dietterich et al.[6] in their drug activity prediction problem and has since been applied to many other situations which include content-based image retrieval and text categorisation. In categorising text as relevant or not, if the text being searched for in a set of sentences is found, then the document is found to be positive and relates to the subject in question. In implementing MIL, the training set consists of labelled "bags", each of which is a collection of unlabelled instances. A bag is considered as positively labelled if at least one instance in it is positive, and is considered negatively labelled if all instances in it are negative. The ultimate goal of the MIL is to predict the labels of new, never-before-seen bags.[7]

A Case for Applying Multiple Instance Learning on Email Communications for Detecting Personal Identifiable Information

Machine learning has contributed significantly to the email communications landscape, especially in the management of emails.[8] There are numerous examples of machine learning solutions. A simple example could be found in the classification or categorisation of an incoming email as either 'spam' or a valid one. This is based on the conditioning of the email filters with several examples to enable the 'learner' differentiate between valid emails versus spam. We have also recently seen Microsoft's attempt to assist in decluttering email inboxes by learning through the patterns of emails and classifying some as 'clutters behind the scenes'.

Given the substantial number of emails exchanged on a daily basis and the inability to control what is included or not included in them, how could organisations effectively identify PII residing in the European Union (EU) or track personal and sensitive information embedded in them?

With GDPR in place now and the Supervisory Authorities actively enforcing the regulations, it is imperative that organisations become more proactive in responding to any investigative requests for information from the regulatory authority as it relates to PII data being held in their technology ecosystem, to avoid hefty financial penalties and other sanctions.

PII collected during transactions or interactions with users or customers would include the following: names, home addresses, email addresses, age, date of birth, answers to security questions to mention but a few. Multiple instance learning algorithms can be deployed to search through the email as a system. Individual instances in the multiple instance learning system (email sent or received by any user on the email exchange) would include general details included in the email such as email address, subject, time stamp, content, and phone numbers or additional details included in the body of the email.

For our multiple instance notation, we adopted the definition by Maron[9] and that of Maron & Lozano-Perez,[10] B^+ to denote a set of positive bags, and the ith positive bag is B_i^+; B^- to denote a set of negative bags and the ith negative bag is B_i^-; c_t to denote the target concept and the rest of them as c. The set of positive bags is the one that has PII included in the email trail. The set of negative bags would be the one that does not include PII. The challenge is how to identify PII through the review of email archives and their data in motion, and those that contain relevant target concepts and allow the decision makers to act on this basis. So how do we investigate PII from corporate datasets?

Cassidy & Westwood-Hill[11] of 'Nuix' (www.nuix.com) in their interesting work around 'removing PII from Enron datasets' investigated those downloaded from www.edrm.net and concluded that there is a 'prevalence of private data in corporate datasets' as evidenced by Table 4.1.

Table 4.1. Result of the PII types identified by Nuix from EDRM Enron PST dataset

S/N	Type of information	Numbers of items containing this type of information
1	Credit card number	60
2	Date of birth	292
3	Highly personal information	532
4	National Identity numbers	572
5	Personal contact details	6237
6	Resume containing substantial personal contact details	3023

The work of Cassidy & Westwood-Hill[11] can be extended further using our approach.

The target concepts would be an email set that contains any type of information identified in Table 4.1 at the minimum. Other related types of personal information include curriculum vitae containing substantial personal details, personal contact details such as telephone numbers, email addresses, payroll identifier, sexual orientation, fax number, Skype ID; national insurance or social security numbers; date of birth, place/country of birth, credit card details and sensitive information such as health records.

We posit that personal and sensitive data can be located using Multi Instance Learning (MIL) algorithm during PII reviews by regulators, law enforcement or independent parties responsible for performing investigative tasks on finding information relating to PII in email data.

We propose a 'target concept' for the email data to be analysed, to be defined as the PII being searched for in email archives. The target concept could also be of a specific PII data class (e.g. 'personal details' where the dataset contains name, phone number, etc). A bag would also be defined as the collection of email exchanges between various users on the network. A bag could also be defined depending on the search criteria as each of the monthly storages of various email exchanges captured. An instance of the email is described as the email sent or received by any individual within the dataset that is being searched.

Where the target concept of PII defined is identified during the search of the email archives, the email batch where this is located is tagged as positive and negative where the search does not give any result. The email trails are searched and classified as either containing personal data or not. The learner is trained with historical emails containing various PII datasets to enable a more accurate classification of in-coming emails to organisations, and scanned to detect if they contain PII data or not.

Conclusion

We have proposed the application of multi-instance learning algorithm to alleviate some of the challenges faced in complying with GDPR requirements on data erasure. As discussed in the main sections of this chapter, we explored the adoption of multiple-instance learning, which is a weak form of a supervisory learning algorithm fit for identifying PII in email communications, given its peculiarity in using bag-based classification. The multiple instance learning algorithm was applied to classify data relating to PII such that relevant data can be traced throughout its lifecycle where it resides and take necessary actions to comply with GDPR requirements. Defining a 'PII bag' facilitates better identification of PII-relevant data which once defined, the learning algorithm can be trained to search for specific PII data.

The framework will enable analysts in organisations to identify time-frames in which a particular email dataset was exchanged, individuals and groups of data objects from multiple perspectives, identify relevant data points in the data journey through the organisation and when these points were deleted based on the data subject's erasure request. The framework would also enable analysts to trace a personal data journey through the organisation and therefore identify where there could be potential data privacy and protection breaches.

Whilst we have only focused on email communications in this chapter, our approach could be extended to any other form of data storage where there is information flow from one point to another.

Future Work

The MIL framework approach defined above can be enhanced with visualisation to develop a visual-based intelligence tool. For example, using a visual-based intelligence approach to demonstrate the flow and journey of data via the data landscape and showing its audit trail. Our solution would be useful to both the supervisory authorities as well as the individual companies using it as a bolt-on to existing e-discovery tools.

The framework designed can also be extended to outside email communications systems to track Covid-19 and trace data gathering, PII as they journey through the organisation's application ecosystems, are both structured and unstructured data types and graphical research data.

In future research, we will be developing visual-based intelligence techniques and strategies to explore the role of visualisation and data analysis, combined with a machine learning framework such as MIL, in demonstrating the GDPR Right-to-be Forgotten compliance as set out and enforced by ICO (UK), other supervisory authorities or any other party that is interested in an evidence-based demonstration regarding PII data.

References

1. *NT1 & NT2 v Google LLC* [2018] EWHC 799 (QB. High Court of Justice [Online]. Available at: https://www.judiciary.uk/wp-content/uploads/2018/04/nt1-Nnt2-v-google-2018-Eewhc-799-QB.pdf [Accessed 27 December 2019].
2. Information Commissioner Office, n.d. [Online]. Available at: https://ico.org.uk/for-organisations/guide-to-the-general-data-protection-regulation-gdpr/key-definitions/ [Accessed 19 May 2020].
3. McCallister, E., Grance, T. and Scarfone, K. (2010). *Guide to protecting the confidentiality of Personal Identifiable Information (PII); Recommendations of the National Institute of Standards and Technology*, s.l.: NIST Special publication 800-122.
4. Information Commissioner Office, n.d. [Online]. Available at: https://ico.org.uk/for-organisations/guide-to-the-general-data-protection-regulation-gdpr/accountability-and-governance/certification/ [Accessed 29 July 2020].
5. Information Commissioner's Office, n.d. [Online]. Available at: https://ico.org.uk/for-organisations/guide-to-data-protection/encryption/scenarios/sending-personal-data-by-email/ [Accessed 19 May 2020].

6. Dietterich, T.G., Lathrop, R.H. and Lozano-Pérez, T., 1997. Solving the multiple instance problem with axis-parallel rectangles. *Artif Intell*, 89(1-2), 31-71.
7. Andrews, S., Hofmann, T. and Tsochantaridis, I. (2002). Multiple instance learning with generalized support vector machines. *American Association for Artificial Intelligence*, 943-944. Edmonton, Canada.
8. Ayodele, T. and Shukun, Z. (2008). *Applying Machine Learning Algorithms for Email Management*. Egypt, IEEE.
9. Maron, O. (1998). *Learning from Ambiguity*. Cambridge: Massachusetts Institute of Technology.
10. Maron, O. and Lozano-Perez, T. (1998). A framework for multiple instance learning. *Advances in Neural Information Processing Systems*, 10, 570-576.
11. Cassidy, A. and Westwood-Hill, M. (2013). Removing personal identifiable information from the Enron data set. *Information and Records Management Society*, September, Issue 175.

CHAPTER 5

Social Media and Data Privacy

Owen Burns

"When sorrows come, they come not single spies, but in battalions."[1]

Introduction

Social media is an integral part of our global society with on-line platforms facilitating communication, sharing of ideas, posting creativity and art all the while making us laugh, cry, inspire, even foster communities. The platforms can unite or divide people and ideas. Users enjoy news, articles, art, music, blogs posts and other information from their preferred sources and in the media style of their choice. Smartphones allow us to access social media and share information wherever, whenever and with whoever we chose. Network posts, shares and Tweets have compounding daily volume growth. Today, social media is only limited by our imagination and willingness to share information. It also has tremendous power to influence and it can have devastating consequences, in the wrong hands.

The market research company Statista, has estimated that 2.34 billion people have social media accounts and this number is expected to grow to over 2.6 billion by the end of 2018.[2] To put this in perspective, there are 7.6 billion people on the planet which means more than 1/3 of the world population now uses social media. Facebook claims to have 2.23 billion monthly active users on Facebook as of June 30, 2018.[3] Putting this into context this is greater than the population of China which is just 1.4 billion.[4] This offers an enticing market for advertisers and businesses due to the presence of an abundance of target prospects with clearly identified demographics.

Email: oburns31@gmail.com

The Business Behind Social Media – How Social Media Companies Work

There are multiple Social Media platforms which may be characterized in a variety of manners depending on how they are being used at any given time. However, according to Hootsuite, they typically fall in the following 10 categories: "Social Networks which focus on connecting with people, media, Sharing Networks for sharing photos, videos, and other media, Discussion Forums to share news and ideas, Bookmarking and Content Curation networks to discover, save, and share new content, Consumer Review networks helpful for finding and reviewing businesses, Blogging and Publishing networks specifically publishing online content, Interest-Based networks for sharing interests and hobbies, Social Shopping networks to shop online, Sharing Economy networks for trading goods and services and Anonymous Social networks for communicating anonymously".[5]

The two most popular categories are Social and Sharing type networks. Social networks include platforms such as Facebook, Twitter, and LinkedIn while sharing networks are known for platforms such as Instagram, Snapchat, and YouTube. Social networks require a profile to confirm the user's identity which typically includes personal information, such as name, where they're from, information about their marital status, place of work, and other interests. Facebook is commonly used for staying in-touch with family and schoolmates by updating personal profiles, posting pictures and brief comments. Facebook is great for following organizations and special interest groups as well. Twitter also has profiles and allows posting of pictures and information but is widely used for its live, bi-directional conversations. Twitter's news feeds have tremendous following and influences as journalists take advantage of the space for long posts and commentary. It might be said Facebook is more for relationships and Twitter is for news and articles. LinkedIn is a business social network forum providing the updated work related profiles and sharing business ideas and material while networking with common business interests. LinkedIn also provides business services such as job searching for a fee.

Sharing networks reveal less personal information in the initial user profile and are focused on sharing images and videos. Social network platforms also have this capacity but with more limited use. Instagram, owned by Facebook, appeals to mobile users for capturing, posting and sharing videos and pictures and impromptu moments. Similarly, Snapchat also appeals to those wishing to post random images but the data on Snapchat is automatically deleted after being viewed and erased from the company servers after 30 days. YouTube is used for hosting, storing and providing on-going video content and has 1.8 billion subscribers.[6] Viewers have an opportunity to post comments after each video. There are many more platforms with comparable features and service and typically target alternate audiences for specific demographics. However, these networks are the most widely used and have the broadest appeal.

These platforms are primarily made available at little or no cost to the viewer or subscriber with a few exceptions for preferred services. The networks make their money by selling ad space to advertisers. The profiles and network information provides an extremely clear demographic allowing media companies to be extremely targeted with their advertising. In contrast, cable or satellite television advertises passively on any given channel without any ad viewing confirmation. Conversely, Social Media not only confirms the audience but also what it is watching, where it is located, who it is sharing information with, its interests, frequency and duration of watching and how often it tunes in.

Marketing companies also buy and sell profile information which monitors behavior such as what the user "likes" and "dislikes" and the sites he or she visits and other activity. This allows the platform to queue up more related information and provides advertisers with additional instances to place ads relevant to the individual's profile creating an on-going revenue stream for the media company. The content shared by the subscriber provides additional information about the user which adds to the profile by portraying varied interests. The profile expands even greater when others allow commenting on shared similar interests. The net result is a greater customer experience with a dynamic and powerful communication network that has become critical to the world's business and social eco system.

However, there is risk of one's personal profile information getting into the wrong hands or used for unintended purposes. Suppose, antidotally, a certain organization decided to target a group of unsuspecting individuals to get them to join the cause. The organization could select certain individuals with profiles deemed vulnerable and more easily influenced using advance analytics and artificial intelligence. The group may then systematically send profound and even fake information to convey the organization's views almost intimidating the individuals in the group to get biased. Sounds too diabolical to be true?

In sharing personal data, we give access to much more information than just our "likes." Users are typically unaware of the intelligence marketing firms gather from their profile as well as from their behavior which is typically presumed private information by the subscriber. Social media subscribers and digital advertisers may define "personal data" differently with varying interpretations. Users may believe private data only refers to their basic profile, while digital marketers in fact track all activity across multiple devices including location, comments, and messages. Article 4 of the GDPR[7] defines 'personal data' meaning "any information relating to an identified or identifiable natural person ('data subject'); an identifiable natural person is one who can be identified, directly or indirectly, in particular by reference to an identifier such as a name, an identification number, location data, an online identifier or to one or more factors specific to the physical, physiological, genetic, mental, economic, cultural or social identity of that natural person." Although social media companies often disclose this practice of tracking and marketing of PII in their terms and condition, the provisions are arguably written in complex legalese with opaque descriptions of what data will be used for. This language is often difficult to understand for the common lay person and provides the social media platform the right to distribute the subscriber's information as they see fit.

Surreptitious – "Done Secretly, without Anyone Seeing or Knowing"[8]

The Electronic Privacy Information Center, "EPIC" explains users are largely unaware of surreptitious monitoring by digital advertisers building profiles; "There is a significant disconnect between the tracking that companies are engaged in on the web and what people know or think is occurring. The public has a limited idea about how every second they are connected to the Internet, their behavior is being tracked and used to create a 'profile' which is then sold to companies for targeted advertising and other purposes".[9] This disconnect creates a false sense of security putting the subscriber at a greater risk of sharing sensitive information.

The practice of tracking and monitoring user's social media activity information across platforms is intended to enhance the user experience. However, this also expands the digital profile, divulging sensitive information to digital advertisers on social media such as location, time away from the home, access to health monitoring apps, and more. The Federal Trade Commission report on "Cross-Device Tracking, 2017" describes the benefits and challenges of this practice citing while there are many positive attributes, there are challenges with the transparency of the media company making known the practice of monitoring in plain language and the advertiser being forthcoming about how the data is being used; "Not only is the practice of cross-device tracking opaque to consumers but so are the myriad entities that have access to, compile, and share data in the tracking ecosystem. While a continuous experience may be intuitive when a consumer logs into the same service on different devices, third-party advertising and analytics companies with which the consumer has no relationship may also track his or her activity across devices".[10]

Subscriber's private data is often collected without their knowledge and distributed without their consent and social media companies queue up ads to the user based on their activity. Users' behavior on one device may trigger certain advertising on their cross-devices especially with shared applications such as social media. It's quite possible that applications such as LinkedIn may be accessed on a personal device but could populate the work computer with relevant advertising on logging into the same social media account or any other device used for logging in. Similarly, the ads generated on their work computer based on web activity involving logging into a social media platform are then accessed by personal shared devices which could generate ads on other shared devices including a home computer. This concept should be unsettling for the employer and the employee since certain information is being tracked and communicated across devices without their knowledge. Additionally, it could be argued that the searches conducted on the work computer are private and confidential and information should not be shared without the expressed consent of the corporation. Cross-device tracking is great for customer experience but could open an array of privacy concerns including matters of business intelligence, confidentiality and intellectual property and trade secrets.

Privacy is an essential element of social media because of the unique personally identifiable information, "PII," required to create profiles when initiating an account. As such, personal profiles are the bases for each service whether for a social networking site such as Facebook and LinkedIn, microblogging with Twitter, video sharing on YouTube and photo sharing sites such as Pinterest, Instagram and Snapchat in each instance, the profile communicates the user's personal identity and unique information for which to build a network. This creates a challenge in global market where various laws and conflicting attitudes towards privacy exist.

Different Views of the EU and US on Privacy

The EU and US have drastically different views on privacy rights which stems from contrasting attitudes towards private information. The HIPPA Journal,[11] states the EU widely holds the right to privacy as a basic human right. Data collected even for non-EU citizens in the EU is subject to the same rights as EU citizens. If someone from outside the EU was traveling there and their data was collected and processed the person would have the same rights and privacy considerations under the GDPR. The American view to privacy and personal information is focused on the type of data. "In a legal sense, the United States does not provide an overall expectation of privacy. The collection and processing of personal data is generally regulated based on the type of data under discussion. This is why, for example, data related to healthcare is subject to the Health

Insurance Portability and Accountability Act, commonly known as HIPAA, and financial data is governed by the Gramm-Leach-Bliley Act, known as GBLA." Data is heavily regulated in these specific fields with various laws and policies for each industry including pharmaceutical, medical, banking, and financial and insurance services.

Another difference is the EU and US in the treatment of Free Speech rules. To demonstrate this, a NY Times article[12] outlines how the EU and US would approach a scenario when someone may have been photographed behaving poorly which somehow makes the local newspaper or on-line trade journal and the subject would like to erase the information to avoid further embarrassment: "In Europe, the so-called right to be forgotten legal decision allows you to ask search engines like Google and Microsoft's Bing to remove links to the news article on European versions of those sites. (The news article remains available on the newspaper's website.) In the U.S., the First Amendment of the Constitution protects freedom of expression, including the right of an individual to speak freely. There is no blanket ruling that allows people to delete or remove negative information about themselves online." It seems unfair to have this information in circulation when the subject was perhaps only having fun at the time and would like to have the article removed. The view on this might change if the subject was not a law-abiding citizen but a criminal caught "red handed" stealing some priceless work of art or some other crime. We might then feel it is justified as a public service to make people aware of the dangerous criminal and perhaps to make others aware of vulnerabilities. The EU would embrace the basic right to privacy and provide some respect towards the subject's privacy. The US would focus on the news or social media company's right to free speech and support the posting. This example could also apply to other information which can then be further distributed around the web or "go Viral" meaning it spreads like a virus from one person to another. There may be little to be done in the US to stop compromising photographs and images from going viral once they are published. It would seem that our digital footprint and activity may not be totally in our control. This attitude is quickly changing for a more general "inherent right" focus with the new California privacy laws.

The California Consumer Privacy Act of 2018 (CACPA) is like the GDPR with a few enhancements. In a CACPA summary prepared by the law firm, Proskauer,[13] the firm noted four basic rights to the consumer's personal information:

"The right to know, through a general privacy policy and with more specifics available upon request, including what personal information a business has collected about them, where it was sourced from, what it is being used for, whether it is being disclosed or sold, and to whom it is being disclosed or sold; the right to "opt out" of allowing a business to sell their personal information to third parties (or, for consumers who are under 16 years old, the right not to have their personal information sold in their absence, or their parent's, opt-in); the right to have a business delete their personal information, with some exceptions; and the right to receive equal service and pricing from a business, even if they exercise their privacy rights under the Act."

These concepts would seem common sense, if not just good business practices. The fact that the laws need to be put in place is causing alarm since it implies companies in the past were not forthcoming with how information is treated nor were willing and cooperative when requested to delete one's data. It seems companies would risk losing a customer or prospect if the consumer requested to have access to his information and demand the company to delete it. It could be bad for the company's public image and possibly lead to a public relations crisis for the company. Still, laws and regulations such as the GDPR and CACPA are put in place for this very reason.

The CACPA provisions to opt out of having personal information sold to third parties and have information deleted are important stipulations, particularly for minors. In the hypothetical scenario mentioned earlier where individuals could be targeted based on their vulnerabilities raises concerns for how minors are being targeted, by whom and with what intent. There should be societal concern to protect this group from predators even if this group intends expressing its views in the short term or in the long term without an adult's consent. Additionally, a minor's digital footprint could start at an early age when he or she may not have the discretion to know what is inappropriate to post on-line nor possesses the insight to understand the implications. Not having the opportunity to clean up one's digital profile could pose an issue for the individual's future on-line identity as he or she ages and matures and could have a negative impact on one's future prospects for a good academic, professional, financial and social life. Negative information could impact individuals when applying for school admissions, jobs, loans and even insurance as certain institutions check an individual's social media profile. CareerBuilders, an on-line executive search site, states 70% of employers check candidates' on-line profile before hiring.[14] Minors, teens as well as adults should have some recourse for poor judgement when posting information on-line.

One of the key aspects of the CACPA is having the ability to opt out and still receive equal services and pricing from a business. This provision differs from other privacy regulations and could have a major impact on how companies are monitoring an individual's personal information. Historically, the opt-in prompt is typically a one-way proposition; one either accepts the terms and conditions when downloading an application or subscribe to a service or is unable to use the product or services. The legalities in the terms and conditions are often difficult to understand and arguably favors the retailer's ability to collect information and distribute at their discretion. Consumers don't have a choice but to accept the terms if they'd like to participate in the service. However, the CACPA states that the user can opt out and still use the service. Moreover, users shall not be penalized with lesser user experience or added cost. This will impact how marketers can benefit from accessing private information and monitor behavior.

CAPCA will impact social media and traditional companies alike. It is believed that other states will follow introducing their own laws which may foster the need for a national privacy policy. Other countries are expected to follow, as well. An article in Forbes[15] cites several market effect predictions including Data Privacy As A Civil Right – "Fast on the heels of GDPR, this law betters it by recognizing that data is the new gold for citizens. Protecting and governing use of data makes our democracy stronger and less vulnerable to global economic and technological forces. This law is a good first step in the journey toward democratizing ownership through data and AI." Companies will need to get their digital house to prepare for changing privacy regulations.

"Something is rotten in the state of Denmark"[16]

Despite the changing privacy laws, the false expectation of users that their social media profile and behavior is being kept private and secure is far from reality. It is clear that a majority of users are unaware of the dangers and implications of using these services. The Cambridge Analytica and Carpenter v. United States, incidents demonstrate how our expectations versus how information is collected, made secure, and used is quite different from what is anticipated.

Facebook, the largest social media giant with over two billion monthly users worldwide, was part of the Cambridge Analytica scandal where purportedly 87 million subscribers' private information was stolen through a deliberate scheme to hijack and use the groups own data against them to influence their opinion during the recent US Election.[17] The scandal demonstrated how nefarious data processors operate under false pretenses to exploit users' private information for personal gain and greed.[18]

In 2016 Aleksander Kogan, an academician with Cambridge University, created an app called "thisisyourdigitallife" which paid hundreds of thousands of people to take a survey to produce information about their personality which would be used for research. The subscriber was requested to sign in through their Facebook account which provided Kogan with access to all the personal data, posts and behavior of the subscriber. The company allegedly also collected the data of the subscriber's "friends" without their permission or knowledge, a practice known as "scraping data".[19] Private information such as users' contact names and information, religious and political affiliations including messages may have been collected. Kogan was later approached by a company called Cambridge Analytica to use the information and technology to gather information for the Trump campaign during the US Presidential Election. Equipped with detailed intimate information, the ensuing micro targeting political marketing campaign played on the individuals' private emotions, fears, and concerns and was dubbed as a "psychological warfare weapon" by Whistleblower Chris Wiley, former Cambridge Analytica employee.[20] Tailored marketing campaigns were created based on the profiles of the subscriber and their unsuspecting connections' vulnerabilities.

While targeted marketing media campaigns are nothing new, the sensitive private data collected without consent provides unfettered insight to vulnerabilities of social media users and their friends. The stolen information continues to circle the Web until all data is deleted or removed by the publisher.

Although Kogan's project was ordinarilly said to be for research purposes, it could be argued that the application, "thisisyourdigitallife" was simply a cover for the true intended purpose, which was to aggregate data for marketing purposes. This is in direct contradiction with, Recital 50 of the EU GDPR.[21] "The processing of personal data for purposes other than those for which it was initially collected should be allowed only where the processing is compatible with the initial purpose for collection." The app stated a purpose, but used data for other objectives and did not describe the procedure for additional data collection.

Facebook founder and president Mark Zuckerberg apologized while testifying in front of the US Congress for the lack of control and failed corporate procedures, but was never fined.[22] As a consequence of the Cambridge Analytica scandal, Facebook stock price dropped $50 billion dollars while the personal data of tens of millions of people still circulated the Internet. There is a need for Corporations to invest in better internal and external controls for managing data and transparency on how users' information may be used.

In the matter, Carpenter v. United States, a criminal was presumed guilty after his location was linked to the scene of the crime from his historical information and geolocation available on his cell phone. This information was collected without issuing a warrant. This landmark case argued whether his fourth amendment rights were violated. It also raised concern on whether our digital profile can be used and accessed by third parties without our consent. The court held that the government requires a warrant when obtaining cell phone location tracking records "A person does not surrender all Fourth Amendment protection by venturing into the public sphere".[23]

Sarah St. Vincent, a national security and surveillance researcher at Human Rights Watch was quoted in Wired[24] "This is a huge victory not only for privacy, but also frankly for reality...When you share your location data via your cell phone, it's not really voluntary. What is critical are exceptions—the lower courts will have to be vigilant about making sure they're not abused." The matter raises the question of how our digital footprint is used including the privacy and ownership of the information. It may be inferred that one's social media history and information also belong to the individual as they identify the subject. In this instance, one's digital footprint is considered to belong to the individual. The subject had an expectation that his data was private and the court agreed.

This raises the question of our expectation about data privacy and security, in the context of what data is collected, how it is being used, and who has access to it. As what became clear in the two matters discussed here, Cambridge Analytica and Carpenter v. United States, we see user expectations of data privacy and security related to social media and the methods used are far from reality. The information we input in our personal profile and the way we use social media platforms are tracked and used by marketers, businesses, and governments and distributed without our knowledge. While this may make the media platform more relevant, convenient, and easier to use, it is our expectation that information will be used for a positive and professional purpose. Essentially the public has blindly entrusted private information to social media companies with the expectation it will be used in for legitimate purposes and in accordance with fair business practices and meet government laws which we feel are common place.

Users may be surprised to know how their information is sold and distributed on a daily basis as a core business model for on-line businesses. Social media companies regularly sell and market user information through "data brokers" or "affiliates" including reputable global companies such as Experian, Acxiom and Epsilon act in terms consistent with privacy disclosure rights of their clients. However, with some oversight, data can be used to mislead and defraud consumers.

To demonstrate the point of how rouge actors regularly take advantage of on-line social media consumers, a Bloomberg Businessweek article dated March 27, 2018 offered information on "How Facebook helps shady advertisers pollute the internet".[25] This article described how ad space is often sold in bulk by the social media companies to affiliate marketers who in turn sell ad space and run ad campaigns on behalf of their clients. Many of these are bogus ads selling knock off products with fake endorsement. For example, an ad for diet may boast an endorsement from the celebrity such as Dr. Oz when in fact he has no affiliation. Subscribers may be duped out of money, fooled into purchasing fake and potentially dangerous products with little or no recourse. The algorithms intended to be used to serve useful content are being exploited to place false information by nefarious actors playing into subscribers' vulnerabilities. Affiliates may also provide access to fake news or "yellow journalism" by making space available for strategically placed propaganda with compelling images and videos, intended to sway the reader for political or commercial gain.

A February 17, 2018 New York Times article cited Jonathan Albright, research director at Columbia University's Tow Center for Digital Journalism, describes how Facebook and Instagram were used to facilitate fake news during the 2016 US election; "Facebook built incredibly effective tools which let Russia profile citizens here in the U.S. and figure out how to manipulate them. Facebook, essentially, gave them everything they needed".[26] Various posts regarding candidates were distributed casting them in inaccurate political positions. This misinformation was intended to divide the US by pitting interest groups against one another serving competing ideals or intended to sway voters to an opposing side. It should be noted Facebook has added 3,000 new privacy specialists for a total strength of 20,000 to monitor fake and misleading information.[27] The Times also stated they've also "changed their advertising policy so that any ad that mentions a candidate's name goes through a more stringent vetting process." While Facebook promises to be more vigilant in screening political ads which may appease the demand for greater corporate responsibility. First Amendment activists are voicing their concern that this may be a step toward censoring content.

Other social media and on-line technology companies have been more outspoken and opinionated about the misuse and abuse of information and on-line media distribution channels. In a keynote address to the European Parliament in October of 2018, Tim Cook, CEO of Apple[28] said the US should have stricter privacy laws, like the GDPR: "Our own information, from the everyday to the deeply personal, is being weaponised against us with military efficiency," he said. "This is surveillance, and these stockpiles of personal data only enrich the companies that collect them." He continued "In many jurisdictions, regulators are asking tough questions. It is time for the rest of the world, including my home country, to follow your lead. We at Apple are in full support of a comprehensive federal privacy law in the United States."

His point highlights how a wide variety of information is being collected and used to manipulate users. We can infer that the unethical and unjust use of ads and fake news influences the masses without their knowledge. Cook uses military imagery such as "stock pile" to give the sense of the dangerous nature of the information being in the wrong hands. He also states it is "our own information" suggesting we should have ownership and control of our profile and make sure it is secure. It is not just our "information" but "something" that should be protected. He makes it clear there exists fierce and strong technology with "military efficiency" implying it is both strategic and tactical which may only be matched by an equal or a more dominant force. Cook is calling for the

US to prepare regulations similar to GDPR in the US. He is contending that the companies have control of consumers' information and are using it indiscriminately to influence individuals. Companies are using information to target advertising and other purposes such as influencing political views as described above. It makes great sense for Cook to state that our information is "being weaponized" as our views and social maraes which are a support to our society are under attack. He leaves the impression that there is a war being waged and all of us are part of it.

If given unfettered access, organizations could potentially manipulate groups of individuals, societies and cultures by directing users' views and even behaviors by playing on their vulnerabilities. Unlike passive advertising and traditional media, this forum would serve up material which can be selective and invoke certain responses. There are several arguments here; one could say it's not healthy to only see one side of any argument or perspective and one should understand alternate aspects to avoid bias and foster tolerance. On the other hand, information could degrade a societal view including the morals and values that support the society. Both arguments raise concern for fake news and other propaganda. Ultimately, the end users should have the right to choose what they'd like to adopt and at the same time, there is a need to be cognizant of the dangers of manipulating marketers and organizations attempting to influence our views.

Why does fake news tend to perpetuate social media despite the heightened awareness and public scrutiny? A study conducted by MIT[29] found that false news stories on Twitter "are 70 percent more likely to be retweeted than true stories are. It also takes true stories about six times as long to reach 1,500 people as it does for false stories to reach the same number of people. When it comes to Twitter's "cascades," or unbroken retweet chains, falsehoods reach a cascade depth of 10 to 20 times faster than facts. And falsehoods are retweeted by unique users more broadly than true statements at every depth of cascade." This would imply that the spreading of fake news is perpetuated by an individual's bias for unique information versus possibly more ordinary, true information. Sinan Aral, a professor at the MIT Sloan School of Management and co-author of a new paper clarifies "False news is more novel, and people are more likely to share novel information…people who share novel information are being in the know." In other words, people are spreading news to gain attention and to seem as though they have an edge on access to information. This desire to get attention or notoriety of having posted "hot news" plays into one's vanity and demonstrates an additional vulnerability of the user profile which further exacerbates the issue of unethically identifying weaknesses and more easily influenced behavior. Twitter and other social media companies have been and continue to monitor the spread of false news but stop short of violating free speech rights.

Free Speech – Challenging the Line in On-Line

Social media companies need to remove fake news and false information to run legitimate and responsible businesses while at the same time make available a forum to share ideas and embrace free speech principles. As per the author Tim Wu, author and professor at Columbia Law School, "What naturally emerges is a debate over the public duties of both "the media," as traditionally understood, and of major Internet speech platforms like Facebook, Twitter, and Google. At its essence, the debate boils down to asking whether these platforms should adopt (or be forced to adopt) norms and policies traditionally associated with twentieth-century journalism.[30] Today, social media companies control who is going to be on the network and what content is appropriate, not necessarily government law or constitutional rights. However, self-governance may not be the answer.

Wu was further quoted[31] as saying "we have to start talking not just about the duty to prevent government from censoring speakers, but the duty of government to protect the main channels of expression. "There is a tradition in American constitutional law that says that the First Amendment creates not just rights but certain duties. Among those duties is the duty to protect speakers." As GDPR and CACPA begin to build the framework around social media data privacy, it would seem governments and regulators will need to also maintain free speech rights to stay consistent with laws and regulations that govern traditional media.

So, where is "the line" in on-line social media? During a rally in Charlottesville, VA in August of 2017 a young woman was tragically killed while counter protesting against a group when one of the protestors drove his car in to the group. The protestors posted crude comments targeting women on their website hosted by Go Daddy. In an interview with CNBC, Go Daddy CEO Blake Irving said he strives to avoid censorship, but the group crossed the line; "We always have to ride the fence making sure we are protecting a free and open internet. Regardless of whether speech is hateful, bigoted, racist, ignorant or tasteless, in many cases we will retain content because we don't want to be censoring and First Amendment rights matter not just in speech but on the internet, as well, except when the line gets crossed. When a speech starts to incite violence we have the responsibility to take it down".[32] Irving stated the company takes a stand when a hate group targets a specific group or person. Google, Twitter and PayPal have similar policies. However, the post itself was not in violation of law, only a breach of the user agreement with Go Daddy.

Similarly, it could be said Professor Kogan did not break the law, rather, he only broke his agreement with Facebook when he sold the data to Cambridge Analytica. This position is reflected in the matter of Sandvig v. Sessions, where two professors went to the Federal court to understand if their practice of releasing bots and scrapping data on social media sites for a research experiment was a violation of the First Amendment. The court ruled that it was a public forum and that because only the agreement was breached, the actions would not be prosecutable under First Amendment rights. Noah Feldman, a Harvard University Law Professor responded in a Bloomberg article "The only crime Kogan could easily be charged with in the U.S. would be a CFAA violation. If that were to happen, his lawyers could now point to the new precedent and say that there is a First Amendment right to be free of prosecution for violating the terms of service and scraping data. What's more, the decision will make it harder to pass new laws to protect user privacy by prohibiting conduct like Kogan's. If data visible to users under terms of service are in fact part of a public forum, the government restrictions on who can gather that data would be subject to the highest level of First Amendment scrutiny".[33] In this case, privacy was the casualty while free speech prevailed. It seems privacy will continue to be compromised as more Social Media companies are held to abide by First Amendment Rights standards.

Corporate Oversight on Private Social Media

Many corporations prohibit or strongly discourage the use of personal social media, as it could divulge private relationships which may have an impact on the business. The ACLU stand on privacy and social media states that, "The privacy line should be clear: All communications not intended to be viewable by the public are out of bounds for employers or school officials. Laws currently in place are inadequate to protect individuals from these flagrant invasions of privacy".[34] Still, businesses often request full access to social media or preview applicant profiles prior to hiring. Financial companies rely on the employee's network to conduct business and as such it becomes part of their intellectual property. This may include trade secrets, confidential information, intellectual property and other proprietary information that belongs to the company. Social networks most often allow other users to view the contacts of other users. Relationships may be inferred by identifying specific contacts with certain companies and thereby presuming the businesses are working together or may in the future. Disclosing these relationships to the competition could have a negative effect on the company.

Alternatively, an innocent personal relationship could potentially implicate someone on inside trading or be perceived to give someone an unfair advantage which may result in regulatory fines and penalties. This could also damage a company's brand and possibly limit its ability to compete in certain markets. Social media could also be an avenue for fraud and intentionally sharing inside information. Having personal social media accounts would make it difficult to legally monitor and track this behavior. In this regard, companies need to maintain clear policies for the employee's social media activities to secure their intellectual property and reduce risk of legal exposure.

Regulating & Monitoring

There is great debate on who should be regulating social media with varying impact on our privacy. Social media companies and marketing associates are currently self-governing and self-policing, while controversial debates continue to unfold over free speech in state and federal court.

Do we need to be protected from ourselves and allow governments create laws to regulate privacy on Social Media? The government already prohibits certain information to be shared when it could have a negative consequence on the third party particularly in regulated markets such as banking, health and finance. Health industries prohibit the use of patient related information including distribution of information and photographs.

The HIPAA Journal[35] states that one of the top HIPPA violations is posting of images and videos of patients without their written consent citing a case where a nursing assistant was terminated and served jail time for posting a patient's photograph on Snapchat wearing underwear. Other common social media HIPAA privacy violations include "Posting of gossip about patients, posting any information that could allow an individual to be identified, sharing of photographs or images taken inside a healthcare facility with patients or PHI visible and sharing of photos, videos, or text on social media platforms within a private group." Each of these violations comes with stiff penalties and fines. Each of these situations may seem to be common sense but the lines may be blurred when the care giver knows the patient or when something humorous takes place and there seems to be a shared appreciation for the situation that plays out. However, the laws are there to protect patients even when they may not be truly culpable to understand the gravity of sharing personal information.

Still, sharing ideas within the medical community can only help medicine, find cures and give relief to urgent care patients. Doctors and medical practitioners including first responders can benefit alike by reviewing videos, read best practices in medical blogs and even watch "how to videos" for treatment or procedures. The challenge is when someone uses poor judgement posting sensitive information and being casual about the entire social media platform viewing the same information. This is in clear violation of HIPAA regulations.

Patients in health care facilities or in the care of health practitioners also need to be made aware of the regulation for posting private information.

It has been made known that social networking has been found to have addictive attributes and users may haphazardly post information without understanding the ramifications due to their distressed state of mind which may put others' privacy at risk and breach HIPAA regulations.[36] In cases where patients are in intense situations users may impulsively post and respond to information based on whims and potentially encroach on libel or slander laws.

Social media networks are presumed to be for like-minded people and comments and statements tend to lack factual backing with assumed support for common sentiments. As stated above, users may perpetuate news without vetting information or censoring for appropriateness. Algorithms may then group users in affiliations and render additional media to support the cause which may influence the user's values and beliefs.[37] Projecting these ideals could enrage some, pacify others, entice or repel people to the cause. Without some oversight, a society's values and beliefs could be persuaded by savvy marketers, or worse, by unmanaged algorithms. Put into context, we make those things vulnerable that are most important to us, such as our relationships and life experiences and the values and beliefs that shape them, by risking our privacy and security. As with regulated products such as prescription drugs and consumables such as cigarettes, entities like communities, lobbyists, and governments need to be vigilant in keeping social media companies transparent and use best practices to protect the users' privacy on social media.

Privacy, Permission, and Security: "Good Fences Make Good Neighbors"[38]

In order to have privacy, as defined by Webster – "the quality or state of being apart from company or observation: freedom from unauthorized intrusion",[39] we need to be able to protect, monitor and secure our private information. Privacy is not security and security is not privacy, but the two intersect when we give specific permissions for the use of our information with clear parameters. Social media privacy may be considered a matter of permissions and limited use. This includes scope of information as well as the duration for which the information will be used.

The GDPR, CAPCA and other laws regulation will help embrace various aspects of privacy as it relates to social media including the basic right to privacy and global industry guidelines. New rules will need to focus on giving the user power to discern on who has access to his information, what information is made available and for how long. This shift will likely have an impact on the internet, technology, marketing and social media companies alike but it's the morally right and ethical solution to maintaining privacy.

Conclusion

As described in this chapter, social media companies need to do a better job with securing our information as well as providing clear parameters with easy to understand terms and conditions to control and monitor information. However, the responsibility to secure privacy inevitably resides with the individual user or group while being discerning about the information made available on social media to avoid profiles from being sold or marketed with or without consent.

References

1. Hamlet. (2018, October 28). Retrieved October 29, 2018, from https://en.wikipedia.org/wiki/Hamlet
2. Number of social media users worldwide 2010-2021. (n.d.). Retrieved from http://www.statista.com/statistics/278414/number-of-worldwide-social-network-users/
3. Company Info. (n.d.). Retrieved from https://newsroom.fb.com/company-info/
4. China Population 2018. (2018). Retrieved from http://worldpopulationreview.com/countries/china-population/
5. C. and H. (2018, May 16). 10 Types of Social Media and How Each Can Benefit Your Business. Retrieved from https://blog.hootsuite.com/types-of-social-media/
6. U.S. YouTube ad advertising revenues 2018 | Statistic. (n.d.). Retrieved from https://www.statista.com/statistics/289660/youtube-us-net-advertising-revenues/
7. Art. 4 GDPR – Definitions. (n.d.). Retrieved October 29, 2018, from https://gdpr-info.eu/art-4-gdpr/
8. Definition of "surreptitious" - English Dictionary. (n.d.). Retrieved October 29, 2018, from https://dictionary.cambridge.org/us/dictionary/english/surreptitious
9. EPIC Submits Comments to FTC on Consumer Tracking Settlement. (n.d.). Retrieved October 29, 2018, from http://www.jdsupra.com/legalnews/epic-submits-comments-to-ftc-on-consumer-06055/.
10. FTC Releases New Report on Cross-Device Tracking. (2017, January 23). Retrieved October 29, 2018, from https://www.ftc.gov/news-events/press-releases/2017/01/ftc-releases-new-report-cross-device-tracking
11. Comparison of European and American Privacy Law. (2018, April 25). Retrieved from https://www.hipaajournal.com/comparison-of-european-and-american-privacy-law/
12. Scott, M. and Singer, N. (2016, January 31). How Europe Protects Your Online Data Differently Than the U.S. Retrieved from https://www.nytimes.com/interactive/2016/01/29/technology/data-privacy-policy-us-europe.html
13. The California Consumer Privacy Act of 2018. (2018, July 13). Retrieved from

https://privacylaw.proskauer.com/2018/07/articles/data-privacy-laws/the-california-consumer-privacy-act-of-2018/

14. Salm, L. (n.d.). 70% of employers are snooping candidates' social media profiles. Retrieved from https://www.careerbuilder.com/advice/social-media-survey-2017

15. Editors, F. (2018, August 20). How Will California's Consumer Privacy Law Impact The Data Privacy Landscape? Retrieved from https://www.forbes.com/sites/forbestechcouncil/2018/08/20/how-will-californias-consumer-privacy-law-impact-the-data-privacy-landscape/#5aa30652e922

16. Hamlet. (2018, June 12). Retrieved October 29, 2018, from http://www.worldcat.org/title/hamlet/oclc/670411733

17. Chaykowski, K. (2017, June 27). Mark Zuckerberg: 2 Billion Users Means Facebook's 'Responsibility Is Expanding'. Retrieved October 29, 2018, from http://www.forbes.com/sites/kathleenchaykowski/2017/06/27/facebook-officially-hits-2-billion-users/?yptr=yahoo

18, 19, 20. Graham-Harrison, E. and Cadwalladr, C. (2018, March 17). Revealed: 50 million Facebook profiles harvested for Cambridge Analytica in major data breach. Retrieved October 29, 2018, from https://www.theguardian.com/news/2018/mar/17/cambridge-analytica-facebook-influence-us-election

21. Recital 50 – Further processing of personal data. (n.d.). Retrieved October 29, 2018, from https://gdpr-info.eu/recitals/no-50/

22. Live updates: Mark Zuckerberg testifies before Congress. (2018, April 11). Retrieved October 29, 2018, from https://www.cnn.com/politics/live-news/mark-zuckerberg-testifies-congress/index.html

23. Center, E. (n.d.). EPIC - Carpenter v. United States. Retrieved October 29, 2018, from https://epic.org/amicus/location/carpenter/

24. Matsakis, L. (2018, June 22). The Supreme Court Just Greatly Strengthened Digital Privacy. Retrieved from https://www.wired.com/story/carpenter-v-united-states-supreme-court-digital-privacy/

25. Faux, Z. and Bloomberg Businessweek. (n.d.). How Facebook Helps Shady Advertisers Pollute the Internet. Retrieved October 29, 2018, from http://www.realclearinvestigations.com/links/2018/03/27/how_facebook_helps_shady_advertisers_pollute_the_internet_110896.html#!

26. Frenkel, S. and Benner, K. (2018, February 17). To Stir Discord in 2016, Russians Turned Most Often to Facebook. Retrieved October 29, 2018, from https://www.nytimes.com/2018/02/17/technology/indictment-russian-tech-facebook.html

27. Balakrishnan, A. (2017, November 01). Facebook pledges to double its 10,000-person safety and security staff by end of 2018. Retrieved October 29, 2018, from http://www.cnbc.com/2017/10/31/facebook-senate-testimony-doubling-security-group-to-20000-in-2018.html

28. Agencies, G. (2018, October 24). Tim Cook calls for US federal privacy law to tackle 'weaponized' personal data. Retrieved from https://www.theguardian.com/technology/2018/oct/24/tim-cook-us-federal-privacy-law-weaponized-personal-data

29. Dizikes, P. and MIT News Office. (2018, March 08). Study: On Twitter, false news travels faster than true stories. Retrieved from http://news.mit.edu/2018/study-twitter-false-news-travels-faster-true-stories-0308

30. Is the First Amendment Obsolete? (n.d.). Retrieved October 29, 2018, from https://knightcolumbia.org/content/tim-wu-first-amendment-obsolete

31. Graham, D. (2018, June 27). The Age of Reverse Censorship. Retrieved October 29, 2018, from https://www.theatlantic.com/politics/archive/2018/06/is-the-first-amendment-obsolete/563762/34. HIPAA Social Media Rules (2018, March 12). Retrieved October 29, 2018, from https://www.hipaajournal.com/hipaa-social-media/

32. Belvedere, M. (2017, August 15). GoDaddy CEO: We booted the neo-Nazi Daily Stormer website for inciting violence. Retrieved October 29, 2018, from https://www.cnbc.com/2017/08/15/godaddy-ceo-we-booted-the-neo-nazi-daily-stormer-website-for-inciting-violence.html

33. Feldman, Noah. (2018, 5 April). Facebook, Cambridge Analytica and a New Free Speech Ruling. Bloomberg.com, Bloomberg, www.bloomberg.com/view/articles/2018=04-05/facebook-cambridge-analytica-and-a-new-free-speech-ruling."

34. Social Networking Privacy. (n.d.). Retrieved October 29, 2018, from http://www.aclu.org/issues/privacy-technology/internet-privacy/social-networking-privacy

35. HIPAA Social Media Rules. (2018, March 12). Retrieved October 29, 2018, from https://www.hipaajournal.com/hipaa-social-media/

36. Andersson, H. (2018, July 04). Social media apps are 'deliberately' addictive to users. Retrieved October 29, 2018, from http://www.bbc.com/news/technology-44640959

37. How Does the Facebook Algorithm Help Shape Our Opinions? (2017, December 29). Retrieved October 29, 2018, from http://www.rewire.org/our-future/facebook-algorithm-shape-opinions/

38. Frost, R. (2015, April 02). The Vantage Point. Retrieved October 29, 2018, from https://www.poets.org/poetsorg/poem/mending-wall

39. Merriam-Webster. Privacy. Merriam-Webster, www.merriam-webster.com/dictionary/privacy.

US Litigators, Does Your Discovery Include EU Data? Strategic, Legal and Technical Considerations under GDPR

Gregory R. Baden, Rachael N. Clark* and Ben Quarmby[1]

Introduction

The proliferation of smartphones and social media has contributed to the meteoric rise in the amount of data generated daily.[2] At the same time, Big Data, artificial intelligence, and other technological innovations are dramatically expanding the types and volume of data corporate entities are able to harness.[3] A substantial portion of that data is now governed by GDPR, which came into force on May 25, 2018. If personal data from the European Union ("EU") is material to litigation in the United States ("US"), US legal teams will need a solid grasp of the GDPR to avoid running afoul of its limitations.

Such teams will have to grapple with many questions. Is the data they are handling within the scope of GDPR? Is the law firm a Controller or Processor? What obligations result from controlling/processing personal data? How does the GDPR impact the rights and obligations of e-discovery

---

[1] Gregory R. Baden - gbaden@gmail.com, Rachael N. Clark - cyberprivacylawRNC @gmail.com, Ben Quarmby - bquarmby@mololamken.com

[2] A Forbes article published days before GDPR took effect, says 2.5 quintillion bytes of data were created, 90% of which was created in the last two years. *See* "How Much Data Do We Create" in References.

[3] Big Data now refers to the ability to study large, complex data sets using technology using predictive analytics. See one company's analysis in references.

---

*Corresponding author: cyberprivacylawRNC@gmail.com

providers and other vendors? And how do these entities manage the risks associated with data subject rights?

The Rise of Big Data, Artificial Intelligence and the Internet of Things

The GDPR reflects a concern about evolving standards and expectations of privacy following the dramatic rise of several key societal and technical developments in the last decade, including Big Data, artificial intelligence ("AI"), and the Internet of Things ("IoT").

In general parlance, "Big Data" is a catch-all term used to describe the large volume of data people generate everyday while conducting their business and social activities. The concept was introduced in the early 2000s, and arises out of the three Vs: large Volumes of data from a variety of sources, accumulating at an unprecedented Velocity, and in a Variety of different formats, including structured and unstructured data, email, video, audio, and others.

That data is generated from many sources, including items related to the Internet of Things, more commonly known as simply "IoT." IoT, broadly defined, is the network of physical devices, vehicles, home appliances, and other items embedded with electronics, software, and connectivity which enable these devices to connect with each other, as well as systems collecting data generated by – or collected by – these devices, and exchange data. Together those devices collect data about our purchases, activities, interests, location, and social networks.

This amounts to a vast data set on which to deploy technology to conduct Big Data analytics tools, i.e. systems capable of parsing through those data sets and identifying information of value to users, consumers, advertisers, marketers, and sales specialists. The more data a company collects, the greater the potential for profit. Big Data analytics tools are beginning to be augmented with newer machine learning and AI.

(a) What does it mean to individual consumers?

It means that failing to use your IoT-connected toaster for two days may lead you to receive an email alert from your online grocer about sales on sliced bread. It means that unsolicited catalogs of baby outfits may find their way under your door less than a year after your purchase of an over-the-counter pregnancy test. And it means that market entities focusing on the data are able to predict with great accuracy your predilections as a consumer, as a member of a social group, as a voter, and as an influence on others.

(b) How much data is being collected?

According to IBM, every day we generate 2.5 quintillion bytes of data—or 2.5 million trillions, much of which will get stored. *See* IBM – Ten Key Marketing Trends.

(c) Who controls this data, and where is it stored?
     There is no simple answer, but it is already clear that Amazon,
     Facebook, Google, as well as a myriad other entities, control and store
     huge amounts of this data in data centers across the United States,
     Europe and Asia, not always in a manner compliant with jurisdictional
     privacy laws.

Most consumer-facing companies in the US now understand that
GDPR represents a potential litigation risk, even if they do not market to
the EU. A rising awareness amongst consumers regarding the amount of
personal data collected and used by companies—an awareness arising at
least in part out of well-publicized data breaches, e.g., Facebook, Sony and
Ashley Madison—means that US litigators cannot ignore GDPR.

The GDPR – Key Concepts

Expansion of EU Directive

The GDPR was intended to make it easier for EU citizens to exercise their
privacy rights; it replaces and expands on EU Directive/95/46/EC. It
applies to all companies collecting personal data from people in the EU,
regardless of where the company is located. It also applies to companies
that process data, regardless of whether payment is exchanged for that
data. Significantly, GDPR now also gives Supervisory Authorities—the
local authorities responsible for enforcing the GDPR in each member
state—the right to levy significant fines.

GDPR Basics

The framework of the GDPR is built around a handful of key terms.
Understanding the meaning and scope of these terms is critical for US
litigators.
     "Personal data" under GDPR is much broader than under the EU
Directive, and significantly broader than under any US federal law or
regulation. The expanded definition of personal data under GDPR is
—"any information that can be related to an identified or identifiable
natural person directly or indirectly," and now explicitly includes location
data and online identifiers (e.g. geo tracking data and IP addresses).
Additionally, Sensitive Data has been expanded to include biometric
identification data.
     GDPR Article 5 articulates several principles governing the use and
collection of data, which require companies seeking to comply with
GDPR to truly understand the lifecycle of data within their organization.
Essentially, data must only be collected for a specified, explicit and
legitimate purpose, and only retained for as long as the specific purpose

applies. Companies are also obligated to minimize the data collected, i.e. collect the least amount of data necessary to fulfill the legitimate purpose, store it for only as long as necessary, and ensure the data is accurate. Finally, GDPR codifies the well-known security principle of ensuring "integrity and confidentiality" through appropriate security measures.

The "Controller" of data under the GDPR generally refers to the company that has primary control of the data collected, i.e. employers, retailers, credit card companies to name a few. The onus for ensuring the privacy and security of that data lies with the Controller, and Controllers are obligated to take steps to ensure third parties have appropriate privacy and security measures in place.

The "Processor," as the name implies, is an entity that processes data, often on behalf of a Controller. Processing in this context is interpreted broadly: it includes transmission, dissemination and storage of data. Like Controllers, Processors are subject to fines for GDPR non-compliance.

Both Controllers and Processors are expected to maintain documentation demonstrating their adherence to documented policies and procedures. They are also under an obligation to implement strict data retention protocols that prevent the data from being used for anything beyond the narrowest specific purpose for which it was provided. This obligation creates some tension between the guiding principles of GDPR, and the broad disclosure policies of US litigation.

GDPR and Litigation in the US

Prior to the adoption and enforcement of the GDPR, the question of how and when to address concerns regarding EU data privacy regulations was often addressed in an inconsistent and ad hoc manner. The reasons for this varied treatment can be traced to two primary contributing factors.

The first factor was the fragmented nature of data privacy regulation in both the US and the EU. The EU has a long history of data privacy focused on protecting the rights of the individual, an effort traditionally led by the Organisation for Economic Co-operation and Development ("OECD"). But the OECD's guidelines and directives were subject to adoption by each of the individual member countries of the EU. While many EU countries adopted legislation to implement them, there were few coordinated enforcement efforts and the risk of large potential penalties was considered low.

By contrast, the US has traditionally taken a very different – but equally fragmented – approach to data privacy. Processing of personal data is permissible and any necessary limitations are to be imposed through a mix of federal and state legislation. Examples include HIPAA (Health Insurance Portability and Accountability Act), which imposes data privacy requirements on personal health data, the Gramm-Leach Bliley Act, which addresses financial data privacy matters, and the

Federal Trade Commission's ("FTC") enforcement of Section 5 of the FTC Act against companies that violated their published privacy policies in a manner deemed to be "deceptive or unfair acts or practices."

Given these fragmented approaches, many companies were content to operate prior to the adoption of the GDPR in a zone of relative low-risk uncertainty. If they followed the applicable US laws in their industry and any country-specific regulations based on the locations of their EU-based operations, data privacy issues could otherwise be addressed on an as-needed basis if and when the company received a complaint.

The second factor was the rate of change in technology and data collection. The explosive growth of industries such as internet search, social media, and internet marketing – each built on the overt and surreptitious mass collection of consumer and personal data – remains very recent. Prior to that, there was little concern that a given company would have access to a detailed data set covering a large group of individuals. To the extent a company collected such data, it was done in the context of the business's interactions with its own customers and prospects, and thus presumably within the bounds of what are regarded as valid bases for collection under the existing data protection laws. In any event, until recently companies simply did not have the technical mechanisms to collect data as they now can after the introduction of IoT devices.

The introduction of the GDPR has helped clarify and unify the privacy landscape. Simultaneously it has also introduced potential tension with the rules framework governing US litigation.

Courts in the US generally favor broad discovery during the course of litigation. But with corporate litigants now controlling vast sets of personal data, broad discovery in cases involving EU personal data is difficult to reconcile with the protections of the GDPR. US litigators will therefore, at least in the early stages of GDPR implementation, have to make some educated guesses as to how best to proceed in order to zealously defend their clients' interests while avoiding fines from the EU.

The European Commission has already indicated that there is only one possible ground for collection and transfer of personal data for a civil legal action in a non-EU state. Such data must be necessary for a legitimate interest pursued by the organization controlling the data. And the legitimate interest[4] of the organization must also outweigh the interests and fundamental rights of the data subject.

---

[4] "Legitimate interest" is the most flexible of the six legal bases for collecting and processing data. The UK's Information Commissioner's Office ("ICO") describes legitimate interest as a purpose "not centered around a particular purpose (eg performing a contract, complying with a legal obligation...)" and not predicated on consent. It is a flexible concept, but companies relying on legitimate interest must perform a balancing test weighing the legitimate interest and the rights of the data subject. *See* References.

US litigants will also look to the standard articulated in *Societe Nationale Industrielle Aerospatiale v. US Dist. Ct. S.D. Iowa* and various district court rulings for guidance on balancing the right to litigation discovery in the US with the risk of fines for GDPR non-compliance. And they will need to keep a close eye on the various Supervisory Authorities to determine how aggressive they are expected to be, particularly when dealing with non-EU entities operating in a purely legal setting.[5]

Key Questions for US Litigants – A Hypothetical Scenario

As US litigation involving GDPR-covered data becomes more prevalent, litigants and the courts will have to resolve key questions regarding the reach and scope of the GDPR. The following hypothetical will help navigate through some of those questions.

FACTS. Leading German car manufacturer Hamburger Motor Wagen (HMW) launched its first fully autonomous motor vehicle—the Solo 100 in May 2018. The Solo 100 is a driverless machine designed to meet the safety and road regulations of all major auto markets. At launch, it was widely expected to sell heavily across Europe, and in the US.

The Solo 100 is a cutting-edge piece of electronic technology. It is controlled from an 8×10 touch screen located between the two front seats. That screen allows the user to regulate the final destination, the route taken, stops on the way, cabin parameters, music, gas levels and fuel efficiency, among many other aspects of the driving experience. It can also offer recommendations—should the user desire them—for any data point, e.g. what music to listen to at any given point, where to stop for gas, what scenic points to visit, all based on past preferences of the owner, as well as upon the aggregated data HMW has collected about the preferences of other owners of the Solo 100. And the list goes on.

User preferences and choices are stored within the on-board hard drives, as well as dedicated servers of HMW located in Germany, to which the car is connected at all times. The Solo 100 offers a safe, pleasant, and smooth ride. And it seems to know everything about you.

---

[5] At the time of writing, there have been mixed signals on this front. The British Supervisory Authority has signaled that it is generally opposed to fines as a means of ensuring compliance. But the European Commission has concurrently filed an *amicus curiae* (friend of the court) brief with the US Supreme Court suggesting that foreign authorities are going to be much more active in defending the GDPR's rights in US courts. Brief of the European Commission on behalf of the European Union as *Amicus Curiae* Supporting Neither Party, *US v. Microsoft Corp.*, No. 17-2 (S. Ct. Dec. 13, 2017) (the "EC Brief").

ISSUE 1. *Does the data stored by the car and on the HMW servers qualify as personal data under the GDPR?*

The data stored by the Solo 100 and on the HMW servers qualifies as personal data, as it falls squarely within the broad definition of that term in Article 4(1).

US litigators may be familiar with the term "personally identifiable information," or "PII," that has been used over the last decade with respect to data privacy law and regulations in the US. At the same time litigators must understand that the term PII and its common usages under US laws are not interchangeable with "personal data" under the GDPR.

PII is defined in the NIST Special Publication 800-122 as "any information about an individual maintained by an agency, including (1) any information that can be used to distinguish or trace an individual's identity, such as name, social security number, date and place of birth, mother's maiden name, or biometric records; and (2) any other information that is linked or linkable to an individual, such as medical, educational, financial, and employment information."

PII appears at first blush similar to "personal data" under Article 4(1)—"'personal data' means any information relating to an identified or identifiable natural person ('data subject'); an identifiable natural person is one who can be identified, directly or indirectly, in particular by reference to an identifier such as a name, an identification number, location data, an online identifier or to one or more factors specific to the physical, physiological, genetic, mental, economic, cultural or social identity of that natural person." But "personal data" is in fact much broader, as it includes "any information *relating to* . . . a data subject . . . who can be identified *directly or indirectly* . . . by reference to an identifier."

The European Court of Justice's ("CJEU") decision in *Breyer v. Germany*, EU:C:2016:779, Case C-582/14 (Oct. 19, 2016) gave some perspective on the scope of the term. Breyer, a German citizen, challenged the German government's practice of storing dynamic internet protocol (IP) addresses of visitors to government websites. Dynamic IP addresses identify the computer that is requesting access to a website. But, unlike static IP addresses that are assigned to a specific known physical address or computer, a dynamic IP address is managed by an internet service provider ("ISP"). And it is assigned dynamically to the ISP's customers depending on when they connect to the internet.

Breyer, like other customers of his ISP, was assigned a different dynamic IP address each time he connected to the internet. He could only be identified as a visitor to a German government website by (i) obtaining a complete record of the dynamic IP addresses assigned to his account by his ISP over a period of time, (ii) matching those addresses to those registered on the website, and (iii) filtering the addresses to account for uses by individuals other than him—for example family members, or guests.

Nonetheless, the CJEU held that "a dynamic IP address registered by an online media services provider when a person accesses a website open to the public constitutes personal data." In reaching its decision, the court lent great weight to the ability to identify an individual "indirectly," noting that "it is not required that all the information enabling the identification of the data subject must be in the hands of one person," and that data can be personal data if the means to identify an individual might "reasonably be used by both the Controller and by 'any other person.'"

The Article 29 Data Protection Working Party's "Opinion 03/2017 on Processing personal data in the context of Cooperative Intelligent Transport Systems (C-ITS)," adopted on October 4, 2017, provides additional guidance on the scope of personal data. It addressed the question of whether data exchanged on a peer-to-peer basis between vehicles and other transportation infrastructure facilities would be considered personal. The Opinion concluded unequivocally that it would. Indeed, the data is directly associated with the sending vehicle, which is in turn strongly associated with a given individual. Because the data includes specific data about the vehicle's operations, including timestamps, location data, and dimensions of the vehicle, it amounts to personal data.

The data collected and managed by HMW in the Solo 100 automobiles and the HMW servers—both the operational data and the personal data may associate with the owners or operators of the cars—would thus in all likelihood qualify as personal data under the GDPR. Any US litigation team undertaking a matter relating to the operation of HMW's cars or, more broadly, HMW's business usage of the data it collects from the cars, must think carefully about the broad scope of the GDPR's definition of personal data to ensure compliance with the GDPR's requirements in the processing of any information discovered.

FACTS. As predicted the Solo 100 is a roaring success in the EU and abroad. By June , 2018, HMW had sold over 500 units in the United States and over 25,000 across the EU.

Unfortunately, the car also made headlines in the United States for the wrong reasons. After customer complaints, HMW subsidiary HMW US was forced to acknowledge isolated reports that some vehicles appear to have gained unauthorized and unexplained access to user data, including data points defined as personal data under the GDPR, which was not provided by the owners. An owner driving into the Costco parking lot was astonished when the touch screen flashed his Costco club card identification number, while another reported that her vehicle informed her that her driver's license needed to be renewed.

Lawyers promptly got wind of this, and by July 2018 HMW US and its parent company in Germany were the targets of several consumer class actions initiated by a handful of plaintiffs' firms.

In order to have the class certified (i.e. to have a court allow the class action to proceed), Plaintiffs must show, among other things, commonality, typicality and adequacy of representation for the class. Counsel for HMW US and HMW (Germany) insist that any discovery into these issues must be limited to vehicles sold in the US. Plaintiffs respond with the argument that the technical issues in question relate to data analytics, automated decision making and other marketing techniques designed and carried out in Germany. In their view, for allowing courts to properly assess and certify a class of owners, the extent of deployment of these marketing techniques in vehicles sold in Europe,needs to be ascertained. They conclude that the need for reliable evidence to this effect is necessary to exercise their legal right to prosecute their case (Article 49(1)(e)). Defendants have moved for a protective order from the Court on the grounds that the data sought by Plaintiffs is protected under the GDPR.

ISSUE 2. *May a judge order discovery of information that is covered by the GDPR?*

A US court assessing whether it may order discovery of the information sought in this case—information that may include personal data subject to the GDPR—will face an unsettled set of precedents and governing regulations. While it is more likely than not that a US court would order the discovery sought from HMW, Plaintiffs may nonetheless find themselves in a German court seeking an order to force HMW to comply with a discover order issued by a US court.

Article 48 of the GDPR contemplates the situation of a non-EU court issuing a ruling that requires a data Controller or Processor in the EU to transfer or disclose personal data to a party not located in the EU. Under Article 48, a US court's discovery order would only be recognized or enforceable if it was "based on an international agreement, such as a mutual legal assistance treaty" (MLAT). While the US has MLATs in place with both the EU generally and Germany specifically, these address discovery sought only in criminal matters. *See* References.

When dealing with general civil discovery requests from the US to EU countries, litigants have traditionally relied on the exercise of US Federal Rule of Civil Procedure 34, which requires the responding party to make an effort in good faith to secure permission to disclose the requested information. However, this would not pass under the terms of GDPR Article 48.

Litigants can also try to rely on Hague Convention letters of request and the rogatory letters process to obtain discovery of evidence located in foreign jurisdictions. But the Hague Convention process is followed in an inconsistent manner among different jurisdictions, and it is unlikely that a court would consider the current MLATs to be sufficient or applicable as contemplated under Article 48 given their focus on criminal matters.

The text of Article 49 of the GDPR may, however, offer an alternative to the apparent limitations imposed by Article 48. Article 49(e) allows for "a transfer of personal data . . . on one of the following conditions . . . the transfer is necessary for the establishment, exercise or defense of the legal claims." Article 48 also provides that its requirements are "without prejudice to other grounds for transfer pursuant to this Chapter." Does relying on Article 49(e) in lieu of Article 48, put the US court on a solid footing to allow the discovery sought by Plaintiffs and the subsequent transfer of the personal data controlled by HWM to the US? Unfortunately, the issue is not so easily resolved.

The European Commission ("EC"), the executive body of the EU with the power to enforce EU-wide legislation such as the GDPR, provided a window into its thinking on this front in an *amicus curiae* brief filed in the *United States v. Microsoft* case argued in 2018. *See* EC Brief. There the EC expressly addressed the issue of a data Controller subject to the GDPR, such as HMW, having a continuing obligation to comply with the GDPR. It explained in particular that any collection and transfer for US discovery obligations must comply with the GDPR ("Production of data stored in the European Union is addressed by EU privacy law") and that "a foreign court order does not, as such, make a transfer lawful under the GDPR." EC Brief at 8, 14.

Similarly, and although it predated the GDPR, the European advisory board on data protection, commonly referred to as the Working Party 29, stated that when considering how an EU party should respond to a US discovery request of personal data, a balance of interest test should be used. That balance should "take into account issues of proportionality, the relevance of the personal data to the litigation and the consequences for the data subject. Adequate safeguards would also have to be put in place . . ." *See* Data Protection Working Party in References. So while a US court might order discovery of GDPR-protected data, the parties to the litigation are not relieved of the obligations imposed by the GDPR. As a result because of this ongoing compliance obligation, HMW is likely to argue for the imposition of stringent data protection arrangements on the Plaintiffs in order to ensure that HMW could continue to meet its obligations as a Controller under the GDPR.

Finally, denying HMW's request for a protective order and ordering discovery with a robust set of data arrangements would be consistent with the Supreme Court's guidance in *Aerospatiale* and subsequent court opinions. *Aerospatiale* requires a comittie analysis that considers the following five factors: "(1) the importance to the . . . litigation of the documents or other information requested; (2) the degree of specificity of the request; (3) whether the information originated in the United States; (4) the availability of alternative means of securing the information; and (5) the extent to which noncompliance with the request would undermine important interests of the United States, or compliance with the request would undermine important interests of the state where the information is located." *Aerospatiale*, 544 US at 544 n.28 (*quoting* the Restatement of Foreign Relations Law of the United States (Revised) § 437(1) (c) (Tent. Draft No. 7, 1986) (approved May 14, 1986) (Restatement).

The first four factors would all point in favor of allowing discovery— the data is necessary to the claims; the request is specific to the data controlled by HMW; certainty of data originating in the US with respect to the Plaintiffs; and there appears to be no alternative means to obtain the data. On the fifth factor, in balancing the discovery order with potential compliance and the order undermining the EU and interests in GDPR compliance, US courts have consistently held that though privacy rights of EU citizens are important, they do not override the "substantial interests of vindicating the rights of American plaintiffs". *See St. Jude Medical S.C., Inc. v. Janssen-Counotte*, 104 F. Supp. 3d 1150, 1161-65, 1168 (D. Or. 2015) (citing cases involving US ordered discovery from foreign jurisdictions, including data subject to Germany's Federal Data Protection Law, which was based on the EU directive on data privacy prior to the enactment of the GDPR and ordering discovery of personal data, holding that there was no blanket protection to the personal data sought under the German Data Privacy statute but requiring all personal data be produced as attorneys' eyes only and, if necessary, filed under seal); *see also In re Auto. Refinishing Paint Antitrust Litig.*, 358 F.3d 288, 304 (3d Cir. 2004) (stating that the court had not "identified a single instance where a German national has been prosecuted, penalized, or sanctioned under German law for complying with discovery orders from a United States judicial or administrative proceeding").

Accordingly, it is likely the US court would deny a defendant's request for a protective order and allow discovery of the HMW data that is covered by the GDPR. Also, it would make allowances in all likelihood for protecting personal data to ensure HMW could continue to meet its obligations under the GDPR.

FACTS. The court ultimately denies the request for a protective order, and rules that discovery of data relating to the European Solo 100s is allowable. Given the amount of data to be reviewed and processed in discovery, counsel for defendants begin making arrangements to transfer the data to the US, review and process it, and present it to the opposing counsel. This entails, among other things, lining up discovery vendors, retaining contract attorneys to review the data, and performing an internal analysis to determine whether the data collection, review, and production is GDPR-compliant.

ISSUE 3. *Are law firms Controllers or Processors? Do discovery vendors qualify? And if so, are law firms responsible for the actions of their discovery vendor agents? Will law firms follow in the footsteps of many corporate entities and start hiring data protection officers?*

Based upon the definitions of "Controller" and "Processor" under Article 4 of the GDPR, law firms receiving information from third parties pursuant to discovery requests will be considered Processors. The litigant from whom the personal data is received, in this case HMW, will be the Controller.

Pursuant to Article 4(7), a Controller is "the natural or legal person ... who, alone or jointly with others, determines the purpose and means of processing personal data." The "purpose and means" of data processing here is to understand how and why HMW obtained certain types of Solo 100 data, and what HMW intended to do with them. HMW collected the data, and remains the Controller of that data.

Plaintiffs' counsel, on the other hand, becomes a Processor—the "natural or legal person ... who processes personal data on behalf of the Controller." That is the case even though, in the context of litigation, the processing might take place on behalf of the Controller but adverse to its interests. As a Processor, the Plaintiffs' law firm must conduct processing activities as defined in Article 4(2).

Discovery vendors engaged by the Plaintiffs' counsel to process the data produced by the defendants will be considered sub-processors under Article 28. Under Article 28(2), the parties must cooperate on the designation of appropriate discovery vendors. Thus, the Plaintiff/Processor, is required to obtain the authorization of the Controller prior to engaging a sub-processor (the discovery vendor). That discovery vendor will be subject to Court-established terms and conditions established for the discovery of personal data pursuant to Article 28(4).

But even though the discovery vendor is bound by those terms and conditions, the Plaintiffs' law firm is still ultimately responsible for the vendor's actions and compliance with GDPR requirements pursuant to Article 28(4). "Wherever the other processor fails to fulfil its data protection obligations, the initial processor shall remain fully liable to the Controller for the its failure." This means that law firms ultimately remain responsible and fully liable to the Controller (i.e., likely the party that produced the data) and thus may have significant risk exposure in cases involving a significant amount of personal data involved.

Given the significant potential risk of liability for non-compliance, it is strongly suggested that law firms appoint a data protection officer under Section 4 of the GDPR. This particularly pertains to, (a) law firms whose regular data collection practices involving clients and potential clients in the EU may give rise to GDPR concerns; and (b) firms whose practice involves the regular receipt and processing of large scale potential personal data from the EU, , such as in the context of class action practice. *See* Article 37(1)b ("the core activities of the Controller or the processor consist of processing on a large scale of special categories of data pursuant to Article 9").

FACTS. A handful of European Solo 100 users have now caught wind of the US-based litigation. Each of these users claims a right to be forgotten in light of Article 17 of the European Data Protection Regulation. In their view, dissemination of their data to US litigants infringes on that right. They have initiated court proceedings in Germany to block the transfer of data. The US law firm for the auto manufacturer, having issued litigation hold notices to its clients, now has to determine whether and how this litigation might impact its client and the process.

ISSUE 4. *How do litigation hold obligations apply in light of the right to be forgotten?*

Article 17 of GDPR codifies the well-known principle of the "right to be forgotten." But there are several exceptions upon which a company may rely to deny a data subject's request for erasure of their data. One such exception is for the "establishment, exercise or defense of legal claims (Article 17 (3)(e)). Accordingly, if litigation is imminent, and the litigation hold is issued and followed in good faith, information subject to the right to be forgotten may nonetheless be retained. Because the litigation hold does not exempt the data covered by the hold from being defined as personal data subject to processing, US companies and litigators need to be diligent in their treatment of data subject to the litigation hold.

That said, the party invoking the litigation hold as a reason for denying a data subject's request to have their data deleted must still promptly notify the data subject of the reason for the denial. It must also be prepared to justify the scope, duration and reason for the litigation hold. Litigation holds should be as narrowly tailored as possible to preserve the necessary relevant information. Organizations should also periodically review the litigation hold so that it may be removed promptly when it is no longer necessary.

FACTS. Separately, Solo 100 owners have submitted a complaint with the independent supervisory authority (SA) established by Germany. After initiating expedited proceedings to prevent dissemination of personal data for use in the US litigation, those owners have obtained an order from the SA determining that personal data ordered to be disclosed by the US court is indeed personal data, and that its disclosure by US-based Controllers in the context of litigation will give rise to fines under the GDPR.

US counsel for the auto manufacturer, having been alerted to the SA proceedings, now seeks guidance from the US court. In particular, it seeks modification of the court order mandating production of the EU data in the litigation.

ISSUE 5. *How is the court likely to balance the respective interests of the US discovery system and the GDPR? Will litigants simply find themselves between a rock and a hard place, forced to choose between judicially imposed sanctions or fines from an EU National authority?*

There is no clear-cut answer to this question at this stage, and little if any precedent from which to determine the likely outcome before a court. The uncertainty on this point is further compounded by the fact that trial-level US judges are likely to have widely varying views on the adequate weight to be given to the pronouncements of a foreign jurisdiction.

That said, the formal imposition of fines—or the threat of such fines—may help tip the scales under the five-factor *Aerospatiale* analysis. For the reasons set forth above, the first four factors of that test—importance of documents, degree of specificity of the request, place of origin of the data, availability of alternatives—may well weigh in favor of allowing discovery. But most judges could be expected to be swayed in their judgment when faced with evidence that compliance with their order would subject a party, a law firm, or an e-discovery vendor to financial ruin.

Courts may ultimately devise procedures intended as a compromise measure, allowing the use of data to permit the US litigation to proceed, while minimizing the scope and impact of disclosure. One could foresee, for example, only a court appointed special master, or an independent expert, alone to receive and process the data in question, disclosing his or her conclusions to the Court and the parties using only anonymized data. That special master or expert could conceivably be based in the European jurisdiction from which the data originates, to avoid any concerns about data crossing international borders.

FACTS. The court, refusing to subject its proceedings to the diktats of a foreign jurisdiction, orders the defendant and its counsel to adhere to the discovery order and produce the requested data. Facing significant fines under the GDPR, the law firm and its discovery vendor turn to their clients to address further steps.

ISSUE 6. *When, and under what circumstances, are discovery vendors and law firms likely to find themselves exposed to GDPR fines? And to what extent is that liability likely to be attributable to their clients?*

Law firms and e-discovery vendors qualify as Controllers and processors of GDPR protected data under our hypothesis, and by extension they are subject to potential fines from European SAs. However, that is not to say that they are likely to be actually subjected to such fines.

As a threshold matter, one should expect law firms and e-discovery vendors to routinely include broad indemnification provisions into their engagement letters specifically contemplating potential fines under the GDPR. Whether those will be recognized by the SA as an allowable transfer of liability is not clear, and may well vary from jurisdiction to jurisdiction. What is certain is that these clauses are going to start appearing in most, if not of all, engagement letters drafted by law firms and e-discovery vendors.

Moreover, even if vendors and law firms behave in ways which warrant fines from the SA, the bottom line remains that they are very unlikely to be subject to any fines, at least in the short term. Indeed, the new GDPR framework applies broadly to hundreds, if not thousands, of entities around the world. Yet it is enforced and regulated by a limited number of SAs with broad powers but limited physical and financial resources.

Are those SAs likely to aggressively enforce the GDPR? Yes, they are. Will they have any difficulty identifying offenders, particularly in the early stages of GDPR enforcement when the boundaries of the regulations are far from clear? Absolutely not. The Amazons, Googles, Facebooks and Netflixes of this world are likely to be squarely in the sights of the SAs from the outset. But that also means that US law firms and e-discovery vendors are not likely to be high on the priority list of these SAs, at least in the early years. So while the threat of fines is real, it may be awhile before any such entities are in fact fined because of their actions in connection with US litigation.

Conclusion

While US litigators and law firms have traditionally given little thought to compliance with EU data privacy regulations, this attitude is no longer permissible in light of the requirements of, and potential fines under, the GDPR. This is particularly true as US litigation grows to routinely involve ever larger and more personal aggregations of Big Data, collected through the use of IoT sensors and devices.

Where litigation over car defects may have once only covered the documents and communications among a manufacturer's engineers and designers, autonomous vehicles add an entirely new dimension of collected data, both with respect to the vehicle's operation as well as the personal data captured from the car's operator. The hypothesis described above is just one facet of a problem that is going to arise time and time again as an increasing number of everyday products collect significant quantities of personal data that may be subject to data privacy regulations. US lawyers must adapt to the changing landscape and recognize that data privacy regulations are no longer a subject to pass along to their specialist colleagues. It must be part of their core strategic planning considerations in data-intensive litigation matters.

References

How Much Data Do We Create. https://www.forbes.com/sites/bernardmarr/2018/05/21/how-much-data-do-we-create-every-day-the-mind-blowing-stats-everyone-should-read/#2566832660ba. Last accessed October 22, 2018.

Big Data Analytics - What it is and why it matters. https://www.sas.com/en_us/insights/analytics/big-data-analytics.html. Last accessed October 22, 2018.

Data Never Sleeps 5.0. https://www.domo.com/learn/data-never-sleeps-5?aid=ogsm072517_1&sf100871281=1. Last accessed October 22, 2018.

IBM – Ten Key Marketing Trends https://www-01.ibm.com/common/ssi/cgi-bin/ssialias?htmlfid=WRL12345USEN. Last accessed October 20, 2018.

Information Commissioner's Office; What is the 'legitimate interests' basis? https://ico.org.uk/for-organisations/guide-to-the-general-data-protection-regulation-gdpr/legitimate-interests/what-is-the-legitimate-interests-basis/. Last accessed October 22, 2018.

Mutual Legal Assistance Treaty Agreement between the United State of America and the European Union, signed June 25, 2003; Treaty between the United State of America and the Federal Republic of Germany on Mutual Legal Assistance in Criminal Matters, signed October 14, 2003.

Data Protection Working Party, Working Document 1/2009 on Pre-Trial Discovery for Cross Border Litigation 9-10 (2009), available at http://ec.europa.eu/justice/article-29/documentation/opinion-recommendation/files/2009/wp158_en.pdf.

The GDPR So Far: Implications for Information Governance, eDiscovery, and Privacy by Design

Gail Gottehrer[1] and Debbie Reynolds[2*]

The General Data Protection Regulation ("GDPR") is a groundbreaking data privacy law that has forever altered how companies view the digital rights of European Union ("EU") data subjects. Although the GDPR is an EU data privacy law, efforts to comply with it have affected, and will continue to impact, technology data design, data governance mechanisms, and the procedures for managing electronic evidence in legal matters worldwide, for the foreseeable future. This chapter will examine how the GDPR, and the decisions issued and enforcement actions taken pursuant to it so far, have affected information governance, eDiscovery, and the role of privacy in the technology design process.

Information Governance

Litigation is reactive. Some companies and their legal departments view information governance or records management as a comparatively low priority task with a high price tag. Although information governance initiatives may not have got the funding they deserve, GDPR is changing these corporate perspectives in all likelihood. The GDPR is demonstrating to companies why it is essential to know what data they have, who they have collected it from, and where it is located. This identifying information was always necessary in an eDiscovery context, but this information has become more crucial because of the potential massive fines stipulated in the GDPR. Under Article 83[3] of the GDPR, companies that handle data in a way that does not align with the GDPR are at risk of having

---

*Corresponding author: datadiva@debbiereynoldsconsulting.com

fines imposed on them that could amount to up to 4% of the company's worldwide annual revenue. Law firms and corporations have done an excellent job of looking at the GDPR from a legal and a risk mitigation standpoint. The challenges of complying with the GDPR, however, go far deeper than understanding the legal risks. Companies must be able to execute their GDPR plan on an operational level by using their technical capabilities to solve problems that could cause GDPR violations. Although the GDPR makes it critical for companies to focus on compliance with its provisions, which is a C-suite level issue, it requires companies to have the technical expertise to understand the regulation, the nature of the data the companies utilize, and the true extent of the operational needs of the companies from a data perspective.

From an eDiscovery viewpoint, it is always important to have procedures in place to enable the identification of data, and to track it by the custodians from whom it was obtained. Documenting the chain of custody is crucial, so attorneys and project managers know, and can prove, who has handled certain evidence and when they handled it. These obligations are familiar to eDiscovery veterans and are likely to make them more comfortable approaching GDPR related matters than those without eDiscovery experience might be. A new consideration that the GDPR brings to eDiscovery professionals, however, is the need for them to understand their role under the GDPR, and determine whether they qualify as data controllers[4] or data processors for purposes of the GDPR.[5]

For many years, eDiscovery experts, and the legal industry think tank called the Information Governance Initiative (IGI),[6] have emphasized the benefits of having a robust information governance program for a company. They have drawn attention to the fact that companies that have immature information governance programs and practices tend to store excessive data, and, as a result, when they are involved in litigation or investigations, often higher eDiscovery costs are incurred, since they cannot easily or effectively target the required data. A favorable by-product of GDPR compliance may be that the robust information governance systems needed to be GDPR compliant, will allow companies to improve their ability to respond to data demands in litigation or regulatory proceedings, including locating information, ensuring proper preservation, and cost and time reduction associated with eDiscovery. The data minimization theme that runs through the GDPR will assist companies on the eDiscovery front by encouraging them to reduce unnecessary information they may have which can be deleted since it is not subject to a legal, regulatory or other preservation obligation. A robust information governance program can help reduce a company's risk under the GDPR as well as its eDiscovery costs and burdens.

Privacy by Design

Privacy by design is one of the most impactful and complicated concepts in the GDPR. Just the thought that a law like the GDPR can affect future technology development is quite astonishing. Privacy by design, as explained in the GDPR, is built on the premise that when technology is being created, developers must build in protection mechanisms for any data of EU subjects that may be affected by the new technology. For decades, developing technology has outpaced legal institutions' ability to regulate it effectively. With privacy by design, however, the GDPR brings an end to that trend and clarifies that technology development must adjust its pace to abide by the laws applicable to it. Privacy by design, as set forth in the GDPR, is a revolutionary concept because it will not only change the way companies develop software, it will require technologies currently in use to adapt to meet the privacy standards of the GDPR. For example, in the rush to meet the May 25, 2018 GDPR timeline, many companies were evaluating their existing software tools to determine whether they were GDPR compliant. Since using GDPR compliant software will be an additional consideration in the future for companies who have high related risks, software developers will have to consider incorporating privacy by design considerations which will be inevitable in the future.

Privacy by design creates challenges for eDiscovery policies and procedures. For example, when eDiscovery professionals are handling data relating to individuals in a case, the objective is to understand who the person is throughout the process and make sure that their data is connected with their identity. Compliance with privacy by design in eDiscovery, however, may entail figuring out the best way to mask an individual's identity throughout the eDiscovery process. In order to comply with the GDPR, a pseudonym may be provided for the individual at the beginning of the eDiscovery process, and the information collected will then be associated with the pseudonym given to that individual. A potential concern with this eDiscovery workflow, which was implemented to comply with privacy by design requirement, is that human intervention is needed to ensure that the information is correctly linked and associated with the right individual. For example, if an individual's identity is pseudonymized as part of a data exercise, it will be critical to make sure that all the data associated with the pseudonymized individual is only associated with that person and not with someone else for tracking purposes.

Privacy by design also affects existing eDiscovery practices relating to the production of documents by making it necessary for personally identifiable information about an EU data subject to be redacted or removed. eDiscovery applications and tools that can redact on an automated basis will be highly sought after by companies updating their eDiscovery workflows to build in the GDPR's vision of privacy by design.

Cases Creating Legal Precedents for the GDPR

Among the cases that have been in the news since the GDPR went into effect, three are notable for their impact on social media sites. The first case addressed whether an administrator of a Facebook fan page could be considered a "controller" and held jointly liable, with Facebook, for failures to protect personal data. The second case answered whether providing a deceased Facebook account holder's heirs' access to her account conflicts with the GDPR and the privacy rights of the deceased person in his or her personal data. A third case (Facebook and Cambridge Analytica), which involved the use of data for multiple purposes by joint controllers and processors.

The European Court of Justice (ECJ) Joint Controller Ruling

On June 5, 2018, the European Court of Justice's Grand Chamber issued a decision in the case of *Wirtschaftsakademie Schleswig-Holstein GmbH v. Facebook Ireland Ltd*, known as the "Facebook Fan Page" case. While the case was filed under the Directive, prior to the implementation of the GDPR, the Court's ruling that companies that administer Facebook fan pages are jointly responsible with Facebook for protecting the personal data of visitors, is equally applicable under the GDPR.

The case involved a German academic institution running a fan page on Facebook and collecting the data of visitors using tools provided by Facebook. As the administrator of the fan page, the academic institution determined the content on it, and that was targeted to attract visitors. Tools from Facebook provided the administrator with demographic data of the visitors, in anonymized form. The administrator had data about its target audience, including data on their age, sex, occupation, and lifestyle and geographical data. This data enabled the administrator to direct its offerings to its target audience.[7]

In 2011, the north-German data protection authority (DPA) ordered the academic institution to take down the Facebook fan page because neither Facebook nor the institution had informed individuals visiting it that cookies were being used to collect personal data about them. The DPA held that the academic institution was responsible for the improper data collection because it controlled data collection through its fan page. The academic institution challenged that determination, arguing it had not asked Facebook to collect personal data on visitors and was not responsible.[8]

The European Court of Justice considered whether "an entity should be held liable in its capacity as administrator of a fan page on a social network ... because it has chosen to make use of that social network to distribute the information it offers." It answered that question in the affirmative, stating that, "the fact that an administrator of a fan page uses the platform provided by Facebook in order to benefit from the associated services cannot exempt it from compliance with its obligations concerning the protection of personal data."[9]

The ECJ held that, by virtue of the actions they take regarding the personal data of individuals, administrators of fan pages are considered "joint controllers" under the Directive:

> "The administrator of a fan page hosted on Facebook ... must be regarded as taking part, by its definition of parameters depending in particular on its target audience and the objectives of managing and promoting its activities, in the determination of the purposes and means of processing the personal data of the visitors to its fan page. The administrator must, therefore, be categorized, in the present case, as a controller responsible for that processing within the European Union, jointly with Facebook Ireland..."

While the ECJ, the administrator, and Facebook were found to be joint controllers, it observed that they were not necessarily equally responsible or liable. It stated that, "the existence of joint responsibility does not necessarily imply equal responsibility of the various operators involved in the processing of personal data," and the level of liability of each party will need to be determined case by case.[10]

Although the ECJ's decision applied to pre-GDPR conduct and interpreted the Directive, its ruling equally applies under the GDPR, as the Directive, and the GDPR defines the data controller and data processor the same way. In addition, the concept of a "joint controller," described by the ECJ, is embodied in Article 26 of the GDPR, which states that, "Where two or more controllers jointly determine the purposes and means of processing, they shall be joint controllers." The GDPR provides for joint controller liability in Article 82(4), which states that, "Where more than one controller or processor, or both a controller and a processor, are involved in the same processing and where they are ... responsible for any damage caused by processing, each controller or processor shall be held liable for the entire damage in order to ensure effective compensation of the data subject."

This ECJ ruling illustrates the complexity, and importance, of entities correctly determining whether they are data controllers or data processors under the GDPR. Facebook and the German academic institution were considered joint controllers, meaning that both companies had shared data controlling responsibilities. Where two companies either have joint responsibilities as data controllers or data processors, it is vital for each company to clearly understand what their roles and responsibilities are as they relate to data controlling and data processing. For example, in the eDiscovery context, if a company provides data to an eDiscovery vendor and instructs the vendor to load the data into a review platform so attorneys can read it, generally, for purposes of the GDPR, the company requesting the service is a data controller and the vendor is a data processor. If an EU data subject submits a data subject access request to the company who is the data controller, the data controller company may turn to the eDiscovery vendor, who is the data processor, for assistance in complying with that data subject access request because the eDiscovery vendor may have possession of the requested data. The assistance requested by the data controller company from the eDiscovery vendor, who is the data processor, may include providing direct data access to the data subject, erasing the data of the data subject, or returning the data to the data subject. The level of coordination that may be required between the data controller and the data processor underscores the importance of companies understanding how their roles are being classified under the GDPR and the obligations that accompany those GDPR specific designations.

Application of GDPR to Personal Data of the Deceased

On July 12, 2018, the German Federal Supreme Court issued its first decision interpreting the GDPR in a case involving the Facebook account of a 15-year-old girl who died in a train accident. When the train conductor sued the girl's parents alleging that she had committed suicide, the parents sought to access her Facebook account to look for indications of whether or not she had committed suicide. The account had been changed to a "memorialized account," and since the girl had not named a legacy contact, her parents could not log in to the account. Facebook denied the parents' request to access the account on the grounds that it was not permitted to give that information to third parties.[11]

The Court ruled that under the general inheritance law provisions of the German Civil Code, the deceased girl's contract with Facebook was transferred by law to her heirs. It further held that Facebook's obligations to maintain confidentiality were not violated by the heirs accessing the account because the other Facebook users who communicated with the deceased girl could not have a reasonable expectation that their communications would be sent only to her and would not be made accessible to third parties; they could only reasonably expect that their communications would be directed only to the deceased girl's user account.

The Court went on to state that the parents' request for access to their daughter's Facebook account did not conflict with the GDPR because the GDPR does not apply to deceased persons.[12] The Court explained that transferring the personal data of the Facebook users who had communicated with the deceased girl did not violate the GDPR because it was justified by Article 6(1)(b) of the GDPR, which provides that processing is lawful if it is necessary for the performance of a contract to which the data subject is a party, and Article 6(1)(f) of the GDPR, which provides that processing is lawful if it is necessary for the legitimate interests pursued by the data controller or by a third-party.

Adopting a different approach to Recital 27, New Zealand has taken the GDPR's invitation to establish rules regarding the processing of the personal data of deceased persons. On July 24, 2018, the Office of the Privacy Commissioner of New Zealand ("OPC") released a statement in which it declared that, "privacy can extend beyond the grave," and therefore, "sometimes it will be inappropriate to release the personal information of the dead."[13]

While acknowledging that New Zealand's Privacy Act does not apply to deceased persons, the OPC clarified that the Act "recognizes that there may be occasions when the information about a dead person needs to be withheld," including situations involving the unwarranted disclosure of the affairs of a deceased individual. It went on to say that certain information, such as mental or sexual health information about a deceased person, "is inherently sensitive," and it could be unfair to release such information to those who are just curious and have no good reason to see it." Accordingly, the rights of individuals requesting information and the privacy rights of deceased people will need to be balanced, and requests for such information will need to be considered on a case-by-case basis.

These decisions, issued in the early days of the GDPR, are instructive because they show that many key determinations under the GDPR, such as the respective liability of joint controllers and the restrictions on disclosing personal data of a deceased person, will be decided case-by-case, subject to the discretion of the regulator handling the case, and the Member State in which the case is brought. This approach increases the challenges associated with GDPR compliance.

The Facebook and Cambridge Analytica Matter

Actions taken by Cambridge Analytica and Facebook, before the GDPR went into effect on May 25, 2018, created intense focus, both in the U.S. and the EU, on the handling of personal data of consumers providing data to Facebook, which in turn was provided to Cambridge Analytica for research, and used by it for political purposes. As in the German Facebook ECJ case, Facebook and Cambridge Analytica might be viewed as joint controllers who shared joint responsibility for data controlling and have some degree of shared responsibility for providing a level of transparency to any EU data subjects that may have been affected by these alternative data uses. Although the U.S. does not currently have a federal law in effect that requires data subject access requests, most social media and search engine providers like Facebook and Google create extensive terms of service documents describing the types of data they collect and what they intend to do with the data. Consumers, however, may not be given specific details about what happens to their data captured by these companies that are then shared with third parties. While the GDPR has created a new level of transparency for the handling of EU data subject information, the same companies are not currently required to provide the same level of transparency to U.S. consumers who use their service platforms.

The GDPR contains derogations, which are special exceptions that can be used for lawful data processing. Some derogations may apply and may be used in eDiscovery matters. For example, if a company can prove that its data use in a legal matter is due its legitimate business interests, the company may not have to request the consent of the individual data subject to do the data processing if the data processing only involves the legitimate business interests and the processing does not exceed the scope of what is considered the legal basis for the legitimate business interests.

Similarly, another derogation concerns a limited number of people that may be affected by certain data handling or a limited timeframe in which the data handling is to occur. For example, if a legal matter only requires a limited number of EU data subjects' data in order to comply with its legitimate business interests, a company may argue that it has a legal basis for using this data for litigation and that it is being done on a limited and irregular basis. However, it is important for companies to know that when they use derogations, they do not extend to the use of the data for other purposes which are outside either initially determined legitimate interests or outside the scope of what the GDPR considers to be a regular stream of data transfer information related to legal matters.

GDPR Trends Likely to Affect Privacy by Design, Information Governance, and eDiscovery

Article 57(1) Compliance Investigations

In July 2018, the Data Protection Authority of the Netherlands ("Dutch DPA") began an investigation of 30 large private companies, selected at random, to verify their compliance with Article 30 of the GDPR, which requires controllers to maintain a record of processing activities under their responsibility and requires them to maintain a record of all categories of processing activities carried out on behalf of a controller. The 30 companies span a range of industries across the Netherlands, including construction, retail, hospitality, travel, finance, communications, and healthcare.[14]

The Dutch DPA is conducting this investigation pursuant to Article 57(1) of the GDPR, which authorizes it to monitor and enforce compliance with the principles of the GDPR. Such investigations can be commenced without a complaint being filed and without any suspicion of non-compliance by a company. If the Dutch DPA finds that a company has not complied with its obligations under the GDPR and that violating Article 30 is not likely to result in a risk to data subjects, the remedies available to it include issuing an "enforcement notice under penalty," which can require a company to comply with the GDPR and demonstrate that compliance by a certain date. If a company fails to demonstrate compliance by the deadline, penalties can be assessed against it for each day it does not comply with the order. In the event the Dutch DPA concludes that the company's failure to comply with Article 30 may result in a risk to the rights and freedoms of data subjects, the remedies available to it could include the imposition of the maximum possible fines in that category.

The Dutch DPA is not expected to name the specific companies it finds to be in violation of Article 30, but instead to provide the results of its investigation in the form of aggregated data, which will identify the number and types of violations in each industry.[15]

It would not be surprising to see more regulators conduct these kinds of investigations, to confirm that companies are complying with their recordkeeping obligations and to send the message that companies need to take the recordkeeping provisions of the GDPR seriously, or face fines. The need to maintain accurate and complete records, and to locate and produce them in response to requests from regulators, will bring attention to the importance of having strong information governance and eDiscovery policies and procedures.

This example illustrates why it is essential in eDiscovery to keep detailed and accurate records of dealing with data of EU data subjects, and also to take a proactive approach to GDPR compliance, so that a company that handles data on a regular basis is in a position to provide a regulator with evidence that it is diligent in its efforts to comply with the GDPR. It is reasonable to assume that the companies that will be heavily fined or affected by GDPR will be the ones that do not take the GDPR's rules and requirements seriously, and companies that fail to institute proactive policies and procedures in their daily operations to ensure that their company is in GDPR compliance.

A GDPR blind spot may be "shadow IT." "Shadow IT" describes situations where employees install applications on company computers and systems without the company's knowledge. If the company is unaware of the use of these applications, it is likely to not have vetted these applications. If the applications are not GDPR compliant, their use could put the company at risk of violating the GDPR. To avoid such situations, it is important for companies to scan their networks and computers to identify any such applications, and assess whether they are GDPR compliant, and remove them if they are not. Training employees about the GDPR and the obligations it imposes on the company, and the potential consequences of violations, is also imperative to reduce the risk of inadvertent GDPR violations.

Data Subjects Exercising Their GDPR Rights

A survey conducted by SAS Institute Inc. of 1,000 consumers in the United Kingdom and 850 consumers in Ireland between May 25, 2018 (when the GDPR went into effect) and June 2018, found that 27% of those surveyed had already exercised their rights under the GDPR and 56% planned to exercise their GDPR rights within the next year.[16]

Most of the consumers surveyed knew the rights afforded to them by the GDPR. 60.8% knew they had the right to access their personal data, 50.3% knew they had the right to be forgotten and to have their personal data erased, and 48.3% knew that they had the right to object to their personal data being used for certain purposes.

Social media companies were identified as the leading targets for erasure requests, with 43.6% of respondents indicating that they had exercised, or planned to exercise their right to have their data removed, from social media companies. 34.4% of those surveyed said they had exercised or planned to exercise their right to have their data removed from retailers, followed by 30% from insurance companies, and 29.7% from banks.

The trend of data subjects being aware of their rights and exercising them makes it critical for companies to be knowledgeable about the data they collect, including its location on their own systems and the processors to whom the data is provided. Companies can anticipate receiving large numbers of access requests from data subjects, which they must respond to promptly. They can also expect to receive many requests for rectification and erasure from data subjects, and to comply with those requests, they will need to know all the places where the data is stored, have a process in place to make the appropriate corrections or to delete data, and have strong recordkeeping policies and procedures in place to document requests from data subjects, their communications with data subjects, and the steps taken to correct or erase data.

Data subject access requests will create a challenge, especially for small or midsize companies, who may not have the resources in place to respond to them. They will also pose a challenge for larger companies who have the data of significant numbers of individuals, and these companies may choose to automate these data subject access processes or make them a self-service type of feature of their software. For example, some social media companies provide data subjects the ability to access their accounts and request information about the data being captured about them. Making this data available in an on-demand fashion puts the impetus on the data subject to locate and use these features in their accounts to find their data or download this information if data portability is desired. After the data subjects have reviewed their data, they can also make requests to have the data deleted or corrected. If the company cannot establish a legitimate reason for not complying with the data subject's request to either delete their data, change it or remove it, EU consumers may contact the data protection authority in their Member State to make a complaint.

Another foreseeable issue is the way in which an individual can make a data subject request to a company with whom they have no formal customer relationship, customer account, or customer agreement. For example, many social media companies have facial recognition tools capable of associating someone's face with their name in photographs even if the individual is not a customer of the service. It remains to be seen what the procedure is for an EU data subject who is not a social media company's customer to request to have his likeness or image data deleted. Nuances around data subject access requests, including questions like how to address data deletion requests made to social media companies by people who are not customers of the service, and how an EU data subject would request rectification or deletion of his data in such a situation, are among the many questions relating to the application of the GDPR that stakeholders in this area will be monitoring.

Increased Data Breach Reporting

According to a July 30, 2018 report in *The Irish Times*, the Irish Data Protection Commission received 1,184 data breach notifications since May 25, 2018, and 743 complaints.[17] This reflected a significant increase from 2017, when the Commission received an average of 230 data breach reports per month, and 2,642 complaints. The GDPR applied to 953 of the data breach notifications and 267 of the complaints received by the Commission since May 25, 2018.[18]

Implementing strong information governance programs will enable companies to identify and respond to potential breaches quickly, and be in a position to effectively assess the extent of the breach, its severity, and the types of data affected. Having policies specifying an employee's ability to access certain data will make companies better able to provide cybersecurity and data protection training to the employees who have access to personal data of data subjects, and to monitor those employees, to reduce the chance of inadvertent breaches.

While the laws of different countries set out different time frames for companies to respond to data breaches, the 72-hour data breach notification period in Article 33 of the GDPR is considered the most stringent in the world[19]. The United States currently has a patchwork of data protection laws, with different state laws requiring data breach notices to be provided within time periods that range from 30 days to several months. Going forward, however, as governments and regulators around the world see companies complying with the 72-hour data breach notification period in the GDPR, many may seek to make the 72-hour notice period the de facto standard in their countries.

In the U.S., not all state data breach notification laws require financial compensation to consumers who have suffered a data breach. In the U.S., companies that suffer data breaches often have to send a letter to consumers about the data breach and often will provide credit monitoring protection for the affected individuals. Although data breaches are costly for companies to recover from in terms of implementing the proper responses to eliminate the risk of having a future data breach, responding to consumers, and also giving free credit protection to consumers, the monetary compensation to consumers is often minimal.

In contrast, under the GDPR, member states' data protection authorities will evaluate data breaches, and will determine the responses that companies provide, and how the data breaches will be remedied. Although there is no private right of action that will result in consumers being financially compensated for data breaches under the GDPR, businesses still may face significant EU government fines for missteps as they relate to data breaches.

Notably, the EU has a cyber security initiative called the NIS Directive which, like the GDPR, has a 72-hour data breach notification deadline, and fines that can be levied against companies that handle data or information concerning public utilities and other vital resources including internet and cloud companies. Businesses who have data breaches could potentially be subject to penalties under both the GDPR and the NIS Directive. The concern for such companies is that a potential data breach in the EU may cause penalties from both the GDPR and the NIS Directive and could create double jeopardy and dual fines in the EU for data breaches. The EU has recognized that since the NIS Directive and GDPR have similar data breach frameworks and fines, it may consider both under appropriate circumstances.

From an eDiscovery standpoint, third-party vendor risk could be a concern for several reasons. For example, companies that conduct eDiscovery data processing or any eDiscovery work that falls under the umbrella of the EDRM (Electronic Discovery Reference Model shown in Fig. 7.1)[20] are likely third-parties for purposes of the GDPR because they are often hired by corporations or law firms to do this work on their behalf. Also, because not every company that does work under the EDRM umbrella can perform every task related to a litigation matter, companies often retain additional third-party vendors. Although it has generally been customary for companies that handle eDiscovery to be transparent contractually about work that is subcontracted, these subcontracted relationships take on greater significance for companies that are subject to the GDPR because the risk of handling data under the GDPR will pass to companies that act either wholly or partially as a data controller or a data processor. Companies are right to be concerned that their third-party vendors create a risk for them under the GDPR. To address these concerns, it is essential that data controllers make sure that third-party vendors who process data for them understand what their role is in handling EU data subject information and understand the reporting and documentation requirements necessary to demonstrate to any EU data protection authority, if asked, how the data was handled in an eDiscovery matter.

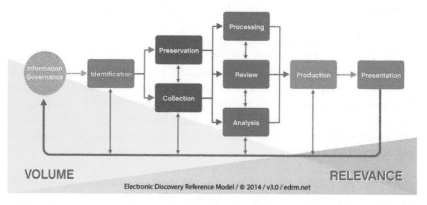

Fig. 7.1. EDRM - Electronic Discovery Reference Model

An example of this would be an eDiscovery vendor outsourcing the data collection to a subcontracted company but continuing to do the eDiscovery data processing themselves. In this scenario, the eDiscovery vendor hired by a company or a law firm is a third-party but is also a data processor and a data controller, especially if they are subcontracting the data collection work to another vendor. The vendor doing the data collection is a joint data processor and also has obligations as it relates to the GDPR. Although companies can get assurances in contracts which cover the legal portion of the GDPR, it can be difficult for data controllers to assure, on an operational level, that their third parties' data processors are complying with these GDPR regulations. An effective way to monitor compliance is to instruct eDiscovery vendors to demonstrate their compliance in practical ways. Companies using software created by or maintained by third-parties will want to obtain assurances they are complying with the GDPR from an operational perspective. It is critical in these situations to partner with companies who understand their joint responsibilities as data controllers or data processors under the GDPR. Companies who look to third parties for this type of service should be prepared to demonstrate any exceptions, like derogations, that may apply to the work of third parties, and which could potentially reduce their risk under the GDPR.

Concern about Third-Party Vendor Risk

According to a Demandbase survey conducted one month after the GDPR went into effect and released in late July 2018, 80% of companies were concerned that their marketing technology vendors could expose them to liability under the GDPR. The 255 marketers surveyed were from mid to large size companies across the world in a variety of industries.[21] When asked if they were concerned that their marketing technology vendors might expose their company to legal risks because they are not GDPR compliant, 9% of respondents described themselves as extremely concerned, while 12% described themselves as moderately concerned, and 20% as somewhat concerned. Thirty-nine percent of respondents said they were slightly concerned about GDPR exposure from third-party vendors, while 20% said that they were not at all concerned.[22]

The GDPR makes clear that controllers need to vet their vendors carefully and to satisfy themselves that they are GDPR compliant. This is likely to create vendors with strong compliance programs and data protection certifications which will distinguish them from their competitors in getting business from companies that are subject to the GDPR.

From an eDiscovery standpoint, third-party vendor risk is something that should not be overlooked. eDiscovery vendors that conduct data processing or other eDiscovery work that falls under the umbrella of the EDRM (Electronic Discovery Reference Model) are likely third-parties because they are often hired by corporations or law firms to process data for them. In addition, as many vendors that perform eDiscovery services under the EDRM umbrella cannot do all the tasks required for a particular eDiscovery matter, often subcontract work to other vendors, creating additional third-party vendor relationships. While eDiscovery vendors are expected to be transparent about any subcontracting they do, or anticipate doing, companies and vendors that hire eDiscovery vendors are wise to increase their scrutiny on the practices of their eDiscovey vendors to ensure they are aware of any subcontracting, and to review their eDiscovery vendor contracts to make sure they include provisions prohibiting, or regulating, any subcontracting.

Challenges to Validity of Consent

The first complaints filed with supervisory authorities in France, Austria, Belgium, and Germany pursuant to Article 77(1) of the GDPR were lodged on May 25, 2018, by "none of your business" – European Center for Digital Rights ("noyb"), an organization run by Max Schrems.[23] In the complaints, noyb alleges that Google, Facebook, Instagram, and WhatsApp unlawfully process personal data of data subjects, in violation of the GDPR, because the consent they obtain from data subjects is "forced" by the controller, rather than freely given by the data subject. Since the processing is based on "forced" consent, and not valid consent, it breaches the data subjects' rights under the GDPR.[24]

Noyb contends that the consent upon which these companies base their processing of the personal data and special categories of personal data of data subjects, covered by Articles 6(a)(1) and 9(a)(2), respectively, is "forced," for the following reasons:

- The imbalance of power between the controller and the data subject leaves the data subject with no choice but to consent to the controller's privacy policy and terms of service. If the data subject's failure to consent would result insignificant negative consequences for him or her, noyb argues, then any consent provided by the data subject is invalid.
- The only way for a data subject to obtain services from these companies is to consent to the processing of their personal data. This "take it or leave it" approach, noyb contends, violates the GDPR.
- The controller requires the data subject to consent to its privacy policy and terms of services as a whole and relies on an "overall bundled consent" to anything contained in the privacy policy. According to noyb, consent based on an "all or nothing" approach like this is not specific, and therefore not valid consent under the GDPR.
- The GDPR requires that a data subject be able to refuse consent without detriment. Noyb claims that unless the data subject consents to the privacy policy and terms of service, these companies do not allow the data subject to use their services.

Noyb's four complaints, filed with the supervisory authorities in France, Austria, Belgium, and Germany, ask these regulators to impose fines of up to $4.3 billion, which, they estimate, is roughly 4% percent of each company's revenue for 2017.

Challenges to the validity of the consent obtained by data controllers are likely to be the most popular types of complaints lodged by data subjects under the GDPR. Companies will need to have effective information governance programs in place to be able to demonstrate that the consent they obtain from data subjects is explicit and freely given based on adequate information, in order to defend themselves against these complaints and satisfy regulators that they have complied with the GDPR.

In the eDiscovery context, attorneys and vendors will need to pay increased attention to tracking the different levels of consent provided by EU data subjects. For example, if a company needs to get consent from ten data subjects in the EU for a particular matter, each of those ten individuals has the right to consent, refuse to give consent or to give only partial consent to the collection of data. Whichever option each data subject chooses should be carefully tracked so that if and when it becomes necessary for the company or its counsel to explain the data collection process, the accuracy and completeness of the data, and the steps taken to comply with the GDPR, they may have to explain the reasons for any gaps in the data.

Although the GDPR impacts a wide range of companies that handle data of EU persons, companies that provide free services in exchange for using the personally identifiable information of individuals are the focus of considerable scrutiny. The nyob cases filed against Google and Facebook raise the concept of "forced consent," as they argue that Internet companies that provide free services do so knowing that the data individuals freely offer is valuable and can be monetized for advertising and other purposes, and, in addition, consumers are not able opt out of all data collection and still use these free services. It remains to be seen how the EU data authorities will handle these so-called "forced consent" situations. The GDPR has given many people a new awareness of the value of the personal information of individuals, not only intrinsically because privacy is a fundamental human right in the EU, but because companies gathering and selling data earn significant revenue from data that individuals provide to them. We may see decisions that lead to companies to give consumers the option to use their service for free and consent to the company using their personal data, or to pay a fee for the service and prohibit the company from using their personal data. It will be interesting to see what consumers decide to do, given that choice. Key factors will most likely include the types of personal data at issue, the importance of the service in their lives, and the amount of the fees.

Consent is not a new concept as it relates to the EU since consent requirements existed in the EU data Directive that preceded the GDPR. The difference with the consent in the GDPR is that GDPR is now a regulation as opposed to a directive and it has substantial penalties for companies who do not comply with consent requirements as they apply to their company's business practices.

In eDiscovery, many companies and law firms have handled the data of EU persons for years and dealt with consent mechanisms effectively. In the U.S., consent of an individual is generally not required, especially if data is taken directly from an employer because the individual's consent may be implied or explicitly provided based on the company's policies about data handling. Accordingly, in the U.S., it is easier for lawyers to obtain data from companies for litigation purposes as opposed to doing so for individuals in the EU who may have to give their express consent and be provided with detailed information about how the data will be used and for what purpose.

States Enacting Laws Similar to GDPR

On June 28, 2018, the state of California enacted the California Consumer Privacy Act of 2018 ("CCPA"). The CCPA was rushed through the legislature when it began to appear likely that the California Consumer Personal Information Disclosure and Sale Initiative ("Initiative") was going to qualify for inclusion on the November 2018 ballot. The Initiative sought to give voters the opportunity to enact a more stringent privacy regime that would enable consumers to demand that businesses disclose the personal information they collect, the purpose for which it is used, and the identities of the entities with whom they share the information, as well as give consumers the right to limit the sharing of their personal information. On June 25, 2018, the California Senate proposed an amended version of the CCPA that sought to strike a compromise between the concerns of the leaders of the Initiative and the business community and ensure that the Initiative would be removed from the November ballot. The legislature passed the bill and sent it to the Governor for his signature, all within a matter of days.

The CCPA incorporates some of the principles in the GDPR. It takes an approach to privacy that is similar to that of Europeans, who view privacy as a fundamental human right. The California Legislature states in the CCPA that the "ability of individuals to control the use, including the sale, of their personal information" is "fundamental" to the right of privacy guaranteed to Californians by the California Constitution.[25]

Like the GDPR, the CCPA provides California residents with certain rights to control their "personal information," which is broadly defined to cover information that "identifies, relates to, describes, is capable of being associated with, or could reasonably be linked, directly or indirectly, with a particular consumer or household." While the CCPA's definition differs from the GDPR's definition of "personal data," both definitions are expansive and designed to include sensitive information that individuals have an interest in controlling. The CCPA provides California residents with certain rights that are similar to, but not the same as, the rights granted to European Union residents by the GDPR, including the right to notice, the right of access, the right to be forgotten, and the right to data portability. The CCPA also adopts some of the GDPR's emphasis on privacy by design, by requiring businesses subject to the CCPA to implement reasonable security procedures and practices appropriate to protect personal information, based on the nature of the information at issue. It is important to note that while there are similarities between the CCPA and the GDPR, the differences between the laws are significant such that compliance with the GDPR does not equate with compliance with the CCPA.

The CCPA was originally scheduled to go into effect on January 1, 2020, but less than two months after it was passed it already faced significant opposition and calls for its overhaul. California State Senator Bill Dodd has introduced a "cleanup bill" to address drafting errors in the CCPA.[26] On August 6, 2018, the California Chamber of Commerce and several dozen companies sent a letter to Senator Dodd addressing what they described as the "unworkable aspects" of the CCPA and its unintended consequences.[27] In order to address these issues, the companies proposed that the effective date of the CCPA be delayed, specifically that the Attorney General not begin the rulemaking process for the CCPA until January 1, 2020, and companies not be required to comply with those rules until 12 months after the Attorney General completes the rulemaking process. The companies also proposed language narrowing the definitions of "consumer" and "personal information." Finally, they indicated that in addition to having input on SB 1211, they are interested in working with the legislature on additional legislation in the fall of 2018 and into 2019 that would address "substantive issues," including the creation of a safe harbor to data breach liability.

SB 1121 was signed by the Governor on September 23, 2018. As amended, the CCPA delayed enforcement by the Attorney General until July 1, 2020 or six months after the publication of the final regulations, whichever was sooner. The amendments also made clear that the private right of action under the CCPA applies only to violations of the data breach section of the CCPA.

California is a trailblazing state as it relates to data privacy law in the U.S. For example, California was the first state in the U.S. to have a data breach notification law. Many years later, almost all of the states in the U.S. have breach notification laws. Although it is an excellent signal to U.S. consumers that the states are taking data breach notification seriously, having different data breach notification laws and requirements in different states makes it very difficult for businesses to comply to these laws and implement standard procedures. However, states are finding it easier to pass consumer privacy laws at the state level than to enact legislation on the federal level. Since California is starting the push toward data privacy laws that are consumer friendly, this may be a bellwether for other states or even spur legislation on a federal level to be implemented in the future. A significant challenge to the California

Consumer Privacy Act which occurred prior to full enforcement were lobbying efforts that were taken to try to persuade the California state legislature government to revise the final version of the law before it went into full effect in 2020. Although some multinational corporations stated they would comply with the GDPR as it relates to EU data subjects, some companies did not welcome legislation in the U.S. that mirrors either the strict operational requirements of the GDPR or the substantial fines that are part of the GDPR. It remains to be seen how influential the California Consumer Privacy Act will be and, whether other states in the U.S. will follow California and enact data privacy laws, and whether the calls for a federal data privacy law will continue or result new legislation being passed.

It is likely that other states will follow California's lead and incorporate concepts and principles from the GDPR into their privacy laws. This trend will create complications for companies subject to the GDPR and state laws in the U.S., such as the CCPA, which may all possibly have inconsistent requirements and impose different obligations on these companies. Companies that do business across the U.S. and in the EU will surely look into ways to create a privacy by design framework that accommodates these different statutory schemes, to the extent possible.

Site Blocking

When the GDPR went into effect, some American newspapers and online services blocked EU internet connections to their sites and made their services unavailable to EU residents presumably to avoid GDPR compliance and potential liability. Approximately one-third of the 100 largest U.S. newspapers decided to block their sites in Europe, including the *Chicago Tribune, New York Daily News, Dallas Morning News*, and *Newsday*. As of the beginning of August, over 1,000 news sites remained unavailable in the EU.[28]

It is unclear whether this is a trend that will continue. Given the vast number of potential customers in the EU, it seems likely that once companies have the benefit of more decisions being handed down interpreting the GDPR and additional guidance being issued by regulators that removes some of the ambiguity in the GDPR as written, companies will have greater clarity on what they must do to be GDPR compliant. Once they have that information, many companies are likely to be more comfortable assessing their potential risk under the GDPR, and more willing to provide goods and services to EU residents.

Although websites blocked visitors from the EU around the time of the full implementation of the GDPR on May 25, 2018, this may not fully protect them from EU subject data requests having GDPR exposure. The

GDPR became law on May 25, 2016, and the penalty phase of the GDPR went into effect two years later, on May 25, 2018. Data from EU data subjects that was accumulated between that two-year period could still be subject to the GDPR even if the company blocked their site from EU data subjects on May 25, 2018. Site blocking could also have the opposite result than was intended. Instead of minimizing the risk of running afoul of the GDPR on May 25, 2018, a company's decision to block its site may cause regulators to take a closer look at their business practices than they otherwise would have. Companies around the world will be watching the EU regulators as they conduct investigations and issues decisions under the GDPR to get an idea of how the EU intends to enforce the GDPR and the types of alleged violations and companies they focus on.

In the eDiscovery world, rather than do the equivalent of site blocking, some eDiscovery companies have either partnered with other organizations with resources and presence in the EU countries or white listed countries that may have stronger data privacy protections than the U.S. Some of these companies had signed up to be part of the EU-U.S. Privacy Shield certification prior to its invalidation in July 2020 by the EU. The EU-U.S. Privacy Shield was a framework by which U.S. companies could transfer EU data to the U.S. under specified circumstances which complied with requirements needed under this agreement between the U.S. and the EU. The EU invalidated the EU-US Privacy Shield because of what it sees as a lack of commitment by the U.S. to fully comply with the agreement. Although it remains to be seen if the EU-U.S. Privacy Shield will be revived between the EU and U.S., this invalidation of the EU-U.S. Privacy Shield certification has created a significant setback for U.S. companies who used this agreement to continue operating their businesses effectively when they needed to transfer data from EU data subjects to the U.S.

Conclusion

In conclusion, data privacy laws being created and enforced will change not only how people think about and handle data in terms of workflow, but will also have an impact on software, technology development and the idea of privacy by design for years to come. The areas of data systems design, information governance, and procedures for managing electronic evidence in legal matters will continue to be impacted especially as the legal world waits to see case precedents being set in the data privacy arena. The world is watching as GDPR is being enforced for indications as to how the EU will decide these cases and also as examples for other countries on how they may start to apply data privacy laws that have similarities to the GDPR.

References

1. Gail Gottehrer, Founder, Law Office of Gail Gottehrer LLC, ggottehrer@outlook.com
2. Debbie Reynolds, "The Data Diva", Founder, CEO, and Chief Data Privacy Officer, Debbie Reynolds Consulting, LLC datadiva@debbiereynoldsconsulting.com
3. Vollmer, N. (2018, September 5). Article 83 EU General Data Protection Regulation (EU-GDPR). Privacy/Privazy according to plan. Retrieved from http://www.privacy-regulation.eu/en/article-83-general-conditions-for-imposing-administrative-fines-GDPR.htm
4. Vollmer, N. (2018, September 5). Article 24 EU General Data Protection Regulation (EU-GDPR). Privacy/Privacy according to plan. Retrieved from http://www.privacy-regulation.eu/en/article-24-responsibility-of-the-controller-GDPR.htm
5. Vollmer, N. (2018, September 5). Article 28 EU General Data Protection Regulation (EU-GDPR). Privacy/Privacy according to plan. Retrieved from http://www.privacy-regulation.eu/en/article-28-processor-GDPR.htm
6. The IGI Mission – Information Governance Initiative. (n.d.). Retrieved from https://iginitiative.com/mission/
7. Bednar, S. and Metelk, J. (2018, June 13). EUROPE: ECJ and responsibility for personal data processing on Facebook fan pages | Privacy Matters. Retrieved from https://blogs.dlapiper.com/privacymatters/europe-ecj-and-responsibility-for-personal-data-processing-on-facebook-fan-pages/
8. Meyer, D. (2018, June 6). Europe's top court has just blown a big hole in Facebook's fan-page terms | ZDNet. Retrieved from https://www.zdnet.com/article/europes-top-court-has-just-blown-a-big-hole-in-facebooks-fan-page-terms/
9. European Court of Justice. (2018, June 5). CURIA – Documents Case C-210/16, Judgement of the Court. Retrieved from http://curia.europa.eu/juris/document/document.jsf;jsessionid=9ea7d0f130daa5580c707a0b4ee09cb787cc77515c22.e34KaxiLc3eQc40LaxqMbN4Pb3iPe0?text=&docid=202543&pageIndex=0&doclang=EN&mode=lst&dir=&occ=first&part=1&cid=325138
10. Facebook has since added a Controller Addendum on its website: https://www.facebook.com/legal/terms/page_controller_addendum
11. Family Law Lexis Nexis. (2018, August 10). German court rules Facebook account can pass to user's heirs after death. Retrieved from https://www.familylaw.co.uk/news_and_comment/german-court-rules-facebook-account-can-pass-to-user-s-heirs-after-death#.W3TiU-hKiUl
12. European Parliament and of the Council. (2016, April 27). EUR-Lex - 32016R0679 - EN - EUR-Lex, General Data Protection Regulation (EU) 2016/679, Recital 27, regarding GDPR rights or deceased persons. Retrieved from https://eur-lex.europa.eu/eli/reg/2016/679/oj
13. Privacy Commissioner of New Zealand ("OPC"). (2018, July 24). Dutch Data Protection Authority: Randomly selected companies will be subject to GDPR-compliance investigations | privacy-ticker.com. Retrieved from https://www.privacy-ticker.com/dutch-data-protection-authority-randomly-selected-companies-will-be-subject-to-gdpr-compliance-investigations/

14. Privacy Ticker. (2018, July 31). Dutch Data Protection Authority: Randomly selected companies will be subject to GDPR-compliance investigations | privacy-ticker.com. Retrieved from https://www.privacy-ticker.com/dutch-data-protection-authority-randomly-selected-companies-will-be-subject-to-gdpr-compliance-investigations/
15. GDPR Report. (2018, August 8). Dutch Data Protection Authority commences compliance verification in randomly selected companies – GDPR Report. Retrieved from https://gdpr.report/news/2018/08/08/dutch-data-protection-authority-commences-compliance-verification-in-randomly-selected-companies/
16. SAS Whitepaper. (2018) GDPR: The right to remain private. Retrieved from website: https://www.sas.com/content/dam/SAS/en_gb/doc/whitepaper1/gdpr-consumer-survey.pdf
17. Edwards, E. (2018, July 30). The Irish Times. DPC receives over 1,100 reports of data breaches since start of GDPR rules. Retrieved from https://www.irishtimes.com/business/technology/dpc-receives-over-1-100-reports-of-data-breaches-since-start-of-gdpr-rules-1.3580240
18. Of those Irish Data Protection Commission received 276 complaints, the most common alleged violation of the GDPR related to allegations of personal data being processed without a legal basis, followed by data subject access requests, and claims of unfair processing.
19. Vollmer, N. (2018, September 5). Article 33 EU General Data Protection Regulation (EU-GDPR). Privacy/Privazy according to plan. Retrieved from http://www.privacy-regulation.eu/en/article-33-notification-of-a-personal-data-breach-to-the-supervisory-authority-GDPR.htm
20. Electronic Discovery Reference Model – EDRM Model. (n.d.). Retrieved from https://www.edrm.net/frameworks-and-standards/edrm-model/
21. Kurzer, R. and Martech Today. (2018, July 31). Report: Majority of companies fear 3rd-party vendors make them vulnerable to GDPR legal risks. Retrieved from https://martechtoday.com/report-majority-of-companies-fear-that-3rd-party-vendors-make-them-vulnerable-to-legal-risks-for-gdpr-non-compliance-218922
22. DEMANDBASE. (2018). Data Privacy & the GDPR; Benchmark Study (August). Retrieved from https://www.demandbase.com/wp-content/uploads/abridged-demandbase-data-privacy-gdpr.pdf
23. Max Schrems is a privacy activist attorney who, as a law student, brought the case that, in 2015, resulted in the Court of Justice of the European Union invalidating the Safe Harbor agreement that had governed data transfers between the European Union and the United States until that time. Electronic Privacy Information Center. (n.d.). EPIC - Max Schrems v. Data Protection Commissioner (CJEU – "Safe Harbor"). Retrieved from https://www.epic.org/privacy/intl/schrems/
24. NOYB.EU. (2018). Complaint Under GDPR Article 77(1) against Google LLC (Android), filed with the French DPA (CNIL). Retrieved from https://noyb.eu/wp-content/uploads/2018/05/complaint-android.pdf;NOYB.EU. (2018). Complaint Under GDPR Article 77(1) against Instagram (Facebook Ireland Ltd), filed with the Belgian DPA (CPP). Retrieved from https://noyb.eu/wp-content/uploads/2018/05/complaint-instagram.pdf;   NOYB.EU. (2018). Complaint Under GDPR Article 77(1) Against WhatsApp Ireland Ltd,

filed with the Hamburg DPA (HmbBfDI). Retrieved from https://noyb.eu/
wp-content/uploads/2018/05/complaint-whatsapp.pdf;NOYB.EU. (2018).
Complaint Under GDPR Article 77(1) GDPR Against Facebook Ireland Ltd,
filed with the Austrian DPA (DSB). Retrieved from https://noyb.eu/wp-
content/uploads/2018/05/complaint-facebook.pdf

25. State of California. (1879). State of CALIFORNIA CONSTITUTION,
    ARTICLE I DECLARATION OF RIGHTS [SECTION 1 - SEC. 32]. Retrieved
    from https://leginfo.legislature.ca.gov/faces/codes_displayText.xhtml?law
    Code=CONS&division=&title=&part=&chapter=&article=I
26. State of California. (2018, September 8). Bill Text - Senate Bill, SB-1121
    California Consumer Privacy Act of 2018. Retrieved from https://leginfo.
    legislature.ca.gov/faces/billTextClient.xhtml?bill_id=201720180SB1121
27. California Business Community. (2018, August 6). Letter to California
    Senator Bill Dodd from business leaders, titled "SB 1121 (DODD) – Business
    Community Requests To Be Included In Ab 375 Clean-Up Legislation.
    Retrieved from http://src.bna.com/A44
28. South, J. and Neiman Lab. (2018, August 7). More than 1,000 U.S. news sites
    are still unavailable in Europe, two months after GDPR took effect. Retrieved
    from http://www.niemanlab.org/2018/08/more-than-1000-u-s-news-sites-
    are-still-unavailable-in-europe-two-months-after-gdpr-took-effect/

The Business Opportunities of GDPR

Kenneth N. Rashbaum, Esq.[1*]

The General Data Protection Regulation ("GDPR") has, in many parts of the US, been demonized as a revenue-draining compliance slog that will hamper the growth and innovation of businesses engaged in global e-commerce. That is a 20th century perspective of information management regulation. The 21st century has brought about a new paradigm: Information is an asset that is easily lost and, therefore, requires protection in order for businesses to grow and thrive. Put more succinctly, information is no longer merely electronic 1s and 0s that describe the company's assets; information *is an asset, and most organizations' most valuable asset.*

The significance of data protection first struck consumers in the wake of well-publicized data breaches by Target, Home Depot and Yahoo, among many more. Consumers and institutional customers (financial services organizations, universities, healthcare organizations, retail establishments and others) want their information protected if given to corporations so that these entities may create new applications and communication platforms by utilizing it. Businesses also have a keen interest in data protection due to the additional need to protect their proprietary information and trade secrets which, in 2018, almost exclusively exist in digital form. These merged interests are at the heart of the way in which GDPR presents opportunities for businesses to grow.

[1] Kenneth N. Rashbaum is a partner at Barton LLP in New York City, where he heads the firm's Privacy and Cybersecurity Practice Group. Ken is also an Adjunct Professor of Law at Fordham Law School in New York City. He may be reached at krashbaum@bartonesq.com.

*Email: krashbaum@bartonesq.com

The GDPR's 99 Articles and 173 Recitals can be summarized in one sentence: Tell the data subject[2] why you are collecting her data and how you will use it; secure the data; and only share it with those whom you trust and who have given a written commitment that they will protect it. The rest is, in essence, commentary and requirements for documentation of these essential safeguards. These themes will be analyzed in order.

The GDPR offers consumers notice of how their information will be used, and a right to request access to their data from all repositories (primary and third-party), and to object to certain uses or all uses and the right to tell the organization to delete all information about them and to remove all links to identify information (the well-publicized, if somewhat limited, right to be forgotten) in addition. Personal information of consumers and even of business partners and employees must be secured appropriately – guarded as one would guard one's product designs or formulae with cybersecurity protections such as encryption, layered malware defenses and periodic penetration testing and vulnerability assessments.

Businesses large and small are increasingly realizing, as they receive questionnaires and service agreements and contract addenda from their customers that request details on how they meet the GDPR's mandates for privacy and confidentiality safeguards and record-keeping, that to thrive in the age of GDPR privacy and cybersecurity thetmust avoid default practices. Safeguards and information management in this regard comprises how they supervise sharing of information with third parties, i.e., how they have performed due diligence to assure that third parties can adequately protect information and the imposition of contractual requirements that require vendors and third party firms to meet the same GDPR standards as the customer. In large measure, how the primary organization manages digital information entrusted to it will be under regulatory scrutiny, and so these organizations are increasingly required to ensure that their service providers, like cloud services, website hosting, marketing, law and accounting firms are compliant with GDPR.

The business opportunities as a result of compliance will be visible with more clarity. Organizations that meet GDPR requirements, which are quickly becoming the gold standard in privacy and cybersecurity practices, will see new areas of business opportunities opening. A robust, well-documented and monitored GDPR program will also be an excellent marketing tool. While this chapter will demonstrate the opportunities for multinational organizations when they have achieved and documented adherence to GDPR standards, there are many more benefits. Many US

---

[2] A "data subject" can be an individual or a business GDPR applies in equal measure to business-to-business ("B2B") digital commerce and to business-to-business ("B2B") interactions.

states[3], and Asian countries,[4] have passed or are actively considering legislation similar to GDPR, and customers in these locations will soon require GDPR "best practice" standards to be followed even for strictly domestic data uses. The opportunities for cost savings through increased efficiencies resulting from data risk assessments required for GDPR compliance should not be overlooked, either. But first, the perspective on compliance – changing the organizational mindset from compliance as a business obstruction to recognition of GDPR standards as a facilitator of business opportunities and in particular, recognizing that new perspective in a data protection agreement that obligates vendors and other business partners to also meet GDPR requirements – must be explored so that it can be clear to those on the front lines who are responsible for day-to-day information management: the business owners.

Before analyzing how businesses that meet GDPR standards can prosper, a short review of the structure of GDPR serves as a background.

Who is Covered by GDPR and Similar Laws?

The harder question to ask would be, "who is not covered?". While the GDPR is law in only the 28 Member States of the European Union[5], the law's reach extends globally to those who sell goods or services to residents of the EU, obtain digital information of or about EU residents, and those who monitor their on line behavior, by using "cookies"[6] or other forms of analytics.[7] Therefore, any organization with a website that analyzes, retains or shares information of EU residents and uses algorithms access to such

---

3 *See*, i.e., California Consumer Data Privacy Act of 2018, available at https:// leginfo.legislature.ca.gov/faces/billTextClient.xhtml?bill_id=201720180AB375 (last visited August 22, 2018), Vermont, Colorado; NYDFS ; The Personal Data Protection Bill 2018 (India), available at http://meity.gov.in/writereaddata/ files/Personal_Data_Protection_Bill%2C2018_0.pdf (last visited August 22, 2018).

4 *I.e.*, India: The Personal Data Protection Bill 2018 (India), available at http://meity. gov.in/writereaddata/files/Personal_Data_Protection_Bill%2C2018_0.pdf (last visited August 22, 2018).

5 The UK Data Protection Act of 2018 is intended to provide GDPR standards for the United Kingdom after the UK has left the EU. It should be noted that certain provisions of the Data Protection Act comprise stricter penalties for violation than those found in GDPR.

6 Cookies are data bits left on the computer of a visitor to a website. These data bits can identify and follow the user around the Internet or may just permit ready identification of the user and her preferences if and when she returned to the website.

7 GDPR Article 3.

information, is covered by GDPR, which has an extraterritorial reach[8]. Put in another way, GDPR affects virtually any organization that has a website, unless that website or other platform is specifically configured to exclude access to and prohibit visits and communications from EU residents. From a business development perspective, organizations that would fit into this narrow category excluding EU residents from one's customer base will be rare and would prove economically counterproductive.[9]

What Activities are Subject to the GDPR?

The scope of activity regulated by GDPR comes readily into focus when one analyzes the Articles regarding the scope and the definitions of terms within those articles. GDPR regulates the "processing of personal data."[10] Article 3 of the GDPR states that the "processing" in question would be that of EU residents, and the processing of data of those residents is covered by the law "regardless of whether the processing takes place in the Union or not"[11] (hence the reach of GDPR is beyond the boundaries of Europe). "Processing" is defined in Article 4 as "any set of operations performed on personal data."[12] So, "processing" includes creation, acquisition, transmission, review and storage (including backup) of personal data. As digital information is the lifeblood of every business, it is not an exaggeration to state that every business engages in "processing." Now, for jurisdictional purposes, does it "process" "personal data?"

What Information is Covered by the Law?

The breadth of the coverage of GDPR through the term "processing" gets a rocket boost from the statutory definition of "personal data." Article 4 defines this term as "any information relating to an identified or identifiable natural person."[13] Unlike US-style data protection laws that are segmented by industry and protect only information pertinent to the activities of those in that industry (i.e., health information under HIPAA[14], account information in SEC or FINRA[15] regulations, education

---

[8] GDPR Article 3 states that the data processor is subject to the requirements of GDPR "regardless of whether the processing takes place in the Union or not".

[9] *See* generally, https://jaxenter.com/avoid-gdpr-geo-blocking-147266.html

[10] GDPR Article 2.

[11] GDPR Article 3.

[12] GDPR Article 4(2).

[13] GDPR Article 4((1).

[14] Health Information Portability and Accountability Act of 1996 at 45 CFR 164.501 *et seq.* (Privacy and Security Rules)

[15] Securities and Exchange Commission (SEC) at Regulation S-P; Financial Regulatory Authority (FINRA) Rule 2010

data under FERPA[16]), GDPR protects *all* information *relating* to the data subject, including communications such as emails or texts written by *or about* that person, or data in databases or other repositories *that concerns* that individual.

The means of identification of the individual for purposes of characterizing the data as personal information is quite broad. It comprises identifiers one might expect, such as a name, address, national identifier number and email or text address, but also those seen in few other regulatory schemes, such as IP addresses. An IP address, the "signature" of the computer used to send the information is "personal data" and therefore is protected under GDPR.

All of this information must be secured as required by Article 32 of GDPR (described in detail below). These provisions arose in large measure in response to the spate of breaches and misuses of personal information in the years leading up to GDPR[17]. But perhaps one of the most groundbreaking aspects of GDPR is the requirement of transparency; that is, letting the data subject know what is being done with her personal data, including giving her a say in those activities by exercising a series of "digital rights." Those corporations under the jurisdiction of GDPR must not only provide a process to accommodate these rights but also a means for accommodation where the request is directed to a third party processor.

Transparency and Notice: What are You Doing with the Subject's Data?

Facebook users were hardly aware that their data would be accessed and processed by a UK company known as Cambridge Analytica, which amassed it to assist the campaign of Donald J. Trump[18]. Even before this story was revealed, though, the Notice and transparency provisions of GDPR[19] had begun to change the paradigm that organizations that collected personal information could use it in whatever ways they wished without advising the data subject. Now, under GDPR, and shortly under the California Consumer Data Privacy Act of 2018[20] data subjects must be told, *at or before the point of data collection* (i.e., on the pertinent website),

---

[16] Federal Education Rights and Privacy Act (FERPA),
[17] GDPR came into full effect on May 25, 2018.
[18] Granville, Kevin, "Facebook and Cambridge Analytica: What you Need to Know as Fallout Widens," *New York Times* March 19, 2018 available at https://www.nytimes.com/2018/03/19/technology/facebook-cambridge-analytica-explained.html (last visited August 22, 2018).
[19] GDPR Articles 3 and 5
[20] California AB 375, available at https://leginfo.legislature.ca.gov/faces/billTextClient.xhtml?bill_id=201720180AB375

whom the data would be sold to or even just shared with, *the purpose* for which a disclosure, sale or transmission or personal information may or will be made.[21] These notices must include the categories of purpose for which the data are processed (including processing for legitimate business purposes, in which case those purposes must be stated); information as to whether automatic decision-making ("profiling" in the US) is utilized and, if so, for what purpose; the period of time for which personal data will be retained and when it will be disposed; and the contact person to whom requests to exercise personal digital rights or to lodge a complaint may be addressed.[22]

Security: Do You take Good Care of the Customers' Data?

GDPR is somewhat typical of non-US data protection schemes in that it has at its core the common-sense maxim that, in the digital age, one cannot have personal information privacy without cybersecurity. These two concepts are inextricably entwined, and this is a critical factor in leveraging GDPR to create business opportunities. Good customer relations in 2018 require that one have in place safeguards for data; in other words, then one is a good steward of the customer's personal information. Article 32 of the GDPR codifies this point in its mandate that the controller[23] "*shall* implement appropriate technical and organizational measures to ensure a level of security appropriate to the risk" (emphasis supplied).[24] These measures include encryption of personal information at rest and in motion (or similar processes to prevent unauthorized disclosure of identifiable information such as anonymization[25] or pseudonymization[26]), documented processes for monitoring the effectiveness of administrative (policy and procedure), technical safeguards and the ability to respond effectively and in a timely manner to a security incident.

Without a doubt, security safeguards are a critical component of consumer confidence in any business, but particularly in those organizations that seek to innovate. They need beta testing of data to ascertain the reliability of their platforms and to refine their applications,

---

[21] GDPR Article 13.

[22] GDPR Article 12.

[23] A "controller" determines the purposes and means of data processing. *See*, GDPR Article 4(7).

[24] GDPR Article 32(1).

[25] Permanent removal from the data of identifiers that could lead to the linkage of the data with information that would lead to the identification of the individual who created the data or who is the subject of the data (i.e., an email, text message or post to social media or a website about an individual). *See* GDPR Article 32.

[26] Temporary removal of the identifiers in a way that could permit reconstitution of the identifiers with the data at a later time. *See* GDPR Article 32.

for business growth. If the organization cannot take good care of the consumer's data, she will not give it to that company and will go elsewhere. Accordingly these organizations will do all they can to assure that their customers' data will be protected in accordance with best practices, for retaining customers and avoiding a bad reputation that accompanies a data breach.

Choose Your Data Partners Wisely: Vendor Management

Rare is the organization that requires no business partners to maintain its information systems, marketing platforms and customer relations management applications. Third party organizations fulfill many roles in the modern business organization. Such tasks include website hosting, security safeguards and monitoring of websites and information systems (i.e., monitors for unusual activity that could be indicative of a cyber attack or reconnaissance by cyber attackers), remote ("cloud" backup and disaster recovery repositories and periodical penetration testing ("ethical" or "white hat" hackers) and vulnerability assessments, often those for which the organization has limited or no capability. These third parties who work with the data of other organizations, are known as "processors," in the context of GDPR.[27] GDPR mandates that organizations may only send personal data to processors with whom they have a contract, often known as a Data Protection Addendum or Agreement, or "DPA," that sets forth representations that the processor will meet the security and privacy safeguards in GDPR[28]; that is, the processor will safeguard the data to the same level of security that is required of the organization that retained the processor. Processors who require the services of other organizations ("sub-processors) must also secure written assurances of compliance with GDPR standards.[29]

These standards do not apply only to technology-based companies. E-commerce companies, healthcare organizations, publishing companies, media companies and even manufacturers are subject to these standards. Further, organizations that retain such processing services that may have access to EU resident's personal data, are subject to additional standards of due diligence, including law and accounting firms; that is, they must document questions asked and answers received that may reasonably indicate that the processor is capable, of meeting GDPR security requirements, technically and administratively. *These bona fides,*

---

[27] GDPR Article 4(8).

[28] GDPR Article 28(3)

[29] GDPR Article 28(4).

and the right of the hiring organization to audit the processor must be documented within the service or engagement agreements to assure that the processor remains in compliance, with the relevant GDPR privacy and security mandates.

The business advantages of meeting GDPR standards should now come into clearer focus. If businesses subject to GDPR may only use business partners that meet GDPR standards, GDPR becomes the bar for service organizations. Meet GPDR standards, more business doors will open. Fail to meet them and the business may well go to those competitors who can and will invest the time and resources to meet the requirements. GDPR compliance, for these service organizations, is not a cost center but, instead, comprises a business advantage and creates business opportunities.

Taking Advantage of the Opportunities: The GDPR Due Diligence Requirements

Due diligence into privacy and security capabilities, and meeting the data safeguard requirements of GDPR, are two sides of one coin. Controllers must know how to assess capabilities of their potential business partners.[30] Those partners, in turn, have to prepare to implement and document the policies, processes and monitoring mechanism of those privacy and security provisions.

Operationalizing the GDPR Business Opportunities

A. What does the customer want?

The end users and the individual customers want to know what is being done with their data, how it is secured, with whom it will be shared and why it will be shared and how they can exercise their rights for limiting the use of, portability or deletion of the data. The organization is required to clearly state guidelines in its privacy policy, but GDPR also requires that these be "operationalized:" put into the daily activities of the organization through policies, procedures, controls for monitoring compliance and documented workforce training. In this way, a virtuous circle is completed.

---

[30] It may be helpful to have third party certify entities assist in this regard. For example, international security standards such as ISO 27001 may in many cases meet the GDPR Article 32 requirement of appropriate security. Many third party organizations can certify ISO 27001 compliance and this third party certification may service as appropriate documentation of technical security safeguards. Other security regimes include SOC2, SOC3 and, for those in the credit card payment matrix, PCI-DSS standards.

However, the above surmises that the privacy policy was prepared a good faith effort to advise the consumers on what will be done with their data in "clear and unambiguous language," as per GDPR _____, so that they can make the ultimate decision as to whether they are comfortable with the data collection and the way it will be used. Prior to GDPR, the term "privacy policy" was almost a cruel irony. Packed with pages of single-spaced legalese text so dense as to be almost opaque to non-attorneys (and even some seasoned lawyers), those "policies" were merely statements of what the company does with data. In essence, they stated "In return for providing you with the service in this application, you agree to give us an unlimited license to use, share and (in some cases) sell your personal data as we deem fit, at our sole discretion. A useful case study involved the developers of an application known as "Unenroll Me," which promised to "clear out your inbox and other storage areas and information the user no longer required. When it was revealed that the developer had collected digital receipts from the ride-hailing service Lyft and sold them to the ride-hailing service Uber, the response of the CEO of UnenrollMe was to point out a provision deep within the company's privacy policy that referred to such a practice and stated "We're sorry that certain users don't like how we monetize this service that we provide for free."[31] The company's reputation, which was heavily dependent upon consumer trust like most organizations, undoubtedly was damaged, perhaps beyond recovery. As of the time of this writing there have been even though no penalty proceedings have been initiated by regulatory authorities in the EU with regard to opaque, confusing, misleading or otherwise deficient privacy policies, it is doubtful that a privacy policy such as that of UnrollMe would have emerged from regulatory scrutiny without criticism and perhaps a significant penalty for the company. Yet, loss of trust by the existing customer base may have been the most long-lasting damage done. Penalties can be paid and Corrective Action Plans can be completed. But trust, once lost, is very difficult to regain.

On the other hand, if consumers feel secure that the company meets GDPR's requirements, they will (hopefully) be confident in giving their data to it. The data, in turn, allows the organization to innovate and grow its data-driver products and services.

B. How can one address the privacy and security of a customer's information when the customer is another business? The Business-2-Business (B2B) opportunities

---

[31] "Unenroll.me, Faces a Backlash Over Widespread Practice: Selling User Data," Isaac, Mike and Lohr, Steve, The New York Times April 24, 2017, available at https://www.nytimes.com/2017/04/24/technology/personal-data-firm-slice-unroll-me-backlash-uber.html (last visited Oct. 27, 2018).

The "customer" is, for service organizations, not the end user (i.e., the individual consumer) but instead the customer is the business that has direct contact with the end user. How can that customer be assured that its third-party business partners can be trusted with its own customers' personal data (the Business-to-Business context)? The GDPR text is a starting point, but GDPR's 99 Articles and 151 Recitals were prepared with the intention to be elastic, covering many industry verticals and to continue to be relevant without the need for regular amendments as technology advances. Accordingly, the GDPR text is not always clearly instructive as to how to meet these "B2B" considerations for every industry. In addition, the requirements of a business for processing another business's personal data are most often highly specific. They are, or should be, addressed in a document commonly known as a Data Protection Agreement (or Addendum), commonly known as a "DPA". These documents are binding contracts required by GDPR, and are usually tailored to the needs of the particular business and its industry vertical by virtue of the description of the services to be provided by the processor, and the commercial terms of the relationship, in a Statement of Work appended to the DPA.

C. Good fences make good neighbors in Business-to-Business: The Data Protection Agreement

This prong of the business opportunity analysis, business to business (or "B2B") is expanding at a rapid pace, and the reason is intuitive. Given the myriad of technical, administrative and record-keeping mandates of GDPR, it is difficult for many small to medium sized organizations to meet the GDPR standards without assistance. This assistance ranges from IT support, consultation of data and website hosting services, legal, accounting and marketing consultants and has led to a multi-billion dollar cottage industry as a result of GDPR compliance support.[32] The opportunity for these support organizations begins with negotiation of the DPA. The way in which this contract is prepared and how the work is monitored can often predict the growth and success of the business relationship.

GDPR Article 28(3) requires that processing of personal data "shall be governed by a contract" that sets out how the information will be processed (in general terms), the purposes of the processing and the standards by which the processor (the support organization) will maintain the privacy and security of the information. This may sound familiar to US lawyers. The US national healthcare privacy law, HIPAA, mandates that before an organization can process protected health information of a healthcare provider or plan (both a "Covered Entity") it must enter into a contract in which the organization providing the service agrees to

---

[32] *See*, generally, https://www.itgovernance.co.ukdpa-compliance-consultancy.

maintain the health information according to the privacy and security standards stipulated by HIPAA.[33] These support organizations are known as HIPAA Business Associates.[34] The HIPAA Rules became effective in 2001, and were amended to strengthen the compliance requirements for Business Associates in 2013.[35]

HIPAA mandates certain clauses that are required in every contract, (known as a Business Associate Agreement) and, except for organizations that try to push the envelope by adding indemnification, injunctive relief, cost-shifting and other provisions not specifically required by HIPAA, the Business Associate Agreement is a fairly routine affair, with little controversy or negative effect on the potential business relationship because there is little discretion in the components of a HIPAA Business Associate Agreement.

The GDPR requirements for organizations providing support that require access to personal data are not quite as prescriptive as those in HIPAA.[36] The HIPAA Business Associate Agreements have been in use for several years and parties to such agreements know what to expect. Generally, the preparation and negotiation of a HIPAA Business Associate Agreement will not create a new business opportunity, and will not endanger an existing relationship. But these are early days for GDPR, and the text regarding the requirements of business partner agreements does not fit all industries or information systems. The pivot points for such agreements, whose discussion may create a better understanding of the obligations of both parties and thereby lead to a stronger, more long-lasting business relationship, include:

a. Data Security

Article 28(3)(c) states that the controllers, organizations who determine the "means and purposes of processing" and retain processors, must secure written assurances from the data processor that it will "take all measures required by Article 32," which comprises data security requirements.[37]

---

[33] See, 42 USC §§164.504(l); 164.308(b)

[34] 42 USC §160.103

[35] HIPAA Omnibus Final Rule, 78 Fed. Reg. 5566 (Jan. 25, 2013)

[36] See Also the New York Department of Financial Services Cybersecurity Regulations, 23 NYCRR 500 at 500.03 and 500.11 that, respectively, required covered entities (banks, insurers, insurance brokers, certain charitable foundations, credit unions and health maintenance organizations and certain elder care centers), respectively, to implement processes to supervise their third party service providers and to include certain provisions such as the right to audit the service provider in the service agreement with that provider.

[37] "Controllers" determine and direct the purpose and means of processing. "Processors," frequently service organizations, carry out processing at the direction of the controller. See, GDPR Article 4.

In other words, the GDPR requires that the controller only use those business partners that secure the data to the same standard of safeguard as the controller. As will be further explained below, a lot is riding on this representation, because the controller may bear responsibility for a processor's data breach due to lax security by the processor if the controller didn't obtain appropriate written assurances that the processor would meet the Article 32 standard. Viewed another way, those organizations that can meet the Article 32 security standard and thereby allow the controller to meet its own security obligations will be best positioned to get the work.

Yet, the processors must exercise caution not to make security representations they cannot meet. They would be well advised to fully examine and, where necessary, update their security safeguards prior to entering negotiations with a controller. Frequently, controllers, to assure themselves that they will have reliable, capable business partners, and vet processors, send detailed multi-page security questionnaires seeking information that would give the controller a profile of how the processor manages data in meeting their due diligence requirement. These questionnaires may include questions about the processor meeting standards such as ISO 27001, SOC2 or SOC3 through third party certifications; whether the processor encrypts data at rest, in motion or both; details the extent and character of the processor's malware defenses (perimeter only, layered, least-privilege or some combination of these); logging access to the systems and whether and, if so, how frequently those access logs are audited; periodic risk assessments, including penetration tests and vulnerability assessments; location of servers; an overview of mobile device management protocols; the existence of security safeguard policies and procedures accessible by the work force; and the extent of periodic work force security training.

If the safeguards and controls are current and tested, the processor may wish to obtain documented backup for its representations with third-party certifications, such as those available pursuant to recognized international security standards such as ISO 27001[38]. Controllers, in their due diligence, may wish to consider requesting review of such certifications (with appropriate protection for that information which may reveal security weaknesses, by clauses requiring that such information be treated with the utmost confidentiality).

b. Subprocessors

To paraphrase the African proverb, it often takes a village to manage

---

[38] Standards that may provide security assurances and third-party certification include SOC2 and 3. The requirements of HIPAA and the CIS Controls, if already met by the organization, may also provide a level of comfort because there is significant overlap between those regimes and GDPR.

the volumes of information generated and received by a multinational organization. Data processors frequently must rely on their own subcontractors, called " sub processors." GDPR envisions the need and use of sub processors in Article 28 (4). Processors may engage sub processors but only on the same terms by which controllers retain processors: sufficient assurances that the sub processors will follow the data protection precepts of GDPR and that they will be responsible for their own acts or omissions. In this regard, controllers must not only inquire about the processors capability to be up to the task, but at the same time must have confidence in the processor's ability to choose its sub processors wisely. The processors that have cultivated and vetted a strong partner ecosystem will be at a distinct business advantage.

c. Security Incident Notification

Notification by the processor to the controller of an actual or threatened data breach is a critical aspect of a DPA, but one that can become very contentious in the drafting it due to overzealousness on the part of counsel or, in some cases, a lack of understanding of the pragmatism built into the GDPR requirements. This can test the drafting and negotiating skills of the most experienced counsel, but resolution can go a long way to creating a strong and lasting commercial relationship.

Given the ecosystem of information management as described above, it is not uncommon for a security incident to originate with a processor or one of its sub processors, a good example being, a processor's employee inadvertently uses the wrong button resulting in a release of personal information to unauthorized recipients, or a sub processor that results in a cyberattack because it failed to apply a cybersecurity patch that could have prevented the attack and resulting breach.

GDPR has caused no small degree of anxiety among controllers by the Article 33 requirement of timing for notification of a security incident to the pertinent supervisory authority. New regulatory schemes often induce over-cautious lawyers to demand unreasonable precautions due to a failure to read the pertinent regulation and relevant guidance documents carefully, and GDPR is no exception.

Article 33 requires that the controller notify the supervisory authority within 72 hours of discovery of a "personal data breach," but that requirement is not absolute. Article 33(1) states that the controller shall notify the supervisory authority "without undue delay, *and where feasible not later than 72 hours* of becoming aware of it" (emphasis supplied). This provision goes on to state that if notification cannot be made within 72 hours, "(the notification) shall be accompanied by reasons for the delay."[39] There is no automatic liability, then, for notification made beyond that 72-hour period.

---

[39] Article 33(1).

Controllers, in their concern about reporting within 72 hours without regard for the "if feasible" language often draft DPAs that state that the processor shall report a personal data breach "immediately" or "within 24 hours" of becoming aware of an actual *or suspected* data breach. "Immediately" is an impossible standard that sets up disputes because a data breach may have occurred weeks or months before it is discovered.[40] In addition, the term "immediate" is subject to a myriad of interpretations. Does it mean right after the introduction of the malware regardless of when it may have happened? When the intrusion was discovered? What if it happens on Christmas Day, when there may be no one available to make or receive such a notification? Even a requirement to advise immediately upon discovery of the data breach is difficult to meet, because the definition of "immediately" is vague: Does it mean the very moment the discovery is made, regardless of the time of day or day of the week? Would four hours, six, or eighteen hours after the moment of discovery be best used to investigate the extent of the attack and salvaging the damage, violate a contract with such a provision?

If this isn't sufficiently headache-inducing, a notification generally does not merely mean only stating that a breach has occurred. It must be accompanied by facts that show how it occurred, and these facts require investigation that cannot be completed within hours, or even days in most cases.

It is in the business interests of processors (and sub processors) to be cognizant of the controller's concerns and to address them rationally, to keep the momentum of the business relationship going and not endangering it by insisting on breach notification standards that, standing alone, may be vague such as "promptly," "as soon as practicable" or "without delay." A defined time limitation for notification following discovery of a breach, with detail about the contents of the notification and an indication of how the processor may assist the controller with the controller's obligations, can instill confidence in the processor, which can lead to more business opportunities for both sides.

d. Audit Rights

The anxiety controllers' experience of data breach notification is often reciprocated by processors' with regard to the controllers' rights to audit and examine how the processors manage and safeguard personal data entrusted to them by the controllers. GDPR Article 28(h) requires the processor to "make available all information necessary to demonstrate compliance with the obligations laid down in this Article and allow for and

---

[40] "Time to Detection Improves While Time to Containment Worsens: Report," Townsend, Kevin, *Security Week* June 21, 2017, available at https://www. itgovernance.co.uk/dpa-compliance-consultancy.

contribute to audits, including inspections, conducted by the controller or another auditor mandated by the controller to it."

Processors may be understandably concerned with the potential intrusion and disruption of their operations by inspections and examination of systems and protocols by the controller. Processors may have other concerns as well, such as the potential disruption of operations that such an audit may cause, or subjective conclusions about the processor's compliance that can lead to expensive disputes. In addition, information regarding how processors manage and protect data may be proprietary. It is also frequently sensitive, to the extent that details of processor's information security, if inadvertently disclosed by the controller, could well expose weaknesses in the processor's defenses (*all* systems have weaknesses) and thereby compromise the processor's ability to conduct business operations. This concern is particularly acute where a controller's counsel may insist on audits of "all processing of personal information," rather than limiting the audit clause to processing of the controller's personal data. Resolution of this question is relatively simple: Inclusion of results of audits by the controller are included within the definition of "Confidential Information" in the agreement with the controller, so that these audit results will be safeguarded by the controller and won't be disclosed without the processor's consent or if required by court order or statute.

Negotiation of these audit rights clauses need not endanger the commercial relationship, or potential relationship, between the processor and the controller. Tracking the audit rights clause to the language of Article 28(3) (h), providing for reasonable notice of an inspection (on site or remote), and treating any information obtained from the audit as confidential can address many of the concerns of controllers and processors.

e. Data Retention

Data retention requirements in a DPA can also be a flashpoint for conflict, but at the same time it can present an opportunity for the processor to show the controller that it is well prepared to meet GDPR obligations and thereby be a long-term business partner of the controller.

Processors are required by Article 28(30(f) to assist controllers in their security obligations as they pertain to data security. While not explicitly set forth in GDPR Article 5 (e), which addresses data retention, states in the text partially out of concern that personal data stored for indefinite periods, which serves no business purpose, can be a source of compromising a data subject if that personal data were taken in a cyber attack.[41]

---

[41] GDPR Recital 39

Much of the personal data of EU residents processed by or on behalf of an organization will be processed by its third-party business partners, which means that these third parties will have significant volumes of an organization's data in their possession. GDPR Article 5(e) requires that such data be kept for a period no longer than that required by the business purpose for which the data was collected and/or otherwise processed, or as required by law. The DPA, then must contain requirements for the processor to abide by this data retention – or, practically minimize or delete it as required.

Keeping data as required by law is a relatively straight-forward exercise. For many years, law firms and consultancies have had lucrative business opportunities in creating retention schedules with requirements that comprise time periods for which data must be kept by mapping the company's data categories to the laws and regulations that mandated that it be kept for specific periods of time. Article 5 of the GDPR, though, turns this paradigm on its head. It mandates that an organization should *delete or destroy* data which no longer has a legal or business purpose instead of retaining it.

How to determine if data should be deleted by a business is only half the question. Perhaps the more difficult inquiry comes in the second half: How does one prescribe criteria, in a policy and process that can be followed consistently, for *retaining* data that the business requires? Put another way, when is retention of personal data necessary for business purposes? Customers often cease to communicate with an organization for long periods, only to resurface months or years later to rekindle the business relationship. This business purpose retention period – the period for which the business must have the information available – can only be determined by the business needs of the controller, who would then communicate these data minimization protocols to the processor so the processor would know when and how the controller wishes its data to be deleted and also how the processor would certify to the controller that this has been done.

Yet, all too often controllers merely parrot the language of Article 5(e) for DPAs and mandate that the processor follow it, without providing any guidance on how this can be accomplished. An effective DPA that defines the roles of both parties should specify that the controller will provide criteria and a process for deletion of data after the business purpose for which it was processed has expired (i.e., the controller will advise the processor as to how that determination will be made). A processor that raises this question in negotiations on the DPA will demonstrate its compliance with GDPR as a business process and thereby instill confidence in the controller that the processor is a reliable business partner in this new and quickly evolving legal and business environment.

Conclusion

When it comes to privacy and cybersecurity as vital components of business strategy the times, as Bob Dylan famously wrote, as "a-changin'." Privacy and cybersecurity are now, and will be for the foreseeable future, tentpole components of the strategy of any business that is engaged in commerce over the Internet – a category that comprises almost every organization, from three-person service providers to the largest internet service providers. There are a number of ironies in the development of the legal matrix of privacy and cybersecurity. Understanding and appreciating them should lead enterprises to get ahead of the sales and marketing curve and thereby develop competitive advantages by meeting the new customer awareness of, and concerns about, the sort of privacy and security issues addressed by GDPR.

The e-commerce landscape has irreversibly changed since the days Scott McNeally, former CEO of Sun Microsystems, dismissed privacy concerns by stating "You have privacy, anyway Get over it,"[42] and Mark Zuckerberg said that privacy is an outmoded social norm.[43] US law and regulations essentially followed this model; that is, apps were (and still are) offered ostensibly without cost, but the real currency is personal data. Any end user license agreement for an app can be downloaded to one's phone, tablet or other device, states "The data may be yours, but in return for providing you with this app you give us a license to do anything we want with it, when its many pages of opaque legalese are distilled to their essence." This has proven to be a very lucrative business model for companies like Google and Facebook and for many small to medium sized enterprises as well. Why should a business change its model that has brought it so much revenue? Well, because its customer base is demanding they do so. As Bob Dylan famously wrote, are indeed "a-changin'," and businesses are beginning to realize the need to recognize this now because, as Mr. Dylan also sang, that "he that gets hurt will be he that has stalled."[44]

Edward Snowden's revelations concerning the extent of US government surveillance on citizens outside the US as well as the myriad of breaches of personal information by and from US companies, some like Yahoo involving hundreds of millions of users, has changed the paradigm. GDPR can be viewed as a direct response to concern in Europe about these excesses of data mining and access, but that's not a surprise as Europe,

---

[42] "Sun on Privacy: 'Get Over It'," Sprenger, Polly, *Wired* January 26, 1999 available at https://www.wired.com/1999/01/sun-on-privacy-get-over-it/.

[43] "Privacy No Longer a Social Norm, says Facebook founder," *The Guardian* January 11, 2010 available at https://www.theguardian.com/technology/2010/jan/11/facebook-privacy.

[44] "The Times They Are a Changin'," Bob Dylan, Witmark Demo – 1963, © Audlam, Inc.

from the time of the 1995 EU Privacy Directives, has had a much keener sense of the importance of privacy.

In the wake of an increasing number of data breaches internet surveillance by government and, finally, disclosures that such breaches (Facebook) and surveillance (Russian, in addition to the US), may have played a role in the election of Donald Trump as US president, consumers have had enough. Put succinctly, GDPR compliance is a means for businesses to show consumers that they are listening to concerns about privacy and security and are doing something about it. US states such as California, Colorado and Vermont have followed this trend with their adaptations of GDPR in data privacy and security law for their respective states.

In the B2B sphere, GDPR business opportunities play out in this regard as clearly as night follows day:

1. Consumers want to know how their data is being used and with whom it's being shared, and want more privacy and data security protections.
2. GDPR and similar US state laws provide a data superstructure that addresses these concerns at a level consumers understand: The law states that the company has to be transparent and must protect their data.
3. For businesses to innovate and create new platforms and services, they must obtain increasing amounts of consumer data. In addition, for these businesses to thrive, consumers must trust that these businesses will appropriately secure and protect their data.
4. The businesses, then, will require any business partner that accesses personal data of its customers, to meet the same GDPR and other privacy and security law standards that pertain to the business.
5. The businesses that meet these standards will get more business from consumers. The providers that can meet these standards will, therefore, get more business from their business customers.

GDPR, and similar laws and regulations in other countries and even in certain US states, then will provide business opportunities for some time. With the continued development of artificial intelligence, which requires millions of data points, these opportunities will only increase. To put a fine point on the business risks for those organizations that are still viewing compliance through the outdated perspective that meeting digital privacy and security standards interferes with business, we must turn to Bob Dylan once again:

> *Admit that the waters around you have grown*
> *And accept that soon you'll be drenched to the bone*
> *If your time to you is worth savin'*

Then you'd better start swimmin'
Or you'll sink like a stone
'cause the times, they are a changin'.[45]

[45] Dylan Bob, "The Times They Are a-Changin," Universal Music, 1963.

Executing Streamlined and Cost-Effective Investigations Across Disparate Data Sources

Daniel S. Meyers*, Esq., Al-Karim Markhani, Esq. and Joseph Pochron

Introduction

Today's fast moving and competitive business-to-business and business-to-consumer environment is driving organizations to engage in a variety of digital transformation processes, often contributing to the proliferation of data sources. Indeed, the information technology infrastructure of businesses today is no longer limited to behind-the-firewall servers and enterprise appliances from traditional providers like Microsoft and IBM. Modern employees demand the ability to access their workspace and collaborate with colleagues in dynamic, diverse environments accessed from the road, from mobile devices and through the cloud. A dizzying array of platforms have arisen to meet this demand. The result is that present-day employees discuss projects on one platform (Teams, Slack, etc.), collaborate through another (Confluence, SharePoint), and manage client relationships through a third (Salesforce, Zendesk, Jira). And that's not to mention the underlying universe of corporate emails, text messages, social media accounts and accounting/finance databases. While this panoply of data sources is a boon to operational efficiency, employee satisfaction and client engagement, it presents a nightmare for legal and compliance professionals. Fortunately, tech-forward platforms and work flows have also arisen to alleviate these tech-forward pain points. This chapter explores tools and techniques to manage a streamlined and effective investigation process across disparate data sources. From knowledge integration platforms to artificial intelligence and machine

*Corresponding author: dmeyers@transperfect.com

learning, companies can access, search and manage their enterprise data in an efficient, defensible, compliant manner.

Disparate Data Sources: A Snapshot of the Modern IT Infrastructure and the Resulting Challenges to an Efficient Investigation

One of the more impactful changes to the investigatory landscape has been the acceleration of new data source adoption in corporations and small businesses alike. Reliance on traditional sources for data storage and communication have changed; customary email and network share storage are being supplemented or undergoing outright replacement by cloud-based platforms, many of which offer a multitude of functions and serve in a hybrid capacity.

The utilization of additional data platforms has impacted the investigatory process at the point of collection in two ways; the need to preserve data from more platforms has grown exponentially and the format of how that data can be preserved has developed into a very real challenge. First though, let's discuss the impact of a seemingly endless variety of data sources.

While email and electronic documents still dominate data preservation, these practices have extended to databases, instant messages, text messages, multimedia files, and social media. Additionally, the breadth of devices capable of storing this data has expanded, and so have the devices companies are choosing for preservation. Most notable is the rise of cloud-based platforms and mobile devices, both fairly new to the investigation process and both presenting unique challenges. Aside from these sources, email, social media, and instant messaging are impacting investigations. The following graphic from a 2017 benchmarking report of in-house lawyers demonstrates the breadth of platforms that fall within the scope of a modern litigation or investigation:[1]

A. Email

The preservation and retention of email has changed significantly over the course of the last few years, due in most part to Microsoft Office365's Security & Compliance platform and the Google Suite of cloud-based business tools, which have continued to evolve into full-fledged investigation and analysis platforms. Importantly, as it relates to email collection for investigation purposes, these platforms have reduced the need for onsite, in-person collections, and provides a universal mechanism for dealing with the preservation of email and certain types of unstructured data. The developments have eased the need for IT departments to spend a great deal of time learning how to export mail, apply legal holds, and

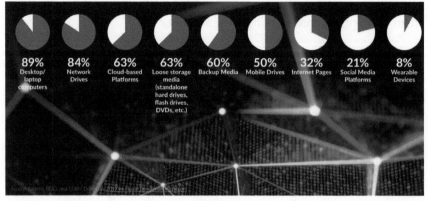

Fig. 9.1.

run targeted searches. In turn, the rise of companies "self-collecting" data has significantly streamlined investigations. According to a 2016 Gartner survey, 78 percent of enterprises used or planned to use Office365, which was a 14% increase since 2014.[2]

B. Instant Messaging

Instant Messaging has been around for quite some time, but utilization in corporate environments has changed, alongwith the need, and ability, to preserve that data. Several factors, including speed, team collaboration and mobile devices, have pushed the popularity of IM applications. Additionally, instant messaging applications are available across a wide variety of devices; the same application can be used on a computer, mobile device, tablet, or through a web browser to name a few. Certain instant messaging applications may offer a retention option, but in large part, the need to collect that data directly from the end-device still dominates collection requests. This can be particularly challenging when the messaging application is primarily used on a mobile device.

C. Mobile Devices

The need to collect data from mobile devices has continued to increase in recent years, undoubtedly impacted by the rise of "bring your own device" (BYOD) or "company-owned, personally-enabled" (COPE) corporate mobile device policies. In fact, a new acronym has emerged – Bring Your Own App (BYOA) that really speaks more about the impact mobile devices have had on data collections. A recent article estimated that over 90% of knowledge workers use 3rd-party applications for work.[3] Many of these applications are not officially approved by IT departments; they are applications the user has unilaterally adopted and put in use, a practice referred to as "shadow IT".

This greatly impacts data collections because retention by the user is not happening often and the mobile device is the main source for preserving this data. Mobile device collections significantly differ from other digital devices and application support is highly dependent on the make, model, and operating system. Furthermore, security plays a prominent role in the success of the data collection. Although recent advances to bypass/crack passwords have occurred, the ability to do so often requires expensive mobile forensic tools or tools that are only available to law enforcement or the military. In short, apart from the device itself, in most instances the password is required for successful data collection.

Application support varies depending on the device. An application like WhatsApp may be supported for extraction on a certain mobile device, but not for another. Additionally, certain applications may not store the data, or a good portion of the data on the mobile device, but rather in the cloud. A recent trend is the evolution of mobile device forensic tools to have the ability to "reach" cloud accounts authenticated on the mobile device to collect data. Undoubtedly, this trend will continue in the future.

D. Social Media

Social media platforms continue to evolve in terms of enabling users to collect and preserve their data. In recent years, tools that would crawl social media sites had been the industry preference. However, due to recent events and privacy concerns, sites like Facebook and Instagram (owned by Facebook) have limited this ability of third party platforms, forcing users to look for alternative options. The majority of sites have a native archive feature that exports site data. The format of data from the archive option is typically the biggest differentiator, but it offers an easy, and cheap, option for data collection.

Since social media sites offer various methods of communication, depending on the site, data collection may occur from a mobile device or computer synced to the account.

E. Cloud-Based Platforms

The popularity of project management and/or project collaboration platforms has had a significant impact on data collection and preservation. These platforms usually are cloud-based, offer several different utilities for project management and communication, and typically present unique preservation issues.

Platforms like Slack, Jira, and Quip provide the user with many operational benefits, including the ability to create projects, edit documents and communicate via instant messaging. This is very efficient for the user but presents challenges for data collection since vastly different file types will be present within one platform.

Additionally, platforms like these primarily run from cloud servers so the timing to export large volumes of data needs to be considered. In many instances, native export options provide a portion of the data, but may not include attachments, which need to be exported separately.

The format of data stored on cloud platforms also needs to be considered. Data from cloud-based platforms usually has limited native options for export, especially when the need is a bulk export. If data is needed for legal review, the export format may not be suitable, and further processing of the data will be required to allow for human review.

In conclusion, the significant proliferation of data sources in recent years has resulted in numerous challenges to an efficient document preservation, collection and investigation process. These challenges not only undermine the efficiency of an investigation, but as discussed in the next section, also create an obstacle to meeting a company's document retention and preservation obligations.

The Legal Obligations to Retain and Preserve Electronic Documents and Data

The duty to retain and/or preserve electronically-stored information ("ESI") arises in a number of contexts. The most common sources of these obligations are (a) document retention requirements imposed by statute and (b) document preservation obligations, triggered when ESI is potentially relevant to a pending or anticipated litigation, arbitration or governmental investigation. This section will survey such obligations under the laws of the U.S. and the U.K.

A. Regulatory Obligations to Retain ESI

1. The United States

In the United States, obligations to retain documents and ESI for pre-determined periods of time come from a panoply of federal, state and municipal laws. For example, under U.S. federal law, employers must retain records regarding employee benefit plans for six years. *See* 29 U.S.C. S. 1027. Likewise, under Section 17(a) of the Securities Exchange Act of 1934, a six-year record retention obligation is imposed on registered brokers and dealers with respect to a wide variety of documents (including all client account terms and all records needed to respond to a SEC audit).

The Internal Revenue Code contains a spectrum of potentially applicable retention periods depending on the action, expense, or event that the document records.[4] U.S. State insurance regulators similarly impose an array of retention obligations depending on the jurisdiction and record type. *See, e.g.,* 11 NYCRR § 243.2(b) (New York imposes a six-year retention period for policy records); 39 Pa.B. 4664 (Pennsylvania imposes a seven-year requirement); 114 CSR 15 (West Virginia imposes a five-year requirement).

Document retention obligations are also imposed by industry-specific associations. As one example, the Rules of Professional Conduct regulating the practice of law contain a variety of obligatory retention periods depending on the relevant U.S. state. *See e.g.,* Colo. RPC S. 1.15-1.16 (imposing six or ten-year record retention provisions depending on record type); New *Jersey* Court R. 1:21-6 (seven-year retention period). As another example, the American Petroleum Institute, a national trade association representing all facets of the oil and natural gas industry in the U.S., has promulgated a standardized Quality Manual that mandates that all member entities retain a diverse array of records for at least five years. Analogous provisions exist in industry standards governing accountants, automobile manufacturers, chemical companies, insurance providers among others

2. The United Kingdom

Likewise, in England and Wales, obligations to retain documents and ESI can be found in all manner of statutes, regulations and directives. Whilst the examples below are by no means exhaustive, their diversity indicates the depth to which document retention is now a function of the modern legal and commercial landscape.

It is well known that companies must retain a copy of the minutes and resolutions from board meetings from the date of the meeting for 10 years – section 248 Companies Act 2006. Failure to comply renders every officer of the company guilty and liable to summary conviction. The same employer is also under an obligation to retain maternity pay records for three years after the end of the tax year in which the maternity pay period ends – regulation 26, Statutory Maternity Pay (General) Regulations 1986 (SI 1986/1960).

Unsurprisingly, there are a raft of obligations relating to medical and safety records. Schedule 3 of the Control of Substances Hazardous to Health Regulations 2002 2002/2677 obliges employers to retain a list of employees exposed to substances which can cause human disease indicating the type of work carried out, the agent to which they were exposed and records of accidents and incidents for a minimum of 40 years.

The Solicitors Regulation Authority Handbook sets out the rules applicable to law firms in England and Wales. As with the U.S. it stipulates at Rule 10 that certain records made under the SRA rules (including but not limited to instructions, transactions, commissions etc.) must be retained for at least six years. In addition to the typical rules for companies, medical records and professional organizations, records must also be retained for everything from environmental purposes to general tax inspection.

3. Document Retention Policies and Schedules

Because the duty to retain documents and ESI is derived from a complex web of statutes and industry standards, many companies invest significant time and resource development, maintaining and periodically updating document retention schedules and policies.

A document retention schedule can be thought of as the "what" behind the company's retention obligations. This is typically a lengthy matrix that breaks down the entity's records by category (*e.g.*, Accounting, Legal, Corporate, Human Resources), with each category being further broken down by record class (*e.g.*, tax documents, contracts, employment applications, etc.). The retention schedule will detail the applicable retention period and cite the legal source of the relevant obligation.

A document retention policy can be thought of as the "how" and "who" of the company's retention obligations. This document explains to employees and corporate stakeholders the scope of their retention obligations and how to comply with them.

The recent proliferation of document *destruction* obligations is further complicating matters – i.e., statutory or industry-based obligations *not* to retain data longer than necessary. As examples, under the GDPR, documents containing personal data shall be retained "no longer than is necessary for the purposes for which the personal data is processed[.]" GDPR Art. 5(1)(e). Likewise, the Payment Card Industry Data Security Standard (PCI DSS) obligates covered entities to "limit data storage amount and retention time to that which is required for legal, regulatory, and/or business requirements." PCI DSS Requirement 3.1.

In conclusion, a company's document retention obligations are varied and multifaceted. They depend on the jurisdiction(s) in which the company operates, its industry and its professional affiliations. The process of identifying applicable obligations is itself a challenge. Effectively implementing those requirements across a disparate matrix of data sources raises the challenge by several orders of magnitude.

B. The Duty to Preserve ESI

The statutory and industry-based document retention obligations described above are constant requirements triggered by jurisdiction and verticals, not by specific events or circumstances that arise and disappear over time. By contrast, the document preservation obligations that apply when an entity is subject to a litigation, arbitration or governmental investigation are ephemeral.

1. The United States

Dispute-based preservation obligations under U.S. law have been aptly summarized by the Sedona Conference[5] as follows: "whenever litigation is reasonably anticipated, threatened, or pending against an organization, that organization has a duty to undertake reasonable and actions in good faith to preserve relevant and discoverable information and tangible evidence." *The Sedona Conference® Commentary On Legal Holds: The Trigger & The Process*, 11 Sedona Conf. J. 265, 267 (2010) ("Sedona Legal Hold Commentary"). Thus, the duty to preserve documents can arise even before a lawsuit is filed so long as a party is on notice that future ligation is likely. *See Cache La Poudre Feeds, LLC v. Land O'Lakes, Inc.*, 244 F.R.D. 614, 621 (D. Colo. 2007).

Once a party's duty to preserve documents has been triggered, the party is obligated to take comprehensive and multifaceted measures. *See Voom HD Holdings LLC v. Echostar Satellite LLC*, 93 A.D.3d 33, 41-42 (1st Dep't 2012) (the party must (i) "take active steps to halt" any "automatic deletion features that periodically purge electronic documents such as emails," (ii) "direct appropriate employees to preserve all relevant records," and (iii) "create a mechanism for collecting the preserved records so that they might be searched by someone other than the employee."); *see also* Sedona Legal Hold Commentary at 267 ("The duty to preserve requires a party to identify, locate, and maintain information and tangible evidence that is relevant to specific and identifiable litigation.").

Implementing such measures across a disparate array of data sources requires a deep understanding of how those data sources operate, and a potentially significant commitment of resources. *See generally* The Sedona Principles, Second Edition: Best Practices, Recommendations & Principles for Addressing Electronic Document Production 17 (The Sedona Conference Working Group Series, 2007) ("Transaction costs due to electronic discovery" can be "overwhelming."); *Concord Boat Corp. v. Brunswick Corp.*, No. LR-C-95-781, 1997 WL 33352759, at *4 (E.D. Ark. Aug 29, 1997) ("Hard disk or tape storage of data is very costly. With corporations spending enormous amounts of money to preserve business-related and financial data . . . they should not be required to preserve every e-mail message at a significant additional expense.").

In recent years, parties to litigation have struggled to satisfy their document preservation burdens with respect to the more technically progressive and innovative data platforms discussed above, resulting in sanctions, fines and reputational harm.

For example, in *Brown v. Tellermate Holdings*, No. 2:11-cv-1122, 2014 WL 2987051 (S.D. Oh. July 1, 2014), the court imposed severe sanctions against a litigant for failing to properly preserve and produce ESI records stored in the company's "Salesforce.com"account. In that litigation, as part of their employment discrimination claim, plaintiffs demanded that the defendant produce reports from Salesforce, a cloud platform that Tellermate used to track employee sales performance. The defendant refused, arguing that it could "only access the salesforce.com database in real time," and thus, if plaintiffs desire historical data, they would need to subpoena Salesforce itself. *See* 2014 WL 2987051, at *1, *5, *20. In reality, however, this argument betrayed a fundamental misunderstanding of the Salesforce platform; "any [defendant] employee with a login name and password could access . . . historical information [on salesforce.com] at any time." *Id*. at 9. The court noted that the defendant's "failure to appreciate" the nature of the defendant's ESI led to a "corresponding failure to take steps to preserve that information" beyond the three- to six-month period it was automatically stored by salesforce.com and as a result, relevant data was lost forever. *Id*. at *9.

As a result, the court imposed a variety of sanctions against the defendant, including a preclusionary order prohibiting the defendantf rom introducing any evidence for performance-related termination of the plaintiffs, effectively eviscerating the defendant's core defense in the litigation. Notably, the *Tellermate* court did not only sanction the litigant for its failure to preserve ESI stored on Salesforce, but also outside counsel. *See* 2014 WL 2987051, at *1 (chastising counsel for falling "far short of their obligation to *examine critically* the information which Tellermate gave them [about ESI]").

2. The United Kingdom

Likewise, in England and Wales, there exist numerous obligations around ESI and sanctions for non-compliance. The most common penalties still come in the form of costs. Parties and their representatives are well aware of the risks and must advise their clients accordingly. For example, in *West African Pipeline Company Ltd v Willbros Global Holdings Inc* [2012] EWHC 396 (TCC), court-imposed cost sanctions were applicable to seven separate breaches ranging from failure to properly gather custodians' data to failure to provide appropriate metadata fields.

The specific obligation to preserve documents in the context of a dispute, emanates from Part 7 of Practice Direction 31B – Disclosure of Electronic Documents in the Civil Procedure Rules – "As soon as litigation is contemplated, the parties' legal representatives must notify their clients of the need to preserve disclosable documents. The documents to be preserved include Electronic Documents which would otherwise be deleted in accordance with a document retention policy or otherwise deleted in the ordinary course of business." This rule, however, is subject to amendment. At the time of publication, new disclosure rules for the Courts of England and Wales are being considered by the Rolls Building Disclosure Working Group in response to widespread industry concern around the scale and complexity of disclosure. The resulting rule changes will no doubt examine the growing number of disparate data sources in which information is contained and how best to deal with them procedurally.

Whilst commonly accepted in progressive jurisdictions, it is worth noting that the definition of a document under the CPR is so broad – "anything in which information of any description is recorded" – that any format of ESI is a document in both rules and case law.

It is well established that the destruction or failure to preserve such documents would draw adverse inferences from a court potentially harming the credibility and veracity of a case. As mentioned above financial penalties for breaches of such obligations are common. Where it appears documents have not been properly preserved, the court has further powers relating to recovering such information, for example to compel forensic recovery of deleted data. On a strict interpretation of CPR r.3.4 (2)(c), breach of such direction practice would provide grounds for strike-out. However, relevant jurisprudence suggests the court will only go this far if such destruction is an attempt to pervert the course of justice - *Douglas v Hello!* [2003] EWHC 55 (Ch). In practice therefore, lawyers are obliged under the procedural rules to notify clients of the need to preserve disclosable ESI from any sources where information relevant to a particular action may be stored. It is of course more important where organizations have routine procedures relating to any electronic information.

The starting point for establishing which sources fall into the scope of disclosure is CPR r. 31.5. The current procedural rules require parties to state where and with whom electronic documents are stored (CPR r.31.5(3)(b) & (c)) 14 days before the first Case Management Conference (CMC). Additionally, US style "meet and confer" obligations are foisted upon the parties before the CMC. This ensures, to the extent possible, no relevant information slips through the net at the earliest stage.

The courts' appreciation for disparate data sources was clear in the recent case of *Glaxo Wellcome UK Limited & Anor v Sandoz Limited & Ors* [2018] EWHC 1626 (Ch). The claimants made an application in relation to the defendants' disclosure, regarding a particular use of a "DocXchange" platform. The application was made in the context of what was already considered to be significant disclosure. The claimants alone sought over 40 custodians, over time periods in excess of 10 years. Even though extensive search terms had been applied, over 400,000 documents were still manually reviewed. The process took six months and cost over £2 million.

The platform in question was set up for various defendants to share information in relation to the inhaler design in question. The issue was that the platform was destroyed when some of the defendants were in the process of joining the action. The defendants' solicitors had provided, on affidavit, information about the platform and its destruction but the judge noted that it was lacking in detail and importantly came from a lawyer, not a technologist who had an appreciation for the information on the platform or reasons for its decommission.

The judge said *"It is not clear from Mr. Howe Q.C.'s evidence, who represents the defendants and accepts the fact that there was a likelihood of documents being held in the platform which were not held elsewhere. There is no uncertainty about that. It follows that there may have been documents falling within CPR 31.6 within the platform which should have been disclosed during the destruction of the system."* Furthermore, *"There is no suggestion from the court that there has been an attempt to consciously mislead. However, the exercise of providing disclosure is underpinned by duties placed on the disclosing party to undertake the exercise with due care. The evidence that has been provided to the court suggests that the defendant did not exercise proper care in this case. The defendants and the defendants' solicitors were plainly aware of their obligation to disclose documents which they had in their control but which they no longer have."*

The judge was in favor of the claimants and made an order on the terms sought. This case is an important reminder that parties must be informed of their duty to preserve documents, as soon as litigation is contemplated. It is also an important reminder that parties and their lawyers must properly explore the format and the source in which any relevant information was or is held, which, as discussed earlier in Section II, is a significant challenge with respect to modern IT infrastructure.

Executing Investigations Across Disparate Data Sources

The foregoing demonstrates that while data sources are expanding and changing rapidly, the legal obligations to retain, preserve and collect such ESI, in the context of litigations, arbitrations and governmental investigations, remain constant. This juxtaposition creates many challenges and mandates new solutions.

A. New Sources, New Challenges

Traditional sources of ESI were often accessed in a similar way. Data from computers and servers were imaged using traditional forensic tools, the file content extracted, processed and reviewed. Preservation methods and defensibility were well understood, and various file types with associated metadata were combined to tell a story. Even scanned paper documents fit well into this work flow.

When mobile devices started to be recognized as important sources of evidence challenges were created by dozens of different cell phone manufacturers, each with a proprietary operating system for their devices. Years of consolidation and standardization in the mobile device industry has helped to solve some of these problems, resulting in a few acceptable phone operating systems which are largely aligned with computer operating systems from a technical standpoint.

In today's technical landscape, we are once again seeing the proliferation of proprietary operating environments, across multiple technologies and business segments. Many new sources of ESI are being introduced almost on a daily basis, and virtually all of them are custom built. Some of these new sources (e.g. cloud-based storage and tools, or distributed ledgers) have some similarities to traditional data sources, driven mainly by the need to maintain backward compatibility. Others (e.g. machine learning, artificial intelligence and distributed processing) represent new concepts with no direct similarity with the traditional process of investigating ESI.

These new data sources sound familiar from last year's science fiction and this year's marketing campaigns. The buzz words and broad technical concepts include: Cloud-based, Blockchain, Cryptocurrency, Machine learning, Artificial Intelligence, Internet of Things and Big Data.

The business processes that utilize these emerging technologies are showing up today across the investigation process. Evidence from IoT sensor nets or decision-making processes for self-driving cars are now part of data investigations and regulatory inquiries. Automated decision making driven by big data, and financial transactions involving cryptocurrency or distributed ledgers are at the center of some court cases. To one degree or another, each of these technical innovations brings challenges to the process of retaining, preserving, collecting and investigating ESI. Furthermore, not each product or system in a given category will introduce the same challenges in the same way as few standards exist with vendors in these technologies. However, we can categorize the challenges and outline typical approaches that can be applied broadly when addressing new or novel data sources in the context of a litigation or investigation.

B. Strategies to Acquire, Normalize and Present ESI from Modern Data Sources

The difficulties in integrating new data sources across the investigation process can be grouped into three categories: acquisition, normalization, and presentation.

1. Acquisition

Traditional data sources have long established methods for surveying, assessing and collecting ESI. Non-traditional data sources often require different approaches to identify relevant data, determining volumes, targeting the required data, and preserving it externally.

In traditional acquisition and preservation, the gold standard was a bit-by-bit preservation or image of the source storage system. This is still commonplace when preserving data in laptops, desktops and storage devices. Email communications have typically been collected into a known container format such as PST. Sources like mobile devices and large file servers are often collected logically, preserving the data and control file structures from the source.

Many new data sources cannot be accessed directly. Their data is typically created and accessed through a software application or some other process. Examples include proprietary chat or communications platforms, and IoT management platforms that control devices connected by the Internet. There are usually a few strategic options for obtaining data:

- Source Application – In some cases, the application that was used to create the data will allow some or all the data to be exported. The export format may be limited, and the export may or may not include metadata or internal control data, useful to determine when and by whom the data was created. The data may also be interpreted or abstracted, as is often the case in IoT, Big Data or AI systems. Some of these data sources may also have an administrative console through which certain data can be exported. Whether such exports are forensically defensible – i.e., capture relevant metadata fields without impacting them during the export process – should be assessed and validated on a platform-by-platform basis.

- Third Party Application – For some cloud platforms, block chain standards, and other types of new data sources, there are third party applications available to help preserve and collect data. Examples include social media platforms (Facebook, Instagram, etc.) and group collaboration tools (Slack, Jira, etc.). These data sources may allow for direct data export, but the third party tools allow more control over the content and format of the data retrieval. Once again, whether such exports are forensically defensible should be assessed and validated on a platform-by-platform basis.

- API – Many cloud-based data sources have an Automated Programming Interface (API) designed into them. This is a feature that allows technology platforms to communicate with each other by passing data back and forth. The data available through an API often exceeds that available via other methods, though it tends to be in a raw and unformatted. APIs range from simple to very complex, and some platforms have multiple APIs with varying degrees of capability. The third party applications previously mentioned often make use of APIs to access data. While most platforms have an API of some kind, the platform owner may not officially allow or support its use. In the absence of a third party tool, using an API to acquire data may require some custom programming or scripting.

- Direct Data Access – For some new data sources, the raw data may be stored in a database or file system. Gaining access can be problematic as these data sources are often multi-tenanted with no easy way to segregate data or access, causing the resource owner to object to this method.

- Access, Security and Debugging Logs – Depending on the nature of the data source and the inquiry, sometimes information such as user access logs, security logs, or event and debugging logs may be relevant. These types of logs are often available for cloud-based data sources, though they may be transitory with fairly small retention periods.

2. Normalization

Managing the combination of data from novel sources and non-standard formats into a body of conventional ESI (e.g., email communications and business documents) can be difficult. Metadata, which often plays a role in understanding digital evidence, can have different meanings. Extracting new data in this context can make its meaning and relationships to other data unclear. The use of search terms and other data reduction techniques may need to be adjusted to accommodate the new data sources.

Indeed, when data from multiple sources is combined in a single investigation for a consolidated view of all available information, there may be certain aspects pertaining to it that need to be adjusted or synchronized to fit with the whole. What is required for each data source should be evaluated separately based on the needs of the case and the role that is expected to play. Areas for consideration include:

- Metadata – The taxonomy and meaning of metadata fields between data sources should be normalized. Different sources may treat fields like MAC dates and owners separately. Time zones should be synchronized. User or custodian names may be represented differently across sources and require synchronization.
- Threading – In modern technology environments, it is not unusual for a conversation about a single topic to take place across multiple platforms. If those conversations need to be threaded together, the user names, data and conversation members will need to be synchronized for continuity.
- Enrichment – If logs or raw data are collected, the data may need to be enriched for it to be properly synchronized. IP addresses may need to be linked with names of people or companies. Internal reference numbers may need to be correlated with other data from a raw data dump. Logs may need to be pre-filtered to include only log entries of interest.
- Volume – If an extremely large amount of volume is collected, as may be the case when handling big data, IoT or AI/MT systems, some

pre-analysis may be necessary. The individual data points may be too voluminous to tell a story, but some basic numeric analytic or summaries (supported by the details) may better meet the needs of the case.

It is also important to understand if the data from a source has been prefiltered or limited in some way. The purpose of normalization is to make sure the data tells a story in a consistent voice, and to cut out any differences that may impact downstream interpretation or analysis.

3. Presentation

In the investigation process, the last step often includes "producing" or "presenting" relevant ESI to an adversary, a governmental agency or an internal compliance committee or board of directors. It may be difficult to format or present information obtained from new technologies. Sometimes there is no mechanism for displaying this data outside of the device or process that created it.

Once the data has been collected and normalized, there needs to be a coherent method for presenting it. Materials collected from traditional sources such as electronic documents, emails or text messages, can be displayed in TIFF or PDF format, or native documents or text files. There are no standard formats for displaying or presenting large amounts of data from IoT sensors, or the decision tree used by an artificial intelligence engines to decide on an action. The review, presentation and production processes should be adjusted to work within the limitation imposed by the nature of the data as well as the methods used to acquire and normalize the data. For example, IoT sensor data may be presented as a numerical and statistical analysis of the body of the data, accompanied by samples of the data itself. The presentation method needs to avoid interpretation of meaning and focus while presenting the data such that it can be understood in the context of the case.

One emerging solution to the integration of disparate data sources is the knowledge integration platform. These tools, generally a cloud-based service offering, can connect directly to multiple data sources simultaneously. Such platforms often use APIs to access the ESI in each data source, either as an on-demand function or continuously. As the platform acquires and aggregates the data, it also addresses the issues of normalization and presentation. Some of these knowledge integration platforms add functionality such as automatic indexing, sophisticated search, and the use of AI to identify the file content, perform sentiment analysis and identify languages present. While these solutions can be extremely useful in managing multi-sourced data collections, they are subject to inherent limitations of the platform or the APIs in use.

Conclusion

There is no end in sight for the introduction of new and diverse data sources into the investigation process. While these technologies mature and evolve at an incredible pace, the underlying legal and regulatory duties to retain, preserve, collect and analyze change at a glacial pace. So, while standards may start to emerge which ease the issues of acquisition, normalization and presentation, the practitioner needs to be prepared to move quickly and understand the available options. As source diversification continues, practitioners will continue to refine the guidelines and methods required to incorporate this data into the investigation lifecycle.

References

1. 2017 In-House Legal benchmarking Report, https://www.bdo.com/insights/business-financial-advisory/2017-in-house-legal-benchmarking-report
2. Microsoft Office365 is Disrupting the eDiscovery Industry in a Major and Permanent Fashion, https://blog.x1discovery.com/2017/05/25/microsoft-office-365-is-disrupting-the-ediscovery-industry-in-a-major-and-permanent-fashion/
3. Strategies for the Bring Your Own App Surge, https://www.gartner.com/smarterwithgartnerbring-your-own-app-strategies/
4. How Long Should I keep Records, https://www.irs.gov/businesses/small-businesses-self-employed/how-long-should-i-keep-records (last visited July 9, 2018).
5. The Sedona Conference is one of the leading think tanks on electronic discovery issues, whose members and authors consist of U.S. judges, private practitioners and legal academics.

Existing and Emerging Biometric Data Technologies[1]

Ami Koldhekar Rodrigues[2], Emily R. Fedeles[3]* and Mari E. Martin[4]

Introduction

As technology advances and more uses are being found for biometrics, regulators are looking for ways to protect individuals while allowing organizations and governments to utilize it effectively. The European Union strives to achieve that balance with the General Data Protection Regulation, while the best efforts of the United States are embodied in the Illinois Biometric Information Privacy Act. This chapter traces biometrics from its origin to its present uses and examines the current landscape of regulation surrounding it, at the same time discussing what has failed to reach fruition and what the future might possibly hold.

---

[1] **Disclaimer:** The views expressed herein are solely those of the authors, should not be attributed to their places of employment, colleagues, or clients, and do not constitute solicitation or the provision of legal or security advice.

[2] Ami Koldhekar Rodrigues
    Chipotle Mexican Grill, Inc., Newport Beach, CA, United States
    ami.rodrigues@chipotle.com

[3] Emily R. Fedeles
    Colgate-Palmolive Company, New York, United States
    emily.fedeles@gmail.com

[4] Mari E. Martin
    Software AG, Reston, VA, United States
    mari.martin48@gmail.com

---

*Corresponding author: emily.fedeles@gmail.com

History of Biometric Data

A. Defining "Biometrics" and "Biometric Data"

The term "biometrics" is derived from the Greek words "bio" (life) and "metrics" (to measure).[1] Traditionally, the term "biometrics" referred to the science of developing mathematical models and methods for statistical analysis applicable to the biological sciences.[2] However, the meaning of the term "biometrics" has changed in the context of its use in the technology industry.[2]

In the field of biometric technology, the terms "biometrics" and "biometric data" are often used interchangeably and inconsistently. Importantly, it is not only those in the technology industry that misuse these terms but scientists and lawmakers also struggle with properly distinguishing and using them consistently due to the lack of clarity around the meaning of each term, particularly "biometrics".[3]

Examples of biometric data include fingerprints, palm veins, face recognition, DNA, palm print, hand geometry, iris recognition, and body odor or scent. This data is classified as "special categories of personal data" under the General Data Protection Regulation ("GDPR").[4] In general, the term "biometrics" may be defined in two ways. First, it may refer to methods for the automated measurement of characteristics of human beings.[5] For example, biometrics may be defined as "the science of establishing the identity of an individual based on the physical, chemical or behavioral attributes of the person".[6] Second, the meaning of the term may focus on biometrics as characteristic biological traits as such and studying them for statistical research purposes.[7] For example, the Association for Biometrics ("AFB") and International Computer Security Association ("ICSA") define the term biometric as "a measurable, physical characteristic or personal behavioral trait used to recognize the identity or verify the claim identity of an enrollee".[8] In an attempt to improve consistency with the use of this term, the International Standard has provided a definition of biometrics that combines aspects of both approaches, defining it as "automated recognition of individuals based on their behavioral and biological characteristics".[9]

Likewise, the Article 29 Working Party ("WP29"), which was the leading data protection advisory body in the European Union ("EU") prior to the implementation of the GDPR, encountered substantial difficulty in consistently and correctly using the term biometrics. Its opinions contain numerous instances in which the terms biometrics and biometric data are used interchangeably.[10] Further, the WP29 improperly stated that the term "biometrics" means the same thing as "biometric technologies".[10]

At least in the context of European data protection law, the term "biometric data" has been defined much more clearly than "biometrics."

In its opinions on biometric data issued in 2003 and updated in 2007, WP29 described biometric data as "biological properties, physiological characteristics, living traits, or repeatable actions where those features and/or actions are both unique to that individual and measurable, even if the patterns used in practice to technically measure them involve a certain degree of probability".[10] Until recently, however, EU data protection law did not contain any specific provisions defining or otherwise addressing biometric data or its use.

However, Article 4 (14) of the GDPR, which came into force on May 25, 2018, is the first provision in EU law to specifically address biometric data or include it within the meaning of the term "personal data" (discussed further in the section titled "Biometric Data under the GDPR" below).

B. Historical Use of Biometric Data

The lack of clarity regarding the precise meaning of the term "biometrics" and the use of a variety of definitions for the same term is due in part to the relatively recent emergence of biometrics as a distinct field.

From this perspective, biometrics did not become a distinct field of study and research until approximately 1870, when Alphonse Bertillon, a police desk clerk and anthropologist in Paris, developed a method of identifying criminals using physical characteristics, such as body dimensions and distinct marks on the body, including scars, birth marks, and tattoos.[11] This system, known as "Bertillonage," became the primary method of criminal identification used in France during the 19th century.[11]

Bertillonage was soon replaced by fingerprinting as a more accurate, efficient, and reliable method of establishing identity. German anatomist J.C.A. Mayer first publicly confirmed that a fingerprint is unique to each person in 1798. In *Anatomical Copperplates with Appropriate Explanation,* which contained drawings of friction ridge skin patterns, he noted that "although the arrangement of skin ridges is never duplicated in two persons, nevertheless the similarities are closer among some individuals".[12]

The use of fingerprints for the identification of criminals was firmly established by 1896, when Sir Edward Henry developed the Henry Classification System for classifying and storing fingerprints and his subsequent creation of the first British fingerprint files.[12] Although the first formal use of fingerprinting methods by police departments did not occur until the late 19th century, the use of finger, hand, and foot prints as marks of identification and authenticity originated in prehistoric times.[12]

Cave paintings in France provide evidence that prehistoric humans appear to have been using biometric data around 32,000 years ago.[13] These paintings contain handprints, some of which are thought to have been intended to identify the individuals who created them.[13] Fingerprints may have been used as personal identifying marks as early as 500 BCE in ancient Babylon. During this period, business transactions were recorded on clay tablets, which also included fingerprints.[5]

The use of fingerprints and handprints as marks of authenticity most likely originated in China at least 2,000 years ago. As in Babylon, the early Chinese routinely recorded their fingerprints in clay tablets and clay seals. According to Joao de Barros, a Spanish explorer and writer, Chinese merchants used fingerprints to settle business transactions, and Chinese parents used fingerprints and footprints to differentiate their children.[1] Clay seals were often used in China even before the first century BCE on official documents and packages.

Finally, a book of law dated to approximately 650 CE describes the use of fingerprints as official signatures on documents related to matters of divorce. Such use of fingerprints to sign and authenticate documents provides clear evidence that the Chinese understood the significance of the uniqueness of fingerprints by this era, at the latest, predating this realization by Europeans by at least 1200 years.[14] This is finally captured under present-day EU law with the inclusion of data based on dactyloscopy within the definition of "biometric data" in Article 4 (14) of the GDPR.

Legal Regulation of Biometric Data

A. GDPR

Unlike the United States, where no comprehensive federal law currently exists regulating biometric data and the general approach to regulating the collection and use of biometric data has, up to this point, been piecemeal and resulted in a patchwork of laws with limited applicability (as described below in the section titled "Biometric Data under the GDPR"), the EU has embraced a fundamentally different approach to not only the regulation of biometric data, but also for data protection and privacy protection in general by adopting the GDPR. The GDPR is intended to establish a comprehensive, harmonized framework for privacy and data protection regulation within the EU. It repeals and replaces its predecessor, the EU Data Protection Directive 95/46/EC, discussed further below.

As a European Commission ("EC") Regulation, the GDPR is directly applicable within all EU Member States, meaning Member States need not implement any enabling domestic legislation for the GDPR to become law in each country. Thus, as of May 25, 2018, the effective date established by the EC, the GDPR became applicable in all 28 Member States of the European Union. Further, the GDPR is applicable to organizations that collect personal data or behavioral information from a data subject in an EU country, regardless of where the organization is located.

i. Biometric Data under the GDPR

Prior to the GDPR, the processing of personal data in the European Union was regulated by what was commonly known as the Data Protection

Directive (officially Directive 95/46/EC on the protection of individuals with regard to processing personal data and on the free movement of such data). Initially adopted in 1995, the Data Protection Directive necessarily failed to address many of the more recent developments in data technology, such as data processing involving geolocation data and the increasingly sophisticated processing of biometric data. Further, because it was a directive and not a regulation, the Data Protection Directive allowed individual Member States to develop their own data privacy legislation that fit within its framework. This resulted in a lack of uniform regulations across the EU.

The GDPR addresses both of these issues. First, as a regulation, it requires the Member States to implement it as is, though it does allow for some derogations in certain areas. Second, it addresses many of the more recent developments in data technology. In a major change from the Data Protection Directive, the GPDR specifically defines and identifies biometric data as subject to its regulations and protections. Under Article 4 (14), the GDPR defines biometric data as "personal data resulting from specific technical processing relating to the physical, physiological or behavioral characteristics of a natural person, which allows or confirms the unique identification of that natural person, such as facial images or dactyloscopic data." As is immediately apparent, this definition of biometric data is quite broad in scope. This broad scope may have been intentionally put in place by the drafters in order to capture future developments which are not yet known in biometric data technology

Although such a broad definition may be useful for such future purposes, it tends to make present-day interpretation of the term somewhat difficult. The definition in Article 4 can be better understood by recognizing that the definition divides biometric data into two categories: first, personal data related to a person's physical or psychological characteristics and second, that related to a person's behavioral characteristics.

The first category of biometric data includes information that largely fits within the traditional concept of biometric data, such as photographs, fingerprints, and DNA. The meaning of biometric data related to a person's behavioral traits is less clear, as is the potential scope of the term. The meaning and application of this term remains to be determined by EU regulators as they determine the scope of the GDPR itself by interpreting the numerous provisions that introduce new concepts into data protection law.

Further, in Article 9, biometric data for the purpose of uniquely identifying a natural person is expressly included within the definition of special categories of personal data. Special categories of personal data are afforded additional protections under the GDPR. For example, under Article 35, the GDPR requires a data controller to conduct a data protection impact assessment if special categories of personal data, including biometric data, are processed on a large scale due to the increased risk to the rights and freedoms of the data subjects.

ii. Global Influence of GDPR

The GDPR appears likely to influence the protections afforded to personal data, including biometric data, by many countries beyond those in the EU. For instance, the EU's closest trade partners have implemented data protection legislation that is unmistakably influenced by the GDPR. This includes those countries that are party to the European Economic Area Agreement ("EEA") but which are not Member States of the EU—namely Norway, Lichtenstein, and Iceland. EC Regulations, including the GDPR, do not apply directly the non-EU members of the EEA. However, in a decision issued on July 6, 2018, the EEA Joint Committee incorporated the GDPR into the EEA Agreement. As a result, the GDPR became legally effective in Liechtenstein, Norway, and Iceland as of July 20, 2018.

Switzerland provides another example of the extraterritorial influence of the GDPR's protections for personal data. Switzerland is neither a member of the EU nor of the EEA and has no general duty to implement EU laws. However, on September 15, 2017, the Swiss Federal Council adopted the final draft revision to the Swiss Federal Data Protection Act ("Swiss Draft DPA"), the aim of which is to align Swiss data protection law with the GDPR.

Under the revised legislation, Swiss organizations must comply with the obligations for data controllers and data in accordance with the GDPR. This ensures that the EC will continue to recognize Switzerland as a third country that provides an adequate level of data protection, as required under the GDPR. Such an adequacy decision significantly facilitates the cross-border transfer of personal data, which is of critical importance to the Swiss economy. Similarly, pending data protection reforms in Argentina and Japan are intended to mirror the protections afforded to personal data under the GDPR allowing these countries to obtain the necessary EC adequacy decision that will permit the relatively unrestricted cross-border transfer of personal data.

Like the GDPR, the Swiss Draft DPA expressly includes biometric data within the definition of special categories of personal data. It also provides similar protections for sensitive personal data, including biometric data. For example, Article 5 (6) requires the data subject to provide express consent to the processing of sensitive personal data. Further, in Article 20 (2) (a), the Swiss Draft DPA includes large scale processing of sensitive personal data as an example of data processing that requires a data protection impact assessment because it is likely to result in a high risk to the rights and freedoms of natural persons.

Notably, the Swiss Draft DPA provides even more stringent protection for sensitive personal data, including biometric data, than does the GDPR.

The draft legislation amends Article 179 of the Swiss Criminal Code to mandate that any person who obtains sensitive personal data which is not generally accessible without authorization shall be punished with a term of imprisonment of up to three years or with a monetary fine.

The GDPR does not provide for criminal penalties for violations of any of its provisions, including those protecting sensitive personal data such as biometric data. However, in Article 84, the GDPR expressly permits Member States to "lay down the rules on other penalties applicable to infringements of this Regulation in particular for infringements which are not subject to administrative fines pursuant to Article 83 ...". Recital 149 is even more explicit: "Member States should be able to lay down the rules on criminal penalties for infringements of this Regulation, including for infringements of national rules adopted pursuant to and within the limits of this Regulation." Thus, although the GDPR itself does not provide for criminal liability for violations of its provisions protecting biometric data, it clearly permits Member States to do so under their national laws.

B. Other Approaches

In the United States, Illinois (740 Ill. Comp. Stat. 14 Biometric Information Privacy Act), Texas (Texas Business and Commercial Code Annotated, §503.001), California (Assembly Bill No. 375, 2018), and Washington have enacted laws specifically regulating the capture and/or collection of biometric data for commercial purposes (Washington State House Bill 1493 – 2017-18). Other states have more limited laws, applicable to either particular categories of entities (e.g., law enforcement authorities or employers) or certain uses of biometric information or specific types of biometric identifiers; still other states are considering the enactment of such laws.

i. Illinois Biometric Information Privacy Act ("BIPA")

BIPA, which was enacted in 2008, regulates the "collection, use, safeguarding, handling, storage, retention, and destruction of biometric identifiers and information".[15] Importantly, the law also creates an individual right of action against businesses that do not meet its requirements.[15] Specifically, the law requires that companies provide written notice—including the purpose of the collection and length of time the identifier will be retained—that a "biometric identifier" or "biometric information" is being collected or stored and obtain a release in writing prior to such collection.[15] BIPA also prohibits a private entity "in possession" of biometric identifiers or information from disclosing and/or profiting from that information without the person's consent.[15] However, disclosure of biometric information may be permitted without consent if such disclosure completes a financial transaction authorized by the individual or if it is required by law or legal process.[15] Additionally, the law regulates biometric information storage and destruction, requiring companies to have a publicly available written policy governing both of these actions.[15]

The individual right of action under BIPA allows a plaintiff to sue for negligent violations—with recovery limited to actual damages or up to $1,000 in liquidated damages—or intentional or reckless violations—with recovery limited to the greater of $5,000 or actual damages.[15] In either situation, a plaintiff may recover attorneys' fees and costs.[15] This individual right of action has paved the way for a flood of putative class action litigation against organizations using biometric information, with claims ranging from the use of biometrics on social media platforms to those used in the workplace or marketplace to authenticate employees or customers, respectively. In fact, between 2015 and 2018, more than 100 lawsuits have targeted employers alone for allegedly violating BIPA.

A 2017 decision temporarily slowed the number of lawsuits being filed alleging BIPA violations. In *Rosenbach v. Six Flags Entertainment Corp.* (2017), a plaintiff sued the theme park on the grounds that it scanned her son's fingerprint without obtaining written consent and without properly disclosing the company's business practices relating to the collection, use, and retention of the fingerprint data. The defendant filed a motion to dismiss stating that Plaintiff was not an "aggrieved party" for purposes of BIPA because she had not alleged an "actual injury".[16] In December 2017, the Illinois Appellate Court issued a unanimous decision issued holding that a plaintiff must allege more than a mere failure to comply with BIPA's notice and consent provisions to state a viable cause of action under BIPA.[16] As a result of this decision, a mere technical violation of the statute will be insufficient to state a cognizable claim. Illinois federal courts have similarly interpreted BIPA as limited by the statute's phrase "person aggrieved."

However, the Illinois Supreme Court reversed the state appellate court's ruling that a mere technical violation of BIPA was insufficient to confer standing to sue and remanded the case to the circuit court further proceedings.[17] The court held that it was "untenable" to interpret BIPA to require proof of actual damages at the pleading stage, because if companies are able to escape liablity as long as they do not cause tangible harm, BIPA is ineffective in giving users greater control over their data and the right to control their own privacy "vanishes into thin air".[17]

The following year, a California federal court rejected the 2017 Rosenbach decision, leaving potential plaintiffs in doubt about how much weight it might carry. In *re Facebook Biometric Information Privacy Litigation* (2018), a class of individuals suing Facebook under BIPA was certified despite Facebook's argument that each class member would need to show that they had suffered a tangible injury to be "aggrieved" and thus eligible for statutory damages under BIPA. In disagreeing with the holding in *Rosenbach*, the court distinguished it and held that an individual need only show a statutory violation—and need not show a resulting tangible injury—to sue.[18] The Ninth Circuit rejected Facebook's motion to have the whole court hear its argument and let the lower court decision stand, and the United States Supreme Court denied Facebook's petition for a writ of certiorari, refusing to decide the circuit split.[19] Following that refusal, a court approved Facebook's offer of $650 million to settle the case.[20]

In spring of 2018, lawmakers proposed a new Illinois bill (S.B. 3053), that would alter BIPA by creating broad new exemptions, including exempting face recognition technology; biometrics captured by employers about their employees; biometrics captured by stores about their patrons; and the many businesses that comply with other privacy statutes, that do not link captured biometrics to confidential information, and that do not store biometrics for more than 24 hours.[21] The bill's sponsor in the Senate, Sen. Bill Cunningham, D-Chicago, has said in support of the bill that "[the technology has bypassed what this law was intended to combat," and that lawmakers do not "want to alter the intent of the original law in any way".[22] Critics of the proposed exceptions decry that the changes "would strip residents of critical protection of their biometric privacy, including their right to decide whether or not a business may harvest and monetize data about their faces and fingerprints".[23]

ii. Texas Business and Commercial Code Annotated, § 503.001

Although the 2009 Texas law regarding biometric identifiers contains safeguards similar to BIPA, it lacks an individual right of action and contains fewer specific requirements.[24] Like BIPA, the Texas regulation limits retention of biometric data and requires a business to store, transmit, and protect biometric data with at least as many safeguards as it uses for other confidential information in its possession.[24] Also like BIPA, it prohibits the collection of biometric identifiers for a commercial purpose without notice and consent.[24] Unlike BIPA, however, there is neither an explicit requirement that consent must be in writing nor a requirement that the notice of collection contain disclosures regarding why biometric data is being collected or how long it will be stored.[24] The Texas Attorney General may bring a civil action for violations of the Texas act, with a maximum penalty of $25,000 per violation.[24]

iii. Washington State House Bill 1493

Washington House Bill 1493, which became effective on July 23, 2017, governs entities that "enroll a biometric identifier in a database for a commercial purpose".[25] Requirements of the law include on mandating that, both prior to enrollment and if the business seeks to sell, lease or otherwise disclose the identifier to a third party, organizations provide notice to individuals and obtain their affirmative consent.[25] The Washington law's definition of "biometric identifier" is somewhat more limited than either of the Illinois and Texas laws, specifically excluding "physical or digital photographs" and "video or audio recordings," which seemingly excludes "face geometry" from its scope.[25] Since the majority of the litigation stemming from alleged violations of the Illinois statute concerns alleged nonconsensual collection and use of "face geometry," this is a notable exclusion in the text of the Washington bill.[25]

The exact form of notice and consent is not spelled out in the law, which instead recognizes that these processes are "context-dependent".[25] The law does not specifically require consent in writing, and contains certain exceptions to the consent requirement for particular disclosures, such as if disclosure is necessary to provide a service or product requested by the individual or if it is made to a third party that "contractually promises" that the biometric identifier will not be further disclosed or enrolled in a database inconsistent with the law.[25]

Unlike the Illinois and Texas laws that refer more generally to the "capture" or "collection" of biometric identifiers, the Washington law differs in the fact that it restricts "enrollment" of such identifiers. To "enroll" a biometric identifier means to capture and convert it such that it can be used to identify an individual (e.g., the kind of fingerprint scanning technology used by Apple's Touch ID, in which a mathematical representation of a fingerprint is derived from its image, but the image itself is neither retained nor can it be reconstructed).[25] The Washington law does not include a requirement for organizations to develop or maintain a written policy concerning data handling practices with respect to biometric identifiers.

iv. California Consumer Privacy Act (A.B. 375)

In June 2018, California became the first U.S. state to pass similar legislation to the GDPR. A.B. 375, which came into effect on January 1, 2020, affords California residents an array of new rights by regulating what business can and cannot do with personal data.[26] The law has a broad definition of "personal information" that includes an individual's personal identifiers, geolocation, internet browsing history, psychometric data, and biometric data.[26] Although the state's attorney general enforces the law, it provides consumers with an individual right of action if organizations fail to maintain reasonable security practices that result in unauthorized access to personal data.[26] The influence of the CCPA and GDPR has resulted in similar legislation in other U.S. states, such as Nevada's Senate Bill 220.

v. Limited Biometric Laws

Both California and Delaware have enacted limited biometric laws prohibiting websites geared toward K-12 schools from selling students' biometric data and restricting the websites' use of that information.[27,28] In North Carolina and West Virginia, a student's biometric data is not to be reported for inclusion in the state's student data system.[29,30] Missouri, Maine, and New Hampshire have laws preventing state agencies from collecting, storing, or using biometric data in connection with ID cards or driver's licenses, but these laws notably do not apply to law enforcement.[31,32,33] New York has a law prohibiting companies from requiring an employee to be fingerprinted as a condition of securing or continuing employment.[34] This law does not apply to employees of New York State, hospitals, or medical colleges.[34]

vi. Other States Considering Similar Laws

Over the past few years, at least eight states have attempted and failed to pass biometric privacy laws to regulate the collection and use of biometric information.[35] Proposed bills in Alaska, California, Idaho, New Hampshire, and Montana all included an individual right of action for the improper use of biometric information.[36,37] In Montana, lobbyists argued that the bill imposed "highly specific notice and consent requirements that would make it unworkable to obtain consent for positive users of biometric data".[38]

In 2016, the Connecticut House passed a bill requiring any "retail business establishment" that captures and stores individuals' facial geometry to display a sign saying "this establishment uses facial recognition technology to capture and store image of the faces of persons on the premises".[39] The bill was not voted on by the senate, and a similar bill also failed in 2017. Alaska, Florida, New Hampshire, and New York all recently modeled proposed laws on BIPA, but they were never brought to a vote.[40,41] Additionally, in 2017, Arizona and Missouri attempted to pass limited biometric laws protecting students' right to privacy, but those bills never made it out of committee.[42]

C. Existing and Emerging Biometric Data Technologies

Existing regulations and the possibility of new regulations creates a bit of an uncertain legal landscape for businesses wishing to integrate the use of biometrics into their practices. Biometric data has and will continue to play an important role in an increasingly digitized world.

When considering the need for biometric data collection, the most common explanation is to enable an identification system that can prevent fraud, ensure physical and digital security of the underlying data which the biometric data authenticates, and streamline transactions. As digital identity and verification of identity become increasingly important, the collection and use of biometric data is likely to continue to grow. Presently, biometric data is most commonly employed in the following areas.

D. Mobile Payments

As individual smartphone usage and transactions conducted on a smartphone continue to increase, so too will the use of mobile payments. Mobile payments replace credit and debit card chips and magnetic stripes and enable point of sale ("PoS") transactions through a contactless terminal. Digital wallet and mobile payment services assist and enable contactless payments with the use of two-factor authentication by using a fingerprint scan, facial recognition, a pin or a passcode. In 2015, ApplePay was introduced, signaling the use of fingerprints combined with near-field technology to authenticate, tokenize, and encrypt the authentication and transaction details proliferated. Since then, a number of banking and financial institutions replicated these technological features to their mobile applications to service new behaviors.[43] Consumer desires and Apple have widened the parameters of biometric authentication by incorporating facial recognition technology. In 2017, tech giant Alibaba launched the "Smile to Pay" feature that allows a customer to pay for goods or services by smiling at the camera to authenticate a purchase. The technology uses 3D cameras and a likeness detection algorithm to block spoofing attempts using other people's photos or video recordings.[44]

The adoption of biometrics allows mobile payments to expand continuously by integrating convenience with the need for security. It is also noteworthy to recognize that mobile payments are not merely limited to the sale of goods and services, but also include money transfer services between two individuals.

E. Online Banking

Similar to mobile payments, the use of biometrics provide comfort to otherwise apprehensive consumers in the area of online banking. Like the facilitation of mobile payments, many U.S. national banks allow already existing Apple Touch ID, Face ID for iPhone X, and Android Fingerprint as forms of biometric authentication. As biometric technologies develop further with refined methods for verification, online banking services will also expand.[43]

F. Immigration Services

Law enforcement and immigration officials consider fingerprints, photographs, and iris scans to be the most reliable source of identification. In the U.S., creating an entry-exit database has been illusive. While the general efforts go beyond the scope of this chapter and are far too complex to explain, a collaborated system implementation across government agencies has proven difficult for reasons that do not even take into account the accuracy and cost of building biometric identification systems and a government-wide technological upgrade to support such systems, which presents its own set of challenges. One of the unique hurdles to an immigration system using sophisticated biometric data verifiers is the possibility of misidentification.[45] Even in the best facial-recognition systems, accuracy plummets as datasets grow.[46] While the other key uses outlined here also have large datasets, the number of individuals whose data would reside in a single government system would far exceed the number residing in a commercial dataset.

G. Government Services

For developing countries and even pockets of developed countries, government services can be difficult to access without the aid of technology and the Internet. Services such as welfare programs, pensions, voting, and those that draw upon proof of residency can be better distributed when identity verification is readily available. Biometric data, when used in smaller application subsets, provides trust in the process of verification, as it is considered unique to each individual and widely thought to have a propensity for fraud.

In India, the Aadhaar Identification Card was introduced in 2018 for citizens of India to verify their state residency. Using an individual's biometric data, a unique 12-digit identification number is generated for the individual. Once issued, this number can be used for a variety of services, such as filing taxes, opening a bank account, buying bonds, obtaining public and private loans, as well as filing any claims for services with the government. As recently as 2018, the Supreme Court of India declared privacy a "fundamental right" and it remains to be seen how the introduction and expanded use of the Aadhaar Identification Card confers further obligations upon the Government of India to secure information used to receive government services.[47]

On a larger scale, China introduced a Social Credit System ("SCS") in 2014, for implementation and mandatory participation by 2020. However, the impact of COVID-19 has delayed full implementation. The Chinese SCS combines an individual's government data with economic data, social data, and creates a "social credit" score to indicate one's reputation. A higher reputation score allows an individual to access discounts on energy and favorable interest rates on loans, while lower reputation scores bar individuals from traveling on airplanes or trains, buying property, or having high-speed Internet.[48]

As China expands the SCS across its provinces, its surveillance cameras will be used not only to monitor actions such as jaywalking or littering to factor into one's social credit score, but also to mass surveil individuals. Such mass surveillance is used to display the faces of jaywalkers or those who renege on their debts. The millions of cameras supplement other systems that track Internet use and communications, hotel stays, train and plane trips, and even car travel in some places. The police department in various provinces in China have also begun using "Black Mirror" glasses that have the capability of taking photographs of individuals to then compare to mugshots within a central database. Though the technology has been widely heralded as being able to monitor criminals, the individual must stand still for several seconds in order to take an effective photograph. While the capabilities are promising, China's national surveillance efforts remain a patchwork as opposed to an all-seeing technological network. Many files remain undigitized and some data is unable to be linked or reconciled with other data. Rather, the efficacy of the system lies in deterring "bad" actions by individuals who fear continued surveillance and ensuing shame. Proponents of the system argue that when individuals are uncertain whether they are truly being monitored, order is more likely to ensue.[49]

H. Workforce Management

To avoid "time theft" and to introduce additional accuracy and reliability in identification, biometric data has begun trending in the areas of workforce management. Biometrics in workforce management have also been considered to benefit employees, as forgotten passwords and password reset requests consume otherwise productive time and reduce queues of employees waiting to log in.[50] This trend is most prevalently seen with regard to workforce management of employees subject to overtime pay and shift work. Unsurprisingly, this trend has also increased for employees who must drive as part of their regular work activities, by monitoring their speeds, seat belt status, and open or closed vehicle doors.[51]

Additionally, employers are leaning towards facial recognition technology and fingerprints in lieu of passwords to log into phones, computers, and access data stored on those devices as well as in the cloud. Current predictions estimate that by 2020, many offices will either do away with passwords or use a combination of fingerprint or facial recognition technology with a password (an enablement of two-factor authentication).[50]

Finally, tools are also being refined to determine unique ways in which an employee can use a device: how the employee holds his or her phone, the types of keystrokes used, whether the employee uses one or two hands to type, as well as how the employee scrolls or toggles between screens. While concerns are abound over employee monitoring, the primary need of this type of technology for companies is to ensure there is no unauthorized access to company data and proper chain-of-custody is maintained in data transmissions and data storage.[51] (Delgado, 2018).

I. The Internet of Things (IoT)

Roughly defined as the interconnection of computing devices embedded in everyday objects via the Internet of Things ("IoT"), enabling sending and receipt of data, and direct integration of the physical world into computer-based systems to provide efficiency, economic benefits, and reduction of human exertion. The recent rise in home automation—such as with home lighting, heating and air conditioning, media and security systems, and lawncare—suggests the rise of individual control in the domestic arena through automation and predictive technology that receives data on an individual's geolocation or calendar to make recommendations.[52]

Because IoT often provides services and goods that automate our home life based on potentially intimate and personal details of an individual's life, the need for complete confidentiality is paramount. Therefore, biometric data, using security by design, can serve as the key to securing the chain of trust.

One recent introduction of biometric data-enabled IoT is in the auto industry, where biometric systems allow car owners to open car doors based on a combination of facial and gait recognition technologies, as well as the integration of biometric sensors integrated into door handles, key fobs, touch screens, and steering wheels that integrate authentication and tailored mobility services.[53]

J. Wearable Devices

Wearable devices, from fitness bands to smart clothing, introduce new modalities in the areas of navigation and stress management. They function as media devices, communication tools, activity trackers, and healthcare aids. Virtual reality ("VR") is also considered an increasingly popular wearable technology, as it combines eye-tracking, facial recognition, and recognizes a user's head, body, and hand movement. The eye-tracking tools can detect a user's emotional state by reading facial muscle movement or pupil dilation and use a range spanning a combination of recreational, educational, therapeutic, and sometimes athletic features for recognition.[54]

Wearable devices range from offering tracking data and analytics for a healthier lifestyle, to providing reminders, and even to improving hearing quality through devices known as "hearables".[55] Wearable devices have proven to be extremely successful in terms of user adoption because they are easy to integrate into everyday life and provide personalized metrics. It is very likely that market growth will be fueled by data collected from wearable devices, as retail experiences will become very personalized to unique individuals, in all probability.

Final Analysis

It is no surprise that the speed of technological change greatly outpaces that of the legislative process, creating a landscape that is unbalanced and ripe for a clash of ideals. As new and creative uses of biometric technologies emerge, varying approaches to legislation will be developed to address the potential problems that accompany these uses. Some onus will be put on the developers of the technologies to self-regulate in a way that will save people from themselves. However, if history is any indicator, the likelihood of self-regulation seems low, placing an even greater burden on the legislators to develop new laws to address these issues.

As discussed above, even before its effective date, the EU GDPR began influencing changes in privacy and data protection laws worldwide. The widespread concern regarding GDPR compliance is due to a number of factors, the most prominent being among them being the global economic power of the EU. According to data published by the World Bank, the International Monetary Fund, and the United Nations, the economy of the EU consistently ranks as one of the three largest in the world, along with that of the U.S. and China, with the relative order of ranking depending on the procedure for measuring such economies. Thus, the EU represents a significant source or potential source of income that businesses may be unwilling to forego as long as the cost of GDPR compliance is reasonable in relation to such revenue.

Further, compared to the national data protection laws that it replaced, the GDPR dramatically increased the potential penalties of a violation. Under the GDPR, a business may be fined up to four percent of annual worldwide turnover for each violation. Further, the GDPR leaves open the possibility for EU Member States to enact national laws providing additional penalties for violations, which may include personal criminal liability. Whether Member States will make use of this option remains to be seen. Given such extensive consequences, including financial insolvency and criminal liability, both EU- and non-EU-based organizations that collect EU personal data are likely to implement significant measures to address GDPR compliance.

References

1. Mitra, S., Wen, B. and Gofman, M. (2017). Overview of biometric authentication. *In*: S. Mitra and B. Wen (eds.). Biometrics in a Data Driven World: Trends, Technologies, and Challenges. Boca Raton, FL: CRC Press. Retrieved from: https://books.google.com/books?id=naKiDQAAQBAJ&printsec=frontcover &dq=the+history+of+biometrics&hl=de&sa=X&ved=0ahUKEwiAr4K86sfcA

hVDT98KHSAhAkAQ6AEIKDAA#v=onepage&q=the%20history%20of%20
biometrics&f=false.

2. Hopkins, R. (1999). An introduction to biometrics and large scale civilian
    identification. *International Review Law Computers & Techology*, 13(3), 337-363.
    Retrieved from: https://doi.org/10.1080/13600869955017.

3. Jasserand, C. (2016). Avoiding terminological confusion between the notions
    of 'biometrics' and 'biometric data': An investigation into the meanings
    of the terms from a European data protection and a scientific perspective.
    International Data Privacy Law, 6(1), 63. Retrieved from: https://ssrn.com/
    abstract=3230339.

4. Regulation (EU) 2016/679 (General Data Protection Regulation) Art. 9.
    Processing of special categories of personal data.

5. Kindt, E.J. (2013). *Privacy and Data Protection Issues of Biometric Applications: A
    Comparative Legal Analysis*. New York: Springer.

6. Jain, A.K. and Ross, A. (2008). Introduction to biometrics. In: Jain, A.K., Flynn
    P. and Ross, A. (eds.). Handbook of Biometrics. New York: Springer. Retrieved
    from: https://books.google.com/books?hl=de&lr=&id=WfCowMOvpioC&o
    i=fnd&pg=PA1&dq=history+biometrics&ots=xqSF-Vz8Ge&sig=AQKUDMN
    k3k0jhqOhvKhm5yiI0kg#v=onepage&q=history%20biometrics&f=false.

7. Bailey, J. (2017). The GDPR's fingerprint: Legal implications of the GDPR for
    the use of biometric data by private parties. Retrieved from: http://arno.uvt.
    nl/show.cgi?fid=143355.

8. Glossary of biometric terms. (1998). Association for Biometrics (AfB) and
    International Computer Security Association (ICSA).

9. Pato, J.N. and Millett, L. (2010). Biometric recognition: Challenges and
    opportunities. Washington DC: The National Academies Press. Retrieved
    from: https://www.nap.edu/read/12720/chapter/3.

10. Article 29 Data Protection Working Party, Opinion 3/2012 (00720/12/EN
    WP193 2012) n7 retrieved from: https://ec.europa.eu/justice/article-29/
    documentation/opinion-recommendation/files/2012/wp193_en.pdf.

11. Yue Liu, N. (2013). Bio-Privacy: Privacy Regulations and the Challenge of
    Biometrics. Abingdon, VA: Routledge.

12. Mayhew, S. (2018). History of biometrics. Retrieved from: https://www.
    biometricupdate.com/201802/history-of-biometrics-2.

13. Clottes, J. (2002). Chavet Cave (ca. 30,000 B.C.). Heilbrunn Timeline of Art
    History. Retrieved from: http://www.metmuseum.org/toah/hd/chav/hd_
    chav.htm.

14. O'Gorman, L. (1998). An overview of fingerprint verification technologies.
    Information Security Technical Report. Retrieved from: https://www.
    sciencedirect.com/science/article/abs/pii/S1363412798800150.

15. Biometric Information Privacy Act, 740 ICS 14 (2008).

16. Rosenbach v. Six Flags Entertainment Corporation (2017 IL App (2d) 170317).

17. Rosenbach v. Six Flags Entertainment Corporation (2019 IL 123186).

18. In re Facebook Biometric Information Privacy Litigation, 2018 WL 1794295
    (N.D. Cal. Apr. 16, 2018).

19. Pester, R. (2020). Patel v. Facebook: Facebook Settles Illinois Biometric
    Information Privacy Act ("BIPA") Violation Suit. JOLT Digest. Retrieved
    from: https://jolt.law.harvard.edu/digest/patel-v-facebook-facebook-settles-
    illinois-biometric-information-privacy-act-bipa-violation-suit.

20. Iovino, N. (2020). Facebook Boosts Facial-Data Settlement to $650 Million to Appease Judge. Courthouse News. Retrieved from: https://www.courthousenews.com/facebook-boosts-facial-data-settlement-to-650-million-to-appease-judge/.
21. Bill Status of SB3053, 100th General Assembly, Retrieved from: http://ilga.gov/legislation/BillStatus.asp?GA=100&DocTypeID=SB&DocNum=3053&GAID=14&SessionID=91&LegID=110583.
22. Marotti A. (2018). Proposed changes to Illinois' biometric law concern privacy advocates. The Chicago Tribune. Retrieved from: https://www.chicagotribune.com/business/ct-biz-illinois-biometrics-bills-20180409-story.html.
23. Schwartz, A. (2018). New attack on the Illinois Biometric Privacy Act. Electronic Frontier Foundation, Retrieved from: https://www.eff.org/deeplinks/2018/04/new-attack-illinois-biometric-privacy-act.
24. Capture or Use of Biometric Identifier, BUS & COM § 503.001 (2009).
25. Capturing Biometric Identifiers, HB 1493 (2017-2018).
26. Ghosh, D. (2018). What you need to know about California's new data privacy law. Harvard Business Review. Retrieved from: https://hbr.org/2018/07/what-you-need-to-know-about-californias-new-data-privacy-law.
27. AB-2799 Privacy: Personal information: preschool and prekindergarten purposes, Ch. 620 (2016).
28. Student Data Privacy Protection Act, 80 Del Laws. C. 149 §§ 8101A–8106A (2015).
29. Protective Provisions and Maintenance of Student Records, Art. 29 Chap. 115C §115C-402.5 (2015).
30. Student Data Accessibility, Transparency and Accountability Act, § 18-2-5h–2654 (2014).
31. Drivers' and Commercial Drivers' Licenses, MO Rev Stat § 302.189 (2015).
32. An Act To Protect the Privacy of Maine Residents under the Driver's License Laws, MRSA §402 (2011).
33. Regulation of Biometric Information, N.H. Rev. Stat. § 359-N:2 (2015).
34. New York Labor Law, § 201-A (2016).
35. Shukovsky, P. (2017). Washington Biometric Privacy Law Lacks Teeth of Illinois Cousin. Bloomberg BNA. Retrieved from: https://www.bna.com/washington-biometric-privacy-n73014461920/.
36. An Act relative to limitations on the use of biometric information, H.B. 523, 2017 Sess. (2017).
37. Establish Montana Biometric Information Privacy Act, H.B. 0518.01, 65th Leg. (2017).
38. Mehrotra, K. (2017). Tech companies are pushing back against biometric privacy laws. Bloomberg Business Week. Retrieved from: https://www.bloomberg.com/news/articles/2017-07-20/tech-companies-are-pushing-back-against-biometric-privacy-laws.
39. An Act Requiring Certain Retail Business Establishments to Display Signs Regarding the Use of Facial Recognition Technology, H.B. 5326, Gen. Assemb. Feb. Sess. (2016).
40. Collection of Biometric Information, H.B. 72, 30th Leg., 1st Sess. (2017).
41. Rosenthal, J. and Oberly, D. (2019). The coming storm of biometric privacy laws: What to expect. Law 360. Retrived from: https://www.law360.com/

texas/articles/1219208/the-coming-storm-of-biometric-privacy-laws-what-to-expect.

42. Relating to Biometric Information in Schools, S.B. 1373, 53rd Leg., 1st Sess. (2017).
43. Conlan-Donnelly, M. (2018). How will biometrics affect the future of banking security. *BizTech Magazine.* Retrieved from: https://biztechmagazine.com/article/2018/03/how-will-biometrics-affect-the-future-of-banking-security
44. Fingas, J. (2017). You can pay at a restaurant by smiling at a camera. Engadget. Retrieved from: https://www.engadget.com/2017/09/03/alipay-facial-recognition-payments/.
45. Face Recognition Technology: FBI Should Better Ensure Privacy and Accuracy, Government Accountability Office, 46, GAO-16-267 (May 2016) http://www.gao.gov/assets/680/677098.pdf (hereinafter "GAO Report").
46. Lafrance, A. (2016). The Ultimate Facial-Recognition Algorithm. The Atlantic. Retrieved from: https://www.theatlantic.com/technology/archive/2016/06/machine-face/488969/.
47. McCarthy, J. (2017). Indian Supreme Court declares privacy a fundamental right, NPR. Retrieved from: https://www.npr.org/sections/thetwo-way/2017/08/24/545963181/indian-supreme-court-declares-privacy-a-fundamental-right.
48. Vanek Smith, S. and Garcia, C. (2018). China Tests 'A Social Credit Score'. NPR. Retrieved from: https://www.npr.org/2018/10/31/662436265/china-tests-a-social-credit-score
49. Mozur, P. (2018). Inside China's Dystopian Dreams: A.I. Shame and Lots of Cameras. The New York Times. Retrieved from: https://www.nytimes.com/2018/07/08/business/china-surveillance-technology.html.
50. Larson, S. (2018). Beyond passwords: Companies use fingerprints and digital behavior to ID employees. CNN Business. Retrieved from: https://money.cnn.com/2018/03/18/technology/biometrics-workplace/index.html.
51. Delgado, A. (2018). Employee privacy at stake as surveillance technology evolves. CBS News Money Watch. Retrieved from: https://www.cbsnews.com/news/employee-privacy-surveillance-technology-evolves/.
52. Ludlow, D. (2017). The smart home seriously needs to wise up if it wants to go mainstream in 2018. TechRadar. Retrieved from: https://www.techradar.com/news/the-smart-home-seriously-needs-to-wise-up-if-it-wants-to-go-mainstream-in-2018.
53. D'Allegro, J. (2018). 8 concept cars that show how technology will dominate the drive of the future. CNBC. Retrieved from: https://www.cnbc.com/2018/11/08/8-concept-cars-shaping-the-technology-dominated-drive-of-the-future.html.
54. Ramgopal, K. (2017). Virtual Reality Companies Are Changing How Athletes See Practice. New York Times. Retrieved from: https://www.nytimes.com/2017/11/24/sports/virtual-reality-athletes.html.
55. Span, P. (2016). No Hearing Aid? Some Gizmos Offer Alternative to 'Speak Up!' New York Times. Retrieved from: https://www.nytimes.com/2016/07/19/health/hearing-aid-alternatives.html.

The Intersection of GDPR, U.S. Discovery and Technology in the Financial Crime Discipline

Camille C. Bent[1] and Kerri-Ann Bent[2]

Introduction

The EU GDPR (Regulation (EU) 2016/679 of the European Parliament and the Council of April 27, 2016 on the Protection of Natural Persons with regard to the Processing of Personal Data and the Free Movement of Such Data, and Repealing Directive 95/46/EC)[1] requires "controllers" and "processors" of personal data to confirm that there is a consensual, legitimate, specific and well-identified purpose that is linked by necessity and proportionality.[2] Financial services firms often act as controllers and/or processors of the personal data they collect on customers and counterparties, and litigators must often do the same. The GDPR obliges controllers and processors to respect and facilitate the multitude of privacy rights granted to individuals, or "data subjects."

When undertaking routine business activity, law firms and banks both assume the role of gatekeeper and banks are also required to adhere to anti-money laundering regulations, which includes the safeguarding of customer identification.[3] Under the GDPR, financial services and law firms alike face similar issues surrounding the ability to obtain, and share personal information, a function that has remained vital to both factions. Practitioners in both disciplines must grapple with certain challenges, particularly with establishing consent under Article 6(1) of the GDPR. Although Article 23 provides financial institutions with some leeway to

---

1   Camille Bent works at BakerHostetler LLP.
2   Kerri A. Bent works at UBS and can be reached on LinkedIn.

fight financial crime under the new GDPR requirements, the right to access information afforded to individuals under Article 15 adds an additional complexity that is both enhanced and encumbered by technology.[4]

In this chapter, we analyze: (a) areas of conflict and compatibility between the GDPR, the current U.S.[42,43] Anti-Money Laundering (AML) regulations and E.U. AML Directives, and U.S. discovery rules, including Federal Rules of Civil Procedure (FRCP) 26 and 34;[44] (b) the challenges faced by law firms and multinational financial institutions that must simultaneously comply with multiple regimes, specifically issues that relate to consent, legal obligation and legitimate interest and GDPR conditions; and (c) case studies which have evidence of the complexities of global GDPR compliance in both the discovery and financial crime contexts.

Last, we consider the impact of technology-driven solutions relating to the right to access and the right to be forgotten, and we provide a comparative forecast of select privacy rights afforded under the California Consumer Privacy Act (CCPA or the Act),[39] which contains many similar provisions to the GDPR and became effective on July 1, 2020.

Lawful Data Processing under the GDPR

Pursuant to Article 6 of the GDPR, data processing is lawful only if one of six conditions are met. This chapter focuses on the application of three of the six conditions required to lawfully process data in the U.S. discovery and financial crimes contexts: (1) consent; (2) legal obligation; and (3) legitimate interests.

Consider the following example: Plaintiff Co. files suit against Defendant Co., a global enterprise with offices around the world, the E.U. included, alleging breach of contract, among other causes of action. Discovery commences, and Plaintiff Co. serves subpoenas on Defendant Co. Defendant Co. fails to respond, so the court signs an order mandating compliance. The subpoena requires Defendant Co. to process and produce emails relevant to the case. The emails were sent by Defendant Co. executives that reside in France. The emails contain confidential information relating to the breach of contract dispute, and they also contain the names and other personal data of the Defendant Co. executives that sent the emails, and that of the E.U. residents who are not employees of the Defendant Co. The parties agree that the GDPR applies to the emails in question, as the activities taken to preserve, gather, analyze and produce the personal data constitute "processing" under the GDPR. The parties also agree that the movement of the data across borders pursuant to the U.S. subpoena constitutes "transfer" of the data under the GDPR. The sections that follow introduce the three conditions: A. consent, B. legitimate interest, C. legal obligation, and present an analysis of whether the Defendant Co. must respond to the subpoena, whether it is prohibited from doing so under the GDPR, and other considerations for Defendant Co.'s counsel.

A. Establishing Consent in the U.S. Discovery Context

Consent is the first of the six conditions listed for lawful data processing under Article 6 of the GDPR. Following GDPR implementation in May 2018, data controllers can no longer assume that consent to process and transfer personal data has been granted; rather, there must be "a statement or ... clear affirmative action" specific to the operation requiring such consent and that can be withdrawn at any time.[4] Article 7 expands on this requirement by providing criteria that the controller must demonstrate to ensure that consent exists. Article 7 specifically requires that: (1) the controller demonstrates that the data subject has consented to the processing of his data; (2) the request for consent be presented in such a way that it is clearly distinguishable from other matters, and in an intelligible and easily accessible form, using clear and plain language; if the declaration is not presented in this manner, it is not valid; (3) the data subject can withdraw his consent at any time, and it must be as easy to withdraw as it is to give consent; and (4) to assess whether consent is given, whether a performance of a contract is conditional on consent that's not necessary for performance of that contract.

Practitioners must evaluate conditions of consent in the context of the relevant U.S. discovery rules. "Parties are entitled to discovery of documents in the 'possession, custody or control' of other parties, Fed. R. Civ. P. 34(a)(1), so long as they are 'relevant to any party's claim or defense,' Fed. R. Civ. P. 26(b)(1)" (2014 WL 61472, at *2). FRCP 26(b)(1) was amended in 2015 to also require proportionality. To determine whether discovery is proportional, courts consider "the importance of the issues at stake in the action, the amount in controversy, the parties' relative access to relevant information, the parties' resources, the importance of the discovery in resolving the issues, and whether the burden or expense of the proposed discovery outweighs its likely benefit."[5]

The case law requires parties to have possession, custody, or control over the evidence to be produced.[6] Possession and custody involve a straightforward inquiry, and thus are not often litigated. In contrast, the inquiry regarding whether a party controls evidence is nuanced, and as a result, more courts have grappled with the question of control. In the Second Circuit for example, control means the right, authority, or practical ability to obtain documents sought upon demand.[7] In the discovery context, control is generally construed broadly. Legal entitlement to the data is insufficient to establish control pursuant to FRCP 34. If "the subpoenaed party makes a showing that it lacks the practical ability to obtain access to documents... a clearer statement of the rule might read: 'control can be found where a party has the practical ability to acquire or access documents by (1) legal entitlement or (2) by any other means."[8]

Therefore, to comply with U.S. discovery laws and the GDPR, the Defendant Co. and similarly situated entities must produce documents that are within their possession, custody and control, and to comply with the production and with the consent condition under the GDPR, they must obtain the consent of the data subjects to process and transfer the data.

In addition to the GDPR and U.S. discovery frameworks that practitioners must consider, it is prudent that they consider who the gatekeepers are within each framework. In the U.S. discovery framework, practically speaking, the gatekeeper is the employer. This is because if the production involves employees' personal data, the unspoken expectation in the U.S. has been full cooperation from employees. The GDPR and its rules of consent will cause this to change.* Existing case law has established that if an employee completes work on behalf of an employer, that work belongs to the employer, and can be used as needed to support or defend the employer in litigation.[9] Most U.S. companies have implemented policies that clearly state that the use of electronic assets and the work associated therewith are company property. In turn, most employees acknowledge or concede that point throughout the course of their employment relationship and generally cooperate with discovery requests. Therefore, in the U.S., there are few overarching restrictions on the collection and use of any data, and consent is either implied or explicit.

In contrast, within the framework of the GDPR, and specifically Article 6, the individual, rather than the company, is the gatekeeper for data access, and, in comparison to existing discovery rules, the conditions that must exist to establish consent to process personal data have become quite robust: "...companies will no longer be able to use long illegible terms and conditions full of legalese... It must be as easy to withdraw consent as it is to give it".[1]

Revisiting our example, when considering whether to reply to the subpoena and process and transfer personal data subject to the GDPR, the

---

* Without doubt, every single employer must process the personal data of each of its employees, including their names, address information, bank account information, and salary data. Beyond employers' minimal requirements, they often automatically accrue and process a mountain of employees' personal data through their everyday use of emails, calendars and other digital applications and equipment. The GDPR provides an exception for the processing of this personal data, as it is "necessary for the performance or preparation of the employment contract." *See* Reference 1. The chapter does not examine this scenario, and instead focuses on personal data that is the subject of litigation.

Defendant Co. must take into account the likelihood of stiff penalties under the GDPR, ranging from up to €10 million in fines for the "lower level" offenses to up to €20 million for the "upper level" offenses.[40] Depending on the size of the production, one viable option the Defendant Co. can consider is to obtain consent from the data subjects. If the Defendant Co. selects this option, to remain compliant with the GDPR and avoid any penalties, it should take the following precautions, in writing, with minimal or no legalese: (1) explain to the data subject the reason for the document and data collection (i.e. discovery, litigation, or investigation); (2) plainly list which documents are being collected (i.e. email, documents related to ABC project); (3) explain how the data will be used (i.e. to review to determine relevance to production requests and/or production to opposing party); (4) obtain clear indication of the custodian's consent for the purposes enumerated above; and (5) inform the custodian of his or her ability to withdraw consent.[10]

Another option that the Defendant Co. may consider is bypassing consent all together and redacting the personal data. However, this option, discussed in more detail below, may not be feasible if the necessary redactions are too numerous or unduly burdensome, or if the personal data itself is relevant to the litigation.

Practitioners may be able to successfully challenge the proportionality of the discovery request. FRCP 26(b) requires the court to consider "whether the burden or expense of the proposed discovery outweighs its likely benefit." Practitioners can argue that the burden of attempting to obtain GDPR-compliant consent far outweighs the benefit of the data, which is subject to refusal by the data subjects to grant it, which results in potential for imposition of severe substantial penalties on their clients.

Obtaining the appropriate consent from the data subject is a prudent option for the Defendant Co. and other similarly-situated entities, but caution should be taken to avoid consent-by-default or mass opt-out consent, as this does not conform to the individualized and informed nature of consent contemplated by the GDPR. The Defendant Co. should also take caution when obtaining consent from employees, as with the inherent power of imbalance, there may be a dispute about whether such consent could ever be "freely given."

Alternatively, as discussed below, the "legitimate interest" condition may obviate the need to obtain consent from employees to collect their data. However, there is little to no case law or other guidance clarifying and understanding what constitutes a legitimate interest. Therefore, obtaining the appropriate consent from the data subject, will often times be the best option for the Defendant Co. and other similarly situated entities before looking at other conditions.

B. Is Consent Required for Data Processing Relating to Financial Crimes?

Financial service firms operating globally must capture and process criminal records and offenses about customers and employees in the course of their regular activities. They must also do so to prevent and detect financial crime (i.e. money laundering, sanctions, data breaches, financial crime, corruption, fraud, insider trading, market manipulation, and breaches of confidentiality).[11] The E.U. AML Directive requires obliged entities to provide notice to customers concerning their AML obligations, but does not require that consent be received.[4] GDPR similarly does not mandate that consent be received in order for financial institutions to process data in compliance with their AML regulatory requirements. The GDPR's "Frequently Asked Questions" section clarifies that, "there are a number of different lawful bases for processing personal data, and consent is just one of them. In some cases, consent will be an appropriate way to legitimize data processing. However, there will be situations when consent is not the appropriate legal basis"[12] (Information Commissioner's Office GDPR FAQs).

Although the GDPR is silent on when consent is required for processing data related to financial crimes[4], two key GDPR articles discuss processing data involving criminal convictions and related information that would be useful in preventing the commission of financial crimes. Articles 10 and 23 provide insight on who can process data and when it can be processed without consent.

Article 23 suspends individual data privacy principles when the essence of fundamental rights and freedoms is implicated and when it is necessary and proportionate to prevent threats to public security. Of particular interest to financial crime practitioners, Article 23 explicitly carves out an exception to the application of individual data privacy rights when it pertains to "the prevention, investigation, detection or prosecution of criminal offences or the execution of criminal penalties, including safeguarding against and the prevention of threats to public security."[1] As discussed in further detail below, Article 23 suggests that consent may not be required if a financial institution can demonstrate a legal obligation, public interest or legitimate interest.

Article 10 similarly provides an opportunity to consider when data may be processed without express consent; however it limits the data controllers' ability to process data by introducing special safeguards for processing sensitive data. Sensitive data is a category of data which is inclusive of biometric information, criminal allegations, proceedings or convictions. Article 10 does not mandate that consent be given; it merely allows sensitive data to be processed under the control of official authority, or when the processing is authorized by the E.U. or E.U. Member State law and provides for appropriate safeguards for the rights and freedoms of data subjects.

Article 10 also explicitly requires that "any comprehensive register of criminal convictions shall be kept only under the control of official authority." Therefore, it would appear that non-official authorities would not be able to lawfully process this type of data without express consent. As a result, law firms and banks should carefully consider how they process and store sensitive data, as the definition of "official authority" is not defined in the regulation and could foreseeably be limited to a public entity or other agency with governmental authority.[13]

C. The GDPR and the Legitimate Interests Condition

With the myriad of data processing mechanisms carried out by financial institutions, express consent may not always be practical. Most banks conduct ongoing automated screening of its customers and associated parties on a daily basis to monitor for AML and sanctions restricted activity.[14] This screening occurs so frequently that it would be untenable to obtain customer consent each time personal data is processed or transferred. Similarly, in the example above, the subpoena may require Defendant Co. to produce hundreds of thousands of documents, many of which contain the personal data of E.U. residents. In these scenarios, practitioners should consider whether another condition for processing data applies.

Article 6(1)(e) permits personal data processing where it is necessary to satisfy the purposes of the legitimate interests pursued by the controller or by a third party. Therefore, although banks and law firms may have a legal requirement, to carry out their AML screening they must first be able to demonstrate its usefulness and purpose by establishing a legitimate interest in collecting or processing personal data. The E.U. AML Directive leaves it up to Member States to define "legitimate interest," but suggests that such information is expected to contribute to "increased trust in the integrity of the financial system by enabling only those who are in a position to demonstrate legitimate interest to become aware of the identity of the beneficial owners".[15]

The European Data Supervisor recently questioned whether certain forms of invasive personal data processing, previously deemed acceptable in relation to anti-money laundering and the fight against terrorism, are necessary and whether they are proportionate.[2] The friction with GDPR's increased individual protection becomes even more palpable when one considers the E.U. 5th AML Directive.[16] This directive provides specific guidance about handling beneficial ownership information, which is critical for preventing money laundering as corporate vehicles, trust arrangements, and shell companies can often be used to evade detection.[3] For instance, it requires that trustees hold adequate, accurate and up-to-date information on beneficial ownership regarding the trust, including the identity of the settlor, the trustee, the protector (if any), the beneficiaries or class of beneficiaries, and any other natural person exercising ultimate control of the trust. Furthermore, trustees are under an obligation to store beneficial ownership information in a central register that is accessible to the public across the E.U. 5th AML Directive.

The Directive clearly calls for increased transparency into personal data, especially pertaining to trusts. However, the regulations also stipulate that when determining the level of transparency of the beneficial ownership information to be provided, E.U. Member States should have due regard to the protection of fundamental rights of individuals, in particular the right to privacy and protection of personal data. Access to beneficial ownership information of trusts and similar legal arrangements should be granted to persons that can demonstrate a legitimate interest.[16]

D. The GDPR and the Legal Obligation Condition

Article 6(1)(e) also permits personal data processing where it is necessary for compliance with a legal obligation to which the controller is subject. The UK Information Commissioner's Office provided the following example of a legal obligation which qualifies as a lawful basis for data processing:

> A financial institution relies on the legal obligation imposed by Part 7 of Proceeds of Crime Act 2002 to process personal data in order to submit a Suspicious Activity Report to the National Crime Agency when it knows or suspects that a person is engaged in, or attempting, money laundering.[4]

Under Article 49(1)(e), data transfers may be permitted in the defense of legal claims. However, the legal authority giving rise to such transfer must be from a Member State or Union law. Therefore, although the GDPR permits data processing where necessary to comply with a legal obligation to which the controller is subject, some European Economic Area (EEA) regulators do not consider a data controller's legal obligations imposed by non-EEA countries to fall within this condition.[17] It follows that the subpoena that the court issued to the Defendant Co. also would not fall within the legal obligations condition to processing data under the GDPR because the U.S. is a non-EEA country. For these reasons, it is considered especially risky to rely solely on the legal obligation condition to process personal data in response to a U.S. discovery request, subpoena or court order.[17]

The hurdle to transfer E.U. customer data outside of the E.U. for financial crime reasons is significantly higher, as the GDPR does not explicitly recognize U.S. law (or any other non-E.U. country law) as a "legal obligation" justifying the processing of E.U. residents' personal data. Thus, it is possible that in the new dawn of GDPR, E.U. data protection authorities may not be swayed by an argument that data needed to be transferred to a jurisdiction with limited data privacy even to satisfy their AML and economic sanctions laws. However, U.S.-based and other foreign financial institutions are more likely to legally process and transfer the data if they can establish overriding legitimate interests and demonstrate adequate data privacy standards.[15]

Article 6 requires that the legal obligation giving rise to data processing be laid out by E.U. law or Member State law.[1] Historically, the E.U. has endorsed information sharing when carried out in the execution of legal obligations related to, AML and Counter Terrorist Financing screening processes. The European Data Protection Supervisor clarified that, AML laws should specify that, "the relevant legitimate ground for the processing of personal data should... be the necessity to comply with a legal obligation by the obliged entities, competent authorities and financial intelligence units."[18]

Similar to E.U. regulations, U.S. financial institutions must aid law enforcement agencies in detecting and preventing financial crimes.[19] AML regulations require banks to know your customers (KYC), and mandate the gathering of client's demographic and identifying information.[20] A typical KYC procedure links users' real-world identity to their accounts and checks users against a whitelist or a blacklist.[27] Therefore, many KYC and sanctions-screening requirements include collection of data that is then filtered, sorted, evaluated, and stored for current and future use.[21] This data-centric process is often exacerbated by the fact that law enforcement may have a legal interest in, and right to, obtain personal customer data, including account information and wire activity maintained by a bank. Another compounding factor is that a financial institution can face significant penalties if they fail to identify and provide the required information. They are also severely penalized if that information is not stored appropriately and leads to a data breach or leak as a result. Thus, in addition to traditional AML enforcement channels, recently enacted laws such as the cybersecurity regulations now call for significant penalties to redress data protection violations.[1]

In the E.U., financial institutions can also generally rely on E.U. AML and sanction laws as a recognized "legal obligation" – i.e., one of the lawful bases – to collect and use customers' personal data within the E.U. The difficulty arises when those E.U. institutions seek to transfer such data to U.S. affiliates, or when U.S. institutions subject to the GDPR collect data about E.U. customers.[15]

D.1 E.U. Data Transfer and the U.S. Privacy Shield

The GDPR places new restrictions on the production of covered personal data to courts, tribunals, and administrative authorities outside of the

EEA, such as the U.S. Department of Justice (DOJ) and the Treasury's Office of Foreign Asset Control (OFAC). Under the GDPR, requests or demands for covered personal data from a non-EEA authority, court, or tribunal are not "recognized or enforceable in any manner" unless they are based on an international agreement, such as a mutual legal assistance treaty (MLAT), in force between the requesting country and the E.U. or Member State.[15]

The GDPR only permits personal data transfers to countries which the European Commission deems to have an "adequate" level of personal data protection. The Commission has determined that several countries ensure an adequate level of protection by their domestic law or of the international commitments they have entered into. For instance, the E.U. recognizes the U.S. Privacy Shield framework, which permits data transfers to companies that have self-certified to the Privacy Shield principles. In the absence of an adequacy decision, transfers are allowed outside non-E.U. states under certain circumstances, such as through standard contractual clauses or binding corporate rules. Provided that the transfer is not repetitive, massive or structural, and no other legal framework can be used; an organization wishing to transfer data outside the EEA can assert one of the derogations listed in GDPR. GDPR also requires that where personal data is transferred to a third country or to an international organization, the data subject shall have the right to be informed of the appropriate safeguards.

E.   The GDPR's Legitimate Interest Condition in the Discovery Context

Litigators face better odds of success demonstrating that the legitimate interests condition applies. Many EEA countries consider the need to defend against a lawsuit, in the US or elsewhere, to be a legitimate interest to process data.[15] Although E.U. regulators have not released guidance about "legitimate interests" in the context of the GDPR as of the close of 2018, the E.U.'s Article 29 Working Party released a non-binding opinion explaining the concept in 2014.[22] The Article 29 Working Party opinion provides that "legitimate interests" is a required basis for processing data under the E.U.'s Data Protection Directive (EDPD).* The wording in the Directive and the GDPR are identical.** The directive notes that the concept of legitimate interest is "open-ended" so it can be "relied upon in a wide range of situations, as long as its requirements" are met.[22] The opinion sets forth three tests: (1) whether the interest or purpose is legitimate; (2) whether processing data in the way envisioned is necessary

---

* Comparing GDPR Article 6(1)(f) with EU Directive 95/46/EC.
** *Id.* The GDPR has additional language relating to protecting the data of children.

to achieve that interest or purpose; and (3) a "balancing act" test, which balances data privacy rights of individuals under the E.U. law with the interests of the data processor.[22]

Applying this framework to the Defendant Co. example, the Defendant Co. could argue that the need to defend a pending lawsuit is a legitimate interest, and processing data is necessary to achieve that goal. In terms of the balancing test, if Defendant Co. redacted the personal data irrelevant to the subpoena or case, it would pass the balancing test in all likelihood. One option is to use technology to redact documents. Traditionally, redaction is often a very labor-intensive, time-consuming, and expensive process that involves the manual review of documents to remove or black out confidential, personal, or otherwise sensitive information. Document review platforms now include several tools that enable parties to streamline the review process, including: "pattern search and redact," which automatically searches for certain patterns, such as those found in Social Security Numbers, credit card information, addresses, etc., and redacts once the pattern is found; redaction of imaged documents, through the use of "optical character recognition," or OCR; native Excel redaction technology, which allows the user to redact a full cell, as well as data within the cell; bulk redactions with context searching; inverse redaction, which permits the user to redact all matches except for certain data the user has identified; and quality control modules, which allows the user to identify all of the data redacted and approve the redactions.[39]

Article 6 also permits processing necessary for the purposes of carrying out legitimate interests pursued by the controller or by a third party. In the context of discovery, the E.U. data protection authorities explained that an order from a foreign court to produce documents does not render that order legal under the GDPR and that in the absence of an agreement between countries for mutual legal assistance, such an order can proceed "only if it qualifies under Article 49".[23]

Article 49(1)(2) provides for limited transfer of individual data where compelling legitimate interests of the data transferring party exist.[1] The following criteria must be met: (1) the transfer is not repetitive and concerns only a limited number of data subjects; (2) the transfer is necessary for compelling, legitimate interests of the data transferring entity that are not overridden by the interests or rights and freedoms of the data subject; (3) the transferring entity has assessed all of the circumstances surrounding the data transfer and has provided suitable safeguards; (4) the relevant data protection authority has been informed of the transfer; and (5) the data subjects have been informed of the intended data transfer. Transfers of information from the E.U. to a 3rd country or international organization are subject to specific rules and will most likely be assessed using the legitimate interest condition.

Article 49 derogations permitting data transfer are to be interpreted strictly. Whereas the data subject must consent to all risks, the transfer must be necessary for important reasons of public interest, or the transfer must be necessary for the establishment, exercise or defense of legal claims.[1] Where none of the derogations are applicable – a transfer to a third country … may take place only if the transfer is not repetitive, concerns only a limited number of data subjects, is necessary for the purposes of compelling legitimate interests…which are not overridden by the interests or rights and freedoms of the data subject. An E.U. Amicus Brief to the Supreme Court explained that the public interest that fits within the list of derogations must be one that is recognized in a member state – for instance the interest to combat serious crimes and thus international cooperation to combat such crimes.

The thresholds and heightened consideration given to the rights of data subjects increases the circumstances where E.U. Authorities may decide data should not be transferred to the U.S. to satisfy a U.S. civil court order, subpoena or discovery request. To date, no judicial determination has confronted GDPR compliance with U.S. discovery rules head on.

These conflicts arise as early as even before a complaint is filed. For instance, under prevailing U.S. rules, a defendant must process data almost immediately once it is sued or has reason to believe that litigation is imminent: it is obligated to preserve documents, including all electronically stored information (ESI), which is potentially relevant to the claims or defenses in the litigation. The party must "suspend its routine document retention/destruction policy and put in place a 'litigation hold' to ensure the preservation of relevant documents".[24] A subpoena recipient must also preserve documents long enough so that they may be collected and produced in accordance with the subpoena's terms.

In our example, the Defendant Co. must send a litigation hold notice to employees/custodians, to inform them of the obligation to preserve relevant information. Under the GDPR, in theory, each recipient has the right to review the preserved material, including historical ESI. One may also make the argument that in addition, persons who have "personal data" contained in the ESI also have a right to review. It remains unclear as to whether this right of review arises before or after the data is matched to specific topics and time periods, or again before the data is produced.

The GDPR has fundamentally changed the implementation of existing procedures, opening new possibilities for their use in discovery and wiping the slate of localized interpretations of their predecessors clean under the old directive. Because the guidance issued under the old directive is also no longer binding, legal practitioners must not assume that what worked under the directive will continue to work under the GDPR.

One practical implication is that when a transfer is needed for response to a discovery request or subpoena, the scope of the request will almost certainly need to be narrowed. European law does not accept the broad concept of responsiveness used in U.S. discovery, so any request must be tightly focused on only the information and custodians directly relevant and critical to the matter in question. Practitioners should also determine whether they can obtain evidence responsive to the subpoena through alternate means, for example, interrogatories or deposition testimony.

The timeline for the Defendant Co. to raise any GDPR-related issues in litigation is as early as possible. Both federal and state rules require that promptly after the pleadings are filed, discovery and meet-and-confer and court conferences must occur. These conferences are not only the Defendant Co.'s first and best opportunity to raise discovery and data issues, but it is the legally acceptable time to do so under the rules of civil procedure. Although conferences occur early in the process, there are several strategies that the Defendant Co. could implement in conjunction with obtaining consent: (1) setting up a rolling production schedule to allow for additional time for obtaining consent or processing the data; (2) introducing confidentiality and information security provisions, including permission to file documents with personal information under seal and provisions governing how the receiving party will protect personal data; and (3) agreements governing the use of redactions to anonymize personal data, to further mitigate the impact of the GDPR.

Legal obligations and legitimate interests may not cover all potential customer data uses; however, they should weigh favorably in achieving GDPR consent in both the discovery and financial crime sectors. It remains to be seen which legal standard will prevail when legal interests and the law give rise to data transfer stems from outside of the E.U. In the case of the Defendant Co, early disclosure will set the tone for the case, on how to treat opposing counsel, among other things.

F. Right to Access Technology-Enhanced Data under the GDPR

Another area for consideration by both financial crimes and U.S. discovery laws in light of the new GDPR requirements is the ability to access technology-enhanced data. The expansive capabilities of technology in data aggregation and data mining can reveal personal data, even family relationships and connections to otherwise anonymous individuals through predictive profiling and matching mechanisms. Within the context of GDPR, it begs the following question: Does an individual's right to access their personal data also extend to obtaining information amplified in an algorithm to populate, parse and predict potential criminal behavior?*

Under Article 15, data subjects have the right to obtain confirmation that personal data concerning them is being processed. Financial institutions increasingly depend on technology to aggregate customer data to build risk profiles and screening models.[1] For instance, using algorithms, artificial intelligence and machine learning, single data points such as a customer's name can be easily scrubbed against hundreds of international watch lists, court cases and other publicly available information to build elaborate connections and customer profiles. Given the increasing technological resources available to financial institutions in aggregating customer data it is not unlikely that the institution could uncover otherwise opaque information via an algorithmic open source data mining process. Advances in technology and the capabilities of big data analytics, artificial intelligence and machine learning have also made it easier to make automated decisions with the potential to significantly impact individuals' rights and freedoms.[25]

The necessity for financial institutions to screen their customers is generally acknowledged; however, the GDPR requires increased transparency on the part of controllers of personal data to assure customers understand the use for which their data is being processed.[41] Article 15 provides a right to access information relating to, "the existence of automated decision-making, including profiling, meaningful information about the logic involved, as well as the significance and the envisaged consequences of such processing for the data subject."[1] On its face, GDPR does not specify the type of information that would be considered "meaningful" nor does it mandate algorithm disclosure. At a minimum, Article 15 requires financial institutions and other data controllers to provide an explanation on how the screening mechanisms carry out their decision-making process. Providing some relief, Recital 63 of the GDPR notes that the right of access "should not adversely affect the rights or freedoms of others, including trade secrets or intellectual property and in particular the copyright protecting the software."[1] Although the Recitals are not legally binding, their inclusion in the GDPR will most likely cause data controllers to offer information that will address general system functionality, but will heavily curtail that information to protect the controller's interests (e.g. trade secrets, intellectual property).[26] In complying with this portion of the GDPR requirements, data controllers

---

* GDPR Article 22 is not discussed in detail here; however, it states that the "data subject shall have the right not to be subject to a decision based solely on automated processing, including profiling, which produces legal effects concerning him or her or similarly significantly affects him or her."

will have to be mindful of exposing internal surveillance mechanisms to nefarious actors and tipping off criminals that may be under investigation.

To protect against this possibility, some E.U. Member States have clarified that protecting data subjects against financial crime threats may outweigh the individual right to access. For instance, the 4th E.U. Anti-Money Laundering Directive makes clear that "access by the data subject to any information related to a suspicious transaction report would seriously undermine the effectiveness of the fight against money laundering and terrorist financing" and requires that Member States "adopt legislative measures restricting, in whole or in part, the data subject's right of access to personal data." Instead, the data subject has the right to request that a supervisory authority confirm the lawfulness of the processing.[4] Nonetheless, there is a strong impetus that the purpose for processing the data is clearly communicated and monitored by the data controller. In fact, the EDPS recently cautioned that "processing personal data collected for one purpose and used for another, completely unrelated purpose infringes the data protection principle of purpose limitation and threatens the implementation of the principle of proportionality."[15] It remains to be seen how much information an individual will be able to obtain under the right to access and whether it will be inclusive of the right to access technology enhanced data. Financial institutions looking for a balance have begun to explore blockchain capabilities such as designing a privacy-preserving KYC (Know Your Customer) scheme on top of Ethereum. It would allow providers of financial services to leverage the potential of blockchain technology to increase efficiency of customer onboarding while complying with regulation and protecting users' privacy.[27] For entities such as the Defendant Co., compliance with the Right to Access conference means regularly informing data subjects of their actions. The Defendant Co. should also reevaluate all relevant processes and implement technology-based solutions whereever possible.

F.1 The Right to Access under the CCPA and Data Portability

Although the U.S. Congress has not implemented a federal privacy law similar in scope or nature to the GDPR, on June 28, 2018, California governor Jerry Brown signed the CCPA into law. The CCPA became effective on January 1, 2020, to provide Californian residents with a variety of new privacy rights, including the right to access the personal information that a business has about them, as well as the purposes for data collection, and the third parties with whom the data has been shared.[39]

The GDPR and the CCPA offer similar protections pertaining to the data subject's right to access. Under Section 1798 of the CCPA, consumers have the right to obtain the following disclosures from businesses: (1) information collected; (2) categories of information collected; (3)

categories of third parties with which the information is shared;[39] (4) categories of sources of the information; and (5) business or commercial purpose for collecting or selling the personal information. Likewise and as discussed above, Article 15 of the GDPR grants data subjects the right to confirm that the controller processed their personal data, and if so: (1) a copy of the personal data; (2) the categories of personal data concerned; (3) the recipients (or categories of recipients) with whom the data might be shared (especially outside of the EEA); (4) any available information about the source (where not collected from the data subject); and (5) the processes of processing.[1]

There are some differences between the rights to access offered by the CCPA and GDPR. The GDPR is more expansive, as it also provides data subjects with rights to information about the retention period and any automated decision-making.[1] The GDPR also provides a right to data portability, which is related to the right to access, but specifically allows data subjects to receive, transmit, and have their personal data transmitted in a commonly used, machine readable format (GDPR Article 20, 2016). The purpose of the right to data portability is to "empower the data subject and give him/her more control over the personal data concerning him/her."[28] Sections 1798.100, 110(a)-(b), and 130 of the CCPA contains similar provisions, under which businesses responding to a consumer's request must provide the information electronically in a readily useable format. The CCPA does not provide consumers with a right to direct the business entity not to share the information with another.[39]

In addition, the CCPA does not restrict the ability to comply with federal, state, or local laws, or to respond to a civil, criminal, or regulatory investigation, subpoena, or summons. It also cannot restrict a business from cooperating with law enforcement agencies or exercising or defending legal claims. Although the CCPA has similar provisions to the GDPR, right to access requests will have limited impact to the financial crime or the U.S. discovery spaces, because these areas fall under express exemptions.[28] However, with all other variables held equal, it will be more difficult for customers to exercise their right to access information in a litigation or a financial crime under the CCPA than under the GDPR.

G. The Right to be Forgotten under the GDPR

In contrast to where we have seen the individual challenges prevailing in obtaining a right to access, the right to be forgotten has typically been upheld in favor of the individual's right to privacy. Under Article 17, data controllers[1] are required to inform E.U. individuals about their "right to be forgotten." Essentially, data controllers must notify individuals about their right to deletion and correction of their personal data. Article 17(3) provides an exemption: a data controller may be exempt from the individual's right to be forgotten if the data processing is "deemed necessary for the exercise of freedom of expression, compliance with a legal obligation, public interests such as public health, scientific or historic research, or the establishment of or defense of legal claims."[1]

While it is understood that a subject may withdraw or object to the processing of its data unless there is a legal obligation which mandates processing, in the financial crime context the right to be forgotten presents a direct challenge with other requirements to preserve data. Generally, a large amount of private data found in financial institutions is not immediately erasable for several reasons, including prevention of money laundering and regulatory enforced data retention requirements.[29]

In fact, the 4th E.U. AML Directive requires retention of customer due diligence information and supporting evidence and records of transactions for five years from the end of the applicable relationship, and E.U. member states can allow for another five-year period "where the necessity and proportionality of such further retention has been established for the prevention, detection, investigation or prosecution of suspected money laundering or terrorist financing."[4] However, it is important to note again that, foreign legal obligations are not recognized as "legal obligations" capable of shielding the controller or processor from complying with the erasure request. However, they may qualify as overriding legitimate interests. Therefore, it remains to be seen if compliance with U.S. financial crime regulatory requirements would override the individual right to erasure when asserted under GDPR.

In the UK, the Financial Conduct Authority attempted to clarify expectations in data retention policies under the GDPR. A spokesman for the Financial Ombudsman Service stated that, requests to delete data should be considered in relation to the firm's "usual data retention policies and if the data is something that can be deleted.[30] A global right to erasure was initially raised in France when the courts there were asked to consider whether the right to be forgotten applies globally (i.e. if Google has to delist information about its users in the UK or EU or if it needs to delist information from google sites everywhere). The case went to the European Court of Justice, and the court subsequently ruled that search engines are controllers of personal data – meaning they are subject to Europe's data laws. Therefore, E.U. citizens were given the right to ask search engines to remove links to articles from search results globally if they contained personal information deemed inaccurate, inadequate, irrelevant or excessive.[30]

In April 2018, two cases in the United Kingdom established significant precedent for the individual right to erasure to be upheld. In their separate claims, two businessmen, whose convictions were 'spent', sought to have reports about their historic offences 'de-listed' from Google's search results when searches are made against their names. Both claims were based on the right to be forgotten and the right to have personal information "de-listed" or "de-indexed" by the operators of an Internet search engine. In the final ruling, the Justice ordered Google to block search results about a past conviction that came up against the businessman's name who had been convicted of a less serious offense. The judge did not uphold the right to be forgotten for the individual who had been convicted of the more serious offense. In distinguishing between the two results, the judge said the 'crime and punishment information' in his case 'has become outdated, irrelevant and is of no sufficient legitimate interest to users of Google Search to justify its continued availability, so an appropriate delisting order should be made'.[30] The impact of this precedent is far reaching when individuals can now request for factual criminal information to be deleted following what appears to be a subjective consideration process with no established framework.

G.1   The Right to Request Deletion of Personal Information under the CCPA

Section 1798.105(a) of the CCPA contains an analogous right to the GDPR's right to be forgotten: the right to request deletion of personal information. To properly comply with both the CCPA's right to request deletion of personal information and the GDPR's right to be forgotten, at a bare minimum, entities must maintain accurate data inventories and data maps.[31]

Many of the technologies in place can ensure compliance with both the GDPR and the CCPA, specifically, pseudonymization and tokenization.[31] Pseudonymization involves replacing confidential, personal or otherwise sensitive data with a pseudonym, and tokenization involves replacing it with a token. Although it is mature technology, using tokenization to delete personal data is not an arduous task if the entity has updated data maps and clearly defined procedures in place. Where an entity has tokenized the identifying elements of an individual's personal data, deleting the personal data simply involves deleting the mapping between the token and corresponding data. Entities should also take care to delete the data from their back up systems as well.

In the discovery/civil litigation context, the legal claim exemption applies in all likelihood. The statutory duty to preserve data and put litigation holds in place will most likely operate to waive the data subjects' right to request deletion of personal data. Nevertheless, because discovery and financial crime concerns are not the only situations in which the right to be forgotten or the right to request deletion may exist, entities should work to implement controls and procedures to ensure compliance with these rights.

Related Case Studies

Because the GDPR was implemented in May 2018, and the CCPA's effective date was January 2020, the case law analyzing the issues presented here are very limited. As a result, the case studies that follow are reflect the few instances that the courts have addressed these issues, and to the instances where they have conflicts with similar foreign privacy laws. Available jurisprudence reveals limitations on the individual's right of access. Several overriding interests and exceptions have been identified that significantly limit both the scope of applicability and content of the explanation. For instance, consider that financial institutions who collect personal data about their customers to ensure that they are not subject to, U.S., E.U. or U.N. economic sanctions programs. Adherence will require institutions to use information that may be subject to GDPR data use restrictions. Foreign parties petitioning the U.S. government to disclose information do not usually result in granting the individual right to access. Consider, the case brought after the U.S. designated six individuals and 68 companies tied to a drug money-laundering network. The designation alleged that a Panamanian-Colombian-Spanish national Waked Hatum and Panamanian-Lebanese-Colombian national, Waked Fares engaged in drug trafficking, money laundering and other financial crimes.[32]

Given the severe implications of the designation, which included asset freezing, Mr. Waked Fares and plaintiffs challenged their designated status and requested a complete un-redacted record demonstrating the basis for their designations.* Before denying relief, the court surveyed the limited case law that addresses the amount of disclosure required from the U.S. government following a sanctions designation. The court recognized that disclosure has its limits. "For example, an unclassified summary may not be possible where the subject matter itself may be classified and cannot be revealed without implicating national security."[32] This often times is the case with terrorist designations where the government may not want to tip their hand to other potential suspects. Although the parties have not

---

* Financial institutions and practitioners can face significant penalties and even personal liability for dealing or otherwise facilitating business activity with restricted parties. Since June 2000, more than 1,900 individuals and entities have been named by OFAC pursuant to the Kingpin Act for their role in international narcotics trafficking. Penalties for violations of the Kingpin Act range from civil penalties of up to $1.075 million per violation to more severe criminal penalties. Criminal penalties for corporate officers may include up to 30 years in prison and fines up to $5 million. Criminal fines for corporations may reach $10 million. Other individuals could face up to 10 years in prison and fines pursuant to Title 18 of the United States Code for criminal violations of the Kingpin Act.

brought a case under GDPR right to access, the challenge faced by non-U.S. persons in obtaining that data is evident from the majority of cases, which similarly hold that, the government may use classified information, without disclosure, when making designation determinations.[33]

The individual right to access their full data record was also denied in the *Holy Land* case where the D.C. Circuit held that, in the context of sanctions' designations, "due process requires the disclosure of only the unclassified portions of the administrative, that the plaintiff failed to establish that "that due process prevents its designation based upon classified information to which it has not had access is of no avail."[34] To date, no financial crime related cases have been adjudicated in the UK since the enactment of the current GDPR regulation.[35] Therefore, in that jurisdiction, it remains to be seen when E.U. national security interests will triumph over the individual right to data privacy.

However, looking at the current U.K. prosecution case trends it seems more likely that the right to privacy will prevail. The *Digital Rights Ireland* case was litigated under GDPR's predecessor; however several key findings remain relevant. In *Digital Rights Ireland* case, the Court of Justice recognized that the fight against international terrorism and serious crime constitutes an objective of general interest. The court also held that, since the legal tools enacted to pursue that objective interfere with the fundamental rights to privacy and data protection, it is necessary, according to the Court, to assess the proportionality of such measures.[2] In support of privacy rights, they reasoned that, the approach to anti-money laundering is risk less risky situations justify less intrusive procedures. A risk-based approach is considered to more in line with the essential principle of proportionality and tends to determine a positive outcome for limiting personal data processing.[2]

Similar challenges have also arisen in the discovery context. One court issued substantial sanctions to one defendant for failure to raise foreign privacy law issues in a timely manner.[36] In that case, the defendant specifically failed to raise neither applicable Macau data privacy laws nor their impact on discovery during the parties' Rule 16 meet and confer on them in the resulting joint stipulation.[36] France's blocking statute makes complying with US discovery requests a crime. "It is well settled that such statutes do not deprive an American court of the power to order a party in its jurisdiction to produce evidence even though the act of production may violate the statute."[37] In *Strauss v. Credit Lyonnais, S.A.*, 2008,[38] the Court also stressed that the interests of the U.S. in deterring international terrorism outweigh French interests in France's "bank secrecy law" and "discovery blocking statute" despite the likelihood that France would pursue criminal penalties against the French bank involved. The EC has already explained that an order from a foreign court to produce documents does not render that order legal under the GDPR and that in the absence of an agreement between countries for mutual legal assistance, such an order can proceed "only if it qualifies under Article 49".[23]

Conclusion: Recommendations/Strategies/Pitfalls

It is undeniable that financial services firms and legal practitioners are facing a new privacy landscape, that continues to evolve. Data controllers will have to analyze and synthesize overlapping legal frameworks including those under the GDPR, U.S. discovery rules, and the CCPA, which can conflict. In many cases, the consent, legal obligation, and legitimate interests' conditions offer viable solutions, but they are not without landmines or technology limitations. Where consent is given, it should also extend to include data preservation requirements. Institutions need to implement appropriate channels to capture requests and to keep the customer informed, especially about which data has been deleted and any exceptions made, including the practices and processes applied to that data. Further, building regular consent reviews into the business process will ensure that the institution keeps an accurate record of when, how, and what you told each individual about consent. On top of that, companies must also allow individuals to be able to easily withdraw their consent at any time which entails having technological capabilities that can readily erase, access, or retrieve relevant customer data and distinguish it from enhanced customer data.

Banks especially need to also take caution as to how criminal convictions will be stored as Article 10 also requires that, "any comprehensive register of criminal convictions shall be kept only under the control of an official authority." To implement an effective data erasure process, institutions need a comprehensive end-to-end view of all processes and systems dealing with personal data, while keeping in mind that this regulation is not just another regulation to deal with, but also a piece of the customer experience.

One thing is certain, banks and legal practitioners will have to implement solutions early in the process to avoid penalties.

Acknowledgments

Thank you to the following for your assistance with this chapter:
Maria de Dios, Certilman Balin Adler & Hyman LLP
Daniel Meyers, TransPerfect Legal Solutions

References

1. General Data Protection Regulation (GDPR). (2016). Retrieved from https://gdprinfo.eu/ (Last accessed on February 9, 2021)
2. Wiewiorowski, W.R. (2017, February 2). Opinion 1/2017 EDPS Opinion on a Commission Proposal amending Directive (EU) 2015/849 and Directive 2009/101/EC: Access to Beneficial Ownership Information and Data Protection Implications. European Data Protection Supervisor (EDPS). http://edps.europa.eu/sites/edp/files/publication/17-02-02_opinion_aml_en.pdf Last retrieved February 15, 2021
3. Kirby, D.J. (2008). The European Union's Gatekeeper Initiative. *Hofstra Law Review*, 37(1), 261-312. Retrieved from https://scholarlycommons.law.hofstra.edu/hlr/vol37/iss1/8/
4. Malish, R. (2018). Financial crime and compliance under GDPR. Nice Actimize. Retrieved from http://www.niceactimize.com/Documents/NICE_Actimize_Financial_Crime_and_Compliance_under_GDPR_White_Paper.pdf
5. Alexander Interactive v. Adorama, 2014 WL 61472 (S.D.N.Y. 2014).
6. New York ex rel. Boardman v. Nat'l Railroad Pass. Corp., 233 F.R.D. 259 (N.D.N.Y. 2006).
7. Gruss v. Zwirn, No. 09 Civ. 6441, 2013 WL 6098482 (S.D.N.Y. 2013); Mariana Islands v. Millard, 287 F.R.D. 204 (S.D.N.Y. 2012); Thai Lao Lignite (Thailand) Co. v. Gov't of Lao People's Democratic Rep., 924 F. Supp. 2d 508 (S.D.N.Y. 2013).
8. In re Application of Natalia Potanina, 2015 WL 4476612 (S.D.N.Y. 2015).
9. Playboy Enterp., Inc. v. Dumas, 53 F.3d 549 (2d Cir. 1995).
10. Schwartz, Barry. (2018, May 16). GDPR and ediscovery – consent. BIA. Retrieved from https://www.biaprotect.com/resources/resource/gdpr-and-ediscovery-consent
11. Brown, S. and Woollett, H. (2017, July 28). Application of article 10 of the GDPR to the financial services' sector in the UK. Society for Computers and Law (SCL). Retrieved from https://www.scl.org/articles/8971-application-of-article-10-of-the-gdpr-to-the-financial-services-sector-in-the-uk
12. Information Commissioner's Office (ICO). (n.d.). General data protection regulation (GDPR) FAQs for small financial service providers. ICO. Retrieved from https://ico.org.uk/for-organisations/in-your-sector/finance/general-data-protection-regulation-gdpr-faqs-for-small-financial-service-providers/
13. Burton, C., De Boel, L., Kuner, C., Pateraki, A., Cadiot, S. and Hoffman, S.G. (2016, January 25). The final European Union general data protection regulation. Bloomberg BNA Privacy & Security Law Report. Retrieved from https://www.wsgr.com/images/content/1/5/v2/15414/BloombergBNA-0116.pdf
14. Financial Conduct Authority (FCA). (2014, November). How small banks manage money laundering and sanctions risk. FCA. Retrieved from https://www.fca.org.uk/publication/thematic-reviews/tr14-16.pdf
15. Cohen Levin, S. and Harris Gutierrez, F. (2018, May 6). Implications of the E.U. general data privacy regulation for U.S. anti-money laundering and economic sanctions compliance. Global Legal Group. Retrieved from /20180621-implications-of-the-EU-general-data-privacy-regulation-for-US-anti-money-laundering-and-economic-sanctions-compliance.pdf

16. European Parliament and Council of the European Union (2018). Directive (EU) 2018/843 of the European Parliament and of the Council of 30 May 2018 amending Directive (EU) 2015/849 on the prevention of the use of the financial system for the purposes of money laundering or terrorist financing, and amending Directives 2009/138/EC and 2013/36/EU (5th Anti-Money Laundering Directive]. Official Journal of the European Union. Retrieved from https://eur-lex.europa.eu/legal-content/EN/TXT/?uri=CELEX%3A32018L0843

17. Practical Law Intellectual Property & Technology. (2018). Conflicts between US discovery and non-US data protection laws. Practical Law. Retrieved from https://1.next.westlaw.com/Document/Id8ece4a8805411e698dc8b09b4f043e0/View/FullText.html?transitionType=SearchItem&contextData=(sc.Search)

18. Buttarelli, G. (2013, July 4). Opinion of the European Data Protection Supervisor of the European Parliament and of the Council on the prevention of the use of the financial system for the purpose of money laundering and terrorist financing, and a proposal for a regulation of the European Parliament and of the Council on information on the payer accompanying transfers of funds. European Data Protection Supervisor (EDPS). Retrieved from https://edps.europa.eu/sites/edp/files/publication/13-07-04_money_laundering_en.pdf

19. Financial Crimes Enforcement Network (FinCEN). (n.d.). FinCEN's mandate from Congress. FinCEN. Retrieved from https://www.fincen.gov/resources/statutes-regulations/fincens-mandate-congress

20. Bank Secrecy Act. (1970). Retrieved from http://uscode.house.gov/statutes/pl/91/508.pdf

21. Barry, W.P. (2017, November 21). A compliance conundrum for financial institutions: U.S. anti-money laundering initiatives and the forthcoming EU general data protection regulation. Bloomberg BNA. Retrieved from https://www.millerchevalier.com/sites/default/files/publications/A-Compliance-Conundrum-for-Financial-Institutions_William-P-Barry.pdf

22. Chepalis, Regina (2018, April 25). How auto-redaction technology can streamline your e-discovery. Complete Discovery Source (CDS). Retrieved from https://cdslegal.com/insights/how-auto-redaction-technology-stream line-ediscovery/.

23. Brief of Privacy International Human and Digital Rights Organizations, and International Legal Scholars as Amici Curiae in Support of Respondent, U.S.A. v. Microsoft Corp., 253 F.3d 34 (2001) (no. 17-2). Retrieved from https://privacyinternational.org/sites/default/files/2018-03/U.S.%20v.%20Microsoft%20Brief%20FINAL.pdf

24. EPAC Tech., Inc. v. HarperCollins Christian Pub., Inc., 2018 WL 1542040 (M.D. Tenn. 2018).

25. Article 29 Data Protection Working Party. (2018, February 6). Guidelines on automated individual decision-making and profiling for the purposes of Regulation 2016/679. The Working Party on the Protection of Individuals with Regard to the Processing of Personal Data. Retrieved from https://ec.europa.eu/newsroom/article29/document.cfm?action=display&doc_id=49826

26. Wachter, S., Mittelstadt, B. and Floridi, L. (2017, June 3). Why a right to explanation of automated decision-making does not exist in the general

data protection regulation. International Data Privacy Law. https://doi. org/10.1093/idpl/ipx005 (Last accessed on February 15, 2021)

27. Biryukov, A., Khovratovich, D. and Tikhomirov, S. (2018, May 9). Privacy-preserving KYC on Ethereum. University of Luxembourg Library. Retrieved from http://orbilu.uni.lu/handle/10993/35915

28. Article 29 Data Protection Working Party. (2017, April 5). Guidelines on the right to data portability. The Working Party on the Protection of Individuals with Regard to the Processing of Personal Data. Retrieved from https:// ec.europa.eu/newsroom/document.cfm?doc_id=44099

29. Banking Hub by Zeb. (2017, November 15). GDPR deep dive—how to implement the 'right to be forgotten.' Banking Hub. Retrieved from https:// www.bankinghub.eu/banking/finance-risk/gdpr-deep-dive-implement-right-forgotten

30. Hopping, C., Afifi-Sabet, K. and IT Pro. (2018, November 23). What is the 'right to be forgotten'? IT PRO. Retrieved from http://www.itpro.co.uk/data-protection/22378/what-is-googles-right-to-be-forgotten

31. Noltensmeyer, John (2018, September 12). Complying with the CCPA's "Right to be Forgotten." Tokenex. Retrieved from https://tokenex.com/complying-with-the-ccpas-right-to-be-forgotten/ (Last accessed on February 15, 2021)

32. Abdul Mohamed Waked Fares et al. v. John E. Smith et al. 249 F. Supp. 3d 115 (D.D.C. 2017).

33. Al Haramain Islamic Found., Inc. v. U.S. Dep't of Treasury, 686 F.3d 965 (9th Cir. 2012).

34. Holy Land Found. for Relief and Dev. v. Ashcroft, 333 F.3d 156, 159 (D.C. Cir. 2003).

35. Information Commissioner's Office (ICO). (2018). Action's we've taken: enforcement action. ICO. https://ico.org.uk/action-weve-taken/ enforcement/ (Last accessed on February 15, 2021).

36. Jacobs v. Las Vegas Sands, Index No. 10-A-627691 (Dist. Ct., Clark Co., Mar. 6, 2015).

37. Societe Nationale Industrielle Aeropostiale v. U.S. District Court for the Southern District of Iowa, 482 U.S. 522(1987).

38. Strauss v. Credit Lyonnais, S.A., 249 F.R.D. 429 (E.D.N.Y. 2008).

39. California Consumer Privacy Act of 2018. (effective 2020, January 1). Retrieved from https://oag.ca.gov/privacy/ccpa

40. GDPR EU.org. (n.d.). Fines and Penalties. GDPREU.org. Retrieved from https://www.gdpreu.org/compliance/fines-and-penalties/

41. Article 29 Data Protection Working Party. (2014, April 9). Opinion 06/2014 on the notion of legitimate interests of the data controller under Article 7 of Directive 95/46/EC. The Working Party on the Protection of Individuals with Regard to the Processing of Personal Data. Retrieved fromhttps://ec.europa. eu/justice/article-29/documentation/opinion-recommendation/files/2014/ wp217_en.pdf

42. European Parliament and Council of the European Union (2015). Directive (EU) 2015/849 of the European Parliament and of the Council of 20 May 2015 on the prevention of the use of the financial system for the purposes of money laundering or terrorist financing, amending Regulation (EU) No 648/2012 of

the European Parliament and of the Council, and repealing Directive 2005/60/ EC of the European Parliament and of the Council and Commission Directive 2006/70/EC [4th Anti-Money Laundering Directive]. Official Journal of the European Union. Retrieved from https://eur-lex.europa.eu/legal-content/ EN/TXT/PDF/?uri=OJ%3AJOL_2015_141_R_0003

43. European Parliament and Council of the European Union (2016). Regulation (EU) 2016/679 of the European Parliament and of the Council of 27 April 2016 on the protection of natural persons with regard to the processing of personal data and on the free movement of such data, and repealing Directive 95/46/ EC [General Data Protection Regulation]. Official Journal of the European Union. Retrieved from https://eur-lex.europa.eu/legal-content/EN/TXT/?q id=1532348683434&uri=CELEX:02016R0679-20160504

44. Federal Rules of Civil Procedure (FRCP) (2017). Retrieved from https://www. uscourts.gov/sites/default/files/civil-rules-procedure-dec2017_0.pdf.

The Human Cultural and Behavioural Factor in Data Privacy

Scott Tees

Introduction

The introduction of the General Data Protection Regulations 2018 (GDPR) has led to organisations having to adapt their understanding and approach to protecting data subject rights, right from the management of processes to focusing more on the rights of individuals and the way their data is processed and stored.

With the sixth GDPR principle requiring data to be processed, "...in a manner that includes taking appropriate security measures as regards risks that arise from processing personal data"[1], it is crucial that there is consistency and parity in every element of the data management process. Organisations now have to re-think their strategy and approaches, particularly with regards to data security.

Training for staff and the evolvement of roles and responsibilities such as the Data Controller, Data Processor and Data Protection Officer, have become commonplace as organisations adapted to this new focus on data privacy and compliance.

Crucial to success in data privacy compliance is the recognition of the roles organisational stakeholders have to play. Studies have shown the importance of human involvement with change and that "Successful transformations begins to involve a large number of people as the process progresses...The more people involved, the better the outcome."[2]

Getting the human factor right is as critical as the regulations and policies themselves, and failure to recognise the importance of the human element could prove fatal to organisational compliance.

Email: scott.tees@decodecybersolutions.com

Such compliance failures are not unique and continue to be visible. In the first half of 2020, statistics showed that phishing attacks, which have historically involved human exploitation, were experiencing a steady increase from 72% in 2017 to 86% in 2020. During the same period, breaches, more associated with technical attacks, such as viruses and malware fell from 33% to 16%.[3]

With the COVID-19 pandemic causing organisations to re-think their cybersecurity strategies, the cybersecurity landscape and its role in data compliance will require re-alignment for it to remain fit for the purpose in the months and years ahead. With most data breaches occurring through human error, the importance of staff engagement and their understanding of the need for them to adhere to data compliance regulations must be at the forefront in shaping future strategy.

Cybersecurity is an area that continually tests data compliance and demonstrates, that despite the progress in policy and regulation, compliance breaches continue to occur as a result of intentional or unintentional human error.

Human Behaviour – Data Privacy in the Online World

The introduction of the General Data Protection Regulations 2018 (GDPR) was undoubtedly a considerable change to how organisations expected to regulate the data they managed. In response, many organisations began to change policies, processes, introducing staff training and awareness as part of this overhaul in regulatory compliance.

Organisational change is not uncommon and has become increasingly routine over the past five years, as organisations prepare and subsequently introduce GDPR into organisational data compliance governance frameworks.

In 2019 a report by the Info Security Group,[4] highlighted analysis of data from the UK Information Commissioner's Office (ICO), which noted that 90% of the 2376 breaches reported to the ICO were a result of mistakes made by people. More worryingly, there was an evident trend in the increase in human error compared to the previous two years, which was recorded at 61% and 87% respectively. Despite the fact that the human factor was being identified as being an area of increasing risk, the steady upward trend in data compliance failures has continued. Even though this issue was a regular feature in the analysis of compliance breaches, very little is being done to understand the cause of the human error.

It is appreciated that not all breaches are intentional, and various mistakes are because of fundamental human error or ignorance of regulatory requirements. In January 2020, a former social worker was prosecuted for passing the personal information of service users to a third-party providing young person placements for a Local Authority. The social worker unlawfully disclosed referrals for residential or foster placements of vulnerable young people aged 16-18 years old. The referrals contained sensitive personal data, including potential identifier information and vulnerability risks of the service user.[5]

Nevertheless, basic errors were continually being made, and organisations were not learning from them. Organisations had, on the face of it, adopted GDPR, however working practices in a number of organisations contradicted this assumption. This view is supported by Dekker[6], who commented on research suggesting that when examined over a period of time, there are associations between human error and the working environment in which they occur. Therefore, to understand why organisations must adopt a better focus on the human error factor to improve data compliance in the online world, it is crucial to understand why it exists in the first place.

Understanding the Human Risk Factor in Online Data Compliance

The decision on how to manage risk within an organisation is generally determined by the broader values and culture within that organisation. If senior managers, line manager and peers adopt an approach of non-compliance or poor practices, then this will reflect on the culture within the organisation. If there is no investment in staff, in areas such as regular training and awareness building, then there is a risk of mirroring that commitment, and becoming passive to compliance requirements.

The approach to GDPR training, noneffective training strategies and the lack of continued investment and support for employees has created a fundamental weakness in data privacy and cybersecurity from the very beginning. The prevailing opinion of the human factor being the most considerable risk to cybersecurity is flawed. The failure to invest in staff as an essential element of data compliance and cybersecurity remains to be the risk. Human error is merely the result of this lack of investment.

Organisational Culture – The Failure to Recognise the Importance of People

In some instances, it is not inconceivable to think that businesses had paid lip service to the introduction of GDPR. Through the minimal investment in any form in ongoing data privacy training, they had ultimately reverted to a process-driven approach, relying more on technical solutions to ensure security and compliance. By not recognising the importance of staff in cybersecurity, organisations posed an unnecessary risk to data compliance.

This was evident almost immediately after the introduction of GDPR when in 2019, only 30% of businesses had taken steps to improve their cybersecurity.[7] These changes included creation of new policies by 60% of businesses, with only 15% introducing extra training or communications. More alarmingly, only 6% created new contingency plans.

It is well documented that the most common breaches involve people targeting (Social Engineering), particularly in the form of phishing attacks or compromising business emails. However, many organisations have not reacted and continued to focus on the process and tech solutions to maintain cybersecurity and data compliance.

The lack of investment could not be attributed to financial constraints. This was evident by the spending projections analysis outlined within the UK Cyber Sectoral Analysis by the Department for Digital, Culture, Media and Sport.[8] Encouragingly the report recorded that the total annual revenue had reached an estimated £8.3 billion within the UK cybersecurity sector, which was an increase of 46% since 2017 (an increase of £2.6 billion from £5.7 billion).

However, analysing the provision of products, as shown in Fig. 12.1 below, only 11% of service focuses on training, awareness, and education.

It would be understandable if technology solutions were the only factor when it came to the protection of data; however, the blame culture of human error would suggest otherwise. Although numerous years of

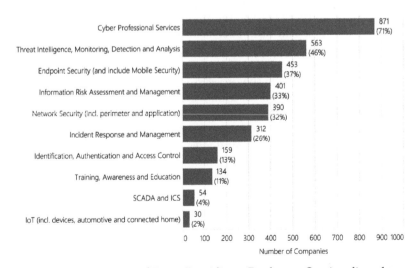

Fig. 12.1. Percentage of Firms Providing a Product or Service aligned to Taxonomy (Source: Perspective Economics)

human error is attributed to online security breaches, most of the financial investment continued to focus on other areas.

Only individual organisations can answer the question why this is the case but what is clear, is that there is a culture which relegates the human factor to a position of lower priority when it comes to data compliance and cybersecurity.

GDPR – The Focus on People

The General Data Protection Regulations 2018 (GDPR) are intended to spell the dawning of a new era in relation to the rights of the data subject. GDPR had introduced a more human focused strategy than its predecessor, 1995 Data Protection Directive, which was a more process-driven ethos. GDPR had evolved from an era of complacency, a lack of understanding of individual rights and the absence of any form of impactive punitive measures.

With data compliance becoming more focused on the individual through GDPR, it would be natural to think that the human aspect would be a critical factor in its preservation. There were indications that this was taken into consideration. Written into the GDPR framework through adjustments to specific roles and responsibilities Data Controllers began to regulate the way personal information was processed, used, transmitted and stored better, including the consideration of the latest technological developments.

In addition, the Data Processor began overseeing more of the delivery of several functions, including, IT processes, security measures to safeguard data, so there was undoubtedly a more structured method for processing data that had been absent up to that point. Furthermore, the Data Protection Officer provided the independent compliance assurance that regulations are being adhered to, including awareness-building and training of staff involved in the processing.

Based on the amount of time, effort and financial investment, organisations have embraced various technical aspects however, many have fallen short when it came to recognising and including the 'human factor' within their compliance strategies. The evident lack of investment on cyber security training and awareness raising, has arguably created an area of risk that has impacted GDPR compliance and potentially contributed to cyber-related compliance breaches that have emanated from fundamental human error.

Organisations had to demonstrate their commitment to this new era of data compliance. Delivering such a strategy should have involved parity of investment, in line with other areas of cybersecurity and data compliance. However, this demonstrates further how organisational focus appeared to deviate from investment in their actual staff to more technical and process compliance measures, rather than ensuring there was a structure that would have facilitated a more holistic approach to their compliance strategies.

The Direction and Estimated Spending on Cybersecurity

Despite the shift towards a more human-focused data compliance framework, it is apparent that the human factor remains not fully recognised and appreciated as part of the solution. This is supported by current organisational spending in the majority of industries.

In a report by the Info Security Group, this gap in staff awareness-building and training was evident. The report noted that in a study by Specops Software, on average, approximately 41% of UK employees, across all sectors had not received appropriate cybersecurity training, which "… is leaving businesses and individuals vulnerable to attack".[9]

This rise in human-related error provided a clear indication of the need to invest in staff as well as technology to safeguard data compliance. If the analysis was evidencing the fact that a considerable amount of security breaches, particularly within large organisations, was a result of human error, the obvious thing to do would be to identify what were the root causes of these errors in the first instance. This would have better informed the direction of spending and risk reduction.

The enormous investment in cybersecurity is outlined in a report by Statista[10], who estimated (pre Coronavirus pandemic) the global spend on cybersecurity to rise as follows:

2017: $137.63 billion
2018: $151.67 billion
2019: $167.14 billion
2020: $184.19 billion
2021: $202.97 billion
2022: $223.68 billion
2023: $248.26 billion

Despite the huge sums of investment this research predicted, the focus continued to centre around technical solutions. Recognising that almost 80% of most cyber-attacks could have been prevented with basic security controls, the UK Government introduced Cyber Essentials and Cyber Essentials Plus accreditation for UK businesses. First introduced in June 2014, both these schemes were intended to help organisations of any size, to protect themselves from the most common cyber-attacks. Cyber Essentials sets out "…five technical cybersecurity controls that all organisations can implement to achieve a baseline of cybersecurity."[11] These five controls are:

- Boundary firewalls and internet gateways
- Secure configuration
- Patch management
- Access control
- Malware protection

Cyber Essentials Plus is still based on the same principle of simplicity, however it requires a physical verification to be conducted.[11] Both levels of certification are intended to:

- Reassure customers that security organisations are working to protect their IT from cyber-attack.
- Attract new businesses with the promise the accredited organisations have cybersecurity measures in place.
- Those organisations have a clear picture of their cybersecurity level.[11]

Even though this business support is welcome, the focus remains on technical solutions, with little training or awareness-raising contained within the programme. This is despite numerous publications continuing to highlight that basic human error remains widespread, despite the upward trend in investment for cybersecurity. One of the main reasons for this upward trend in online security breaches was a result of the measures taken by organisations for safeguarding data being merely a process to show compliance for regulation rather than a commitment to change.

The need to adapt to these new regulations was evident, particularly with the more punitive measures that accompanied GDPR, particularly the rise in financial penalties organisations would face should they breach regulations. In addition, reputational damage and private lawsuits could also result from compliance breaches.

When considering these incidents, it is evident that despite the introduction of GDPR, and efforts to introduce solutions, including cybersecurity, there has been no evidence of a dramatic change in compliance. It may have resulted in more breaches being detected and more significant fines being imposed; however, the causes, particularity human error remain.

Case Study

The following case study is an example of how, by including the human factor in cybersecurity, organisations can enhance their data compliance.

A large organisation with over 39,000 staff were experiencing issues with scam emails, which had resulted in considerable financial losses and had the potential to impact on their data compliance. Efforts to improve staff awareness were not delivering the required response and outcomes. A 3rd party vendor was asked to review their prevention activity and make recommendations to address the matter.

Stage 1

The consultant met with IT security teams to better understand the issues they faced, including analysing the emails, which were the primary method of breach. It was established that the scams they faced were in the form of Business Email Compromise (BEC) which is generally used to trick people into conducting some sort of action, such as authorising false payment requests, which was the case in these incidents.

Stage 2

Recognising the main entry point for the breaches was via the staff, individual meetings and group workshops were conducted with staff members. This assisted with establishing their level of understanding and awareness of the threat, with several key issues being identified, which included:

- A lack of awareness of the types of risks and methods used by threat actors.
- No regular basic training on data privacy or cyber security threat awareness.
- Staff members were unable to recognise potential threats.
- In the absence of an incident response plan, staff were not aware of how to react once a potential threat was identified.

In addition to these fundamental issues, through further analysis, it was noted that an organisational culture existed which left it critically exposed to potential data compliance breaches. This included:

- Standard practices in some offices, whereby a junior member of staff had the login details for other team members in the office. This was to allow them to start work earlier than their colleagues and log onto their desktop computers. The intention was to give the individual a degree of responsibility by helping to save her colleagues time by logging onto their computers and having them ready to use when they arrived into work.
- Some basic training, circulation of bulletins and emails which staff could not understand due to technical language used in the content. This resulted in documents and emails being discarded without being read and more importantly understood.
- Lack of quality assurance processes in place, which resulted in bogus payments being made.
- A lack of organisational cybersecurity standardised processes and procedures.

Stage 3

Having identified the core issues, the consultant worked with key individuals including Senior Management, Operations Managers, IT Department and Human Resources to create an improved strategy and framework in relation to enhancing their cybersecurity program. This included:

- Improving organisational culture towards cybersecurity through regular training.
- Ensuring staff were central to organisational cybersecurity and consequentially data compliance.
- Improving the communication of threat and risk to staff by removing technical terminology from correspondence and making the content easier to understand.
- Regular meetings of key representatives from the IT departments, Human Resources, and management departments to allow a more holistic approach to cybersecurity.
- Improved organisational culture by including subject matters such as online bullying, hate crimes, sexual harassment, and general online conduct, both at and away from the workplace. This was to improve behaviour and create respect in the online workplace as would be expected in the physical environment. It also created an ethos of inclusion which reflected in their attitude towards cybersecurity and data compliance.

Stage 4

Having assisted with the restructuring, the consultant continued to link in with the organisation, sharing threat intelligence and also met with practitioners to measure the effectiveness of the new approach.

The feedback from the 3rd party consultant's activities have been a success and the culture in the organisation has evolved in such a way that cybersecurity is now an agenda item and subject to regular conversation, something that would certainly not have been the case 12 months ago and galvanised their data compliance.

The New Normal

On the 23rd March 2020, the UK went into lockdown because of the COVID-19 pandemic. Like many other countries worldwide, working from home became the 'new normal'. Whereas pre-lockdown IT solutions were the primary cybersecurity safeguard in relation to data compliance, these unprecedented circumstances catapulted the human factor in relation to online data compliance to the fore.

Staff were now responsible for implementing workplace security measures in their home while organisations scrambled to address this risk to prevent cybercriminals from exploiting this newfound opportunity.

On the 24th March 2020, just one day after the UK went into lockdown, John Clay, Director of Global Threat Communications at Trend Micro, delivered a webinar regarding current online threat and risk. Clay highlighted that the most significant challenges facing organisations during lockdown were 'spam and phishing emails which would be targeting either individuals or their employees.[12] In addition, when presenting the 'Human and technology mix – critical challenge', his view was that 'The Human is the weakest link...we cannot patch humans... social engineering is growing'.

The realisation of how crucial the human factor was in relation to cybersecurity and data compliance had arrived, and organisations were not ready, despite GDPR being in force for almost two years.

Working from home was now standard practice with organisations such as Twitter stating that they will allow staff to work from home 'forever' if they wish.[13] The switch to home working may have been easier to accommodate and more importantly, secure for some than it is for others. However, what cannot go unnoticed is that these adopted ways of working can potentially exacerbate the human vulnerability aspect of cybersecurity and its role in data privacy.

The initial responses to GDPR appear to have resulted in quick-win measures being introduced, with most of the focus falling on technological solutions when it comes to cybersecurity. The one fundamental component that had not been invested in, to the degree of technical and policy advances could now come back to haunt those organisations that had just 'ticked a box' in relation to their compliance measures. The human factor was now a central focal point.

Acknowledgement of staff and the importance of the role they have, with ensuring compliance should have been at the forefront of organisational cybersecurity strategy whilst implementing the changes. This is particularly important when factoring in the frequency of use, reach and accessibility of the online world. With online staff management of data being a core function within businesses, it is not inconceivable that more consideration should have been given to the impact of these changes and staff reaction to them, particularly in relation to contingency planning and establishing a business as usual.

Awareness of the potential increase and methodology of attack an employee may face should have been adopted earlier on. This failure to have staff as part of cybersecurity solutions created an unsteady foundation on which to build cybersecurity strategies that adhered to GDPR. It was crucial that the end-user, the human beings using the IT were part of the solutions and not just the technically adept members of staff.

Prior to the impact of the COVID-19 pandemic, highlighting the threats to organisations in 2020, Trend Micro predicted that "…methods such as extortion, obfuscation and phishing remained successful attacks"; however, new risks would emerge such as the migration to cloud computing which "…exacerbates human error".[14]

Organisations may have viewed the online space as a thing and did not recognise it as another place where they work, socialise and interact with other human beings, similar to the interactions they have in the physical world. They saw the online space as a safe space, offering a degree of risk that would be best dealt with through technical solutions. They were aware that some looked to exploit the vulnerable. As with the police in the physical world, it was not solely the responsibility of the IT Department to keep people and online communities safe. Everyone has a role to play; however, the lack of awareness training and abdication of responsibility to technical experts created a false sense of security in the online world. It also creates a culture of staff not taking ownership to deal or report an issue, viewing it as someone else's responsibility.

Organisations must learn from experiences throughout the COVID-19 pandemic. Policy, process, and procedure must change to reflect matters such as home working, threat awareness amongst staff and good cyber hygiene, both technical and physical, to safeguard data compliance. Organisations will also have to be mindful of the risks involved as and when they potentially begin to introduce some form of hybrid office and home working model as a new form of working practice.

Pre-COVID-19 research heightened matters such as interconnected devices and the reduction of security that was ordinarily provided within the corporate networks, as areas of risk. Home security and integrity would not reflect organisational practice and ultimately increase risks. The tick in the box mentality must be replaced by structure, training and most importantly inclusion of every member of staff if we are to influence attitudes to cybersecurity to ensure data compliance is more than a technical solution.

Conclusion

The ethos of the General Data Protection Regulations 2018 is commendable. The intention was to improve data compliance by moving away from a process-driven culture and giving power to the individuals in relation to their data, placing more accountability onto those utilising the data.

When analysing compliance, particularly in relation to cybersecurity and adherence to compliance requirements, there are flaws. Organisations appear to have resorted to what comes naturally to them. Creating processes and ticking boxes to demonstrate their compliance. What they have not done is to include the most crucial element in ensuring its success, the their staff.

Referencing human error as ones of the greatest threats to cybersecurity and data compliance is still a common default position. Staff are a crucial component to ensuring data compliance, yet training and awareness within organisations remains minimal, often at the expense of servicing compliance requirements instead of safeguarding data itself. While spending on technological solutions continues to grow, human investment has been stagnant.

One side effect of the enforced changes resulting from COVID-19 has been the focus on staff working from home and the security and compliance issues that this has created. These are matters that had greater staff recognition been taken into account whilst preparing for GDPR, may not be as so impacting as they now are. Arguably, had staff been actively involved as part of the solution, human error may not be as much of an issue.

Nevertheless, there are many unanswered questions as to what the future will hold for us in the 'new normal'. If working from home is part of this, then to ensure data compliance, there will be a need for a considerable amount of re-structuring, revisiting and re-thinking of cybersecurity strategies, which encompass the human element.

Future Work

The COVID-19 pandemic has resulted in a global pause in our daily routine. However, as organisations adapt and return to some form of business as usual, numerous considerations must be made in relation to data compliance. The most obvious of these is the regularity which staff will work from home. However, this could also be viewed as staff sleeping, socialising, and having family time in the office, so consideration must be given to the safeguarding of data and ensure that compliance requirements are maintained.

When it comes to cybersecurity, correlated matters, including home security, secure network access and a lack of clarity between work and social use of laptops and similar devices are all areas that will require consideration in policy, process and risk evaluation.

Most importantly, COIVD-19 has demonstrated the vulnerabilities caused by not having the human factor as part of organisational cybersecurity. Some elements of corporate culture has created the general default for cybersecurity to be the responsibility of the IT department. Now employees have been thrust into being an essential part of security, with organisations now relying on them to ensure they have suitable home-based security measures in place and awareness of the opportunities the pandemic has given to cybercriminals. Increases in phishing attacks, online scams and successful attacks caused by poor home security are just some examples of why the human factor is so critical in ensuring data compliance through good cybersecurity.

Moving forward, there must be clarity as to data protection compliance and reverting away from relying on process management. Organisations must demonstrate ongoing compliance measures, including staff awareness training, and testing. This will help ensure that measures organisations have allegedly taken are not merely geared towards appearing to do the right thing. Adopting and continuing to act upon the data compliance requirements, such as GDPR require ongoing education. This is particularly relevant when it comes to cybersecurity, as the type of threat and risks are being more focused on exploiting the human factor, which is an area of underinvestment, and an area of overexposure to data compliance breach.

Consideration must also be given to staff appreciating the difference between public and private spaces when working from home. It may require homes being considered as external vendors, requiring IT support and security to allow them to manage data appropriately and in line with regulations. Organisations must appreciate and take steps to address this obvious increased risk stemming from staff moving between the office and home working environment. Such exposure was identified in a report by Data Breach Today[15] that highlighted the evident risk to data privacy and protection while in situations such as the coronavirus lockdown. 'Devices changing between work and personal use depending on the time of day, means that corporate credentials could be phished from an attacker targeting a victim through a personal social media platform or third-party messaging app'.

Utilising the considerable amount of information that they have already gathered, cybercriminals will continue to look for new and innovative methods of illicitly accessing data, by exploiting the new ways of working and utilising new environments such as the employee's home as a key focal point for compliance breaches.

Organisations will have to create frameworks that raise the awareness of staff on how attackers will target them and the sophisticated methods they deploy to trick people. This includes making staff aware of and understanding the evolving use of advanced social engineering techniques, such as AI outlined in Stupp.[16] An established framework and the continuous education of people are essential in preventing the loss of data in such attacks. People will be, '…prime targets for this kind of fraud since they are often in calls, conferences, media appearances, and online videos'.[17]

The human factor was captured by Dr. James Cuffe, who is a cyber-anthropologist lecturing at University College Cork and Director of the Ethnographic and Human-Centred Research Group at The University

College Cork. When presenting at the Cyber Ireland South Chapter Meeting on the 16th June 2020, Dr. Cuffe stated that, 'The security industry can only go so far in treating security as a problem that can be solved by engineering alone. Until we couple technology with a better understanding of the human users, there is a limit on how much progress we can ultimately make'.[18]

To improve compliance in data privacy, the new normal must begin with, the Human Factor.

References

1. Great Britain (2018). Data Protection Act. London: Stationary Office.
2. Kotter, J.P. (1995). *Leading Change: Why Transformation Efforts Fail.* Harvard Business Review, p. 64.
3. Department for Digital, Culture Media and Sport (2020). *Cybersecurity Breaches Survey 2020.* London.
4. Info Security Group (2019). 90% of UK Data Breaches Due to Human Error in 2019. Info Security Group, 15 June 2020, <https://www.infosecurity-magazine.com/news/90-data-breaches-human-error/>
5. Information Commissioner's Office, ICO, 2020, 13 June 2020, <https://ico.org.uk/>
6. Dekker, S. (2002). *The Field Guide to Human Error Investigations.* Ashgate.
7. Department for Digital, Culture Media and Sport (2019). *Cybersecurity Breaches Survey 2019.* London.
8. Department for Digital, Culture, Media and Sport (2020). *UK Cybersecurity Sectoral Analysis 2020, Research report for the Department for Digital, Culture, Media and Sport.* London, IPSOS Mori.
9. Info Security Group (2020). 41% of UK Workers Haven't Received Adequate Cybersecurity Training. Info Security Group, 15 June 2020, <https://www.infosecurity-magazine.com/news/uk-workers-not-recieved/>
10. Statista (2020). *Global Spend on Cyber Security. Statista,* 18 June 2020, <https://www.statista.com/statistics/595182/worldwide-security-as-a-service-market-size/#:~:text=Cybersecurity%20market%20revenues%20worldwide%202017%2D2023&text=The%20global%20cybersecurity%20market%20size,network%2C%20and%20data%20from%20cyberattacks>.
11. National Cybersecurity Centre, 2020, Cyber Essentials, 14 June 2020, <https://www.ncsc.gov.uk/cyberessentials/overview>
12. Clay, J. (2020). Coronavirus is the Latest Lure for Attackers [Webinar], Available at https://event.on24.com/wcc/r/2224498/02E4A9E3C2DC8D42BE53454B4723852B?mode=login&email=scott.tees@decodecybersolutions.com (24 March, 2020).
13. BBC News, May 2020, Coronavirus: Twitter allows staff to work from home 'forever', BBC News, 11 June 2020, <https://www.bbc.co.uk/news/technology-52628119>

14. Trend Micro (2020). *Trend Micro Security Predictions for 2020*. Trend Micro Research.
15. Data Breach Today (2020). COVID-19 Drives Spike in Mobile Phishing Attacks: Report, Data Breach Today, 7 June 2020, <https://www.databreachtoday.com/covid-19-drives-spike-in-mobile-phishing-attacks-report-a-14381?rf=2020-06-05>
16. Stupp, C. (2019). Fraudsters Used AI to Mimic CEO's Voice in Unusual Cybercrime Case. *The Wall Street Journal*. 12 June 2020, <https://www.wsj.com/articles/fraudsters-use-ai-to-mimic-ceos-voice-in-unusual-cybercrime-case-11567157402>
17. Tung, L. (2019). Forget email: Scammers use CEO voice 'deepfakes' to con workers into wiring cash. April, 2020, <https://www.zdnet.com/article/forget-email-scammers-use-ceo-voice-deepfakes-to-con-workers-into-wiring-cash/>
18. Cuffe, J. (2020). Key factors in Human Behaviour for Cyber-Security [Webinar], Available at <https://www.cyberireland.ie/key-factors-in-human-behaviour-for-cyber-security/?utm_source=Master+Audience&utm_campaign=8768952db9-EMAIL_CAMPAIGN_2020_04_22_03_08_COPY_01&utm_medium=email&utm_term=0_38208d3cd5-8768952db9-396951202&mc_cid=8768952db9&mc_eid=f6f8a0834c> (16 June, 2020).

eDiscovery under the GDPR – Can Portable Solutions Provide Needed Innovation?

Claudia T. Morgan* and Shaun E. Werbelow[1]

Introduction

With great anticipation, the European Union's new General Data Protection Regulation ("GDPR") went into effect on 25 May 2018. During the two years since the GDPR was first agreed upon in April 2016, there has been no shortage of published material examining the GDPR's potential business impact and how affected parties can best prepare for the GDPR's ultimate implementation. These important topics have at times overshadowed similarly important legal issues that the GDPR will require practitioners to address. One such issue is the impact that the GDPR will have on U.S. eDiscovery.

Under the GDPR, any entity that collects or processes personal data of EU residents must comply with the regulation's provisions. This is the case regardless of whether the entity is located in the EU or elsewhere. On a basic level, electronic discovery (often referred to as "eDiscovery" for short) involves identifying, collecting, and producing electronically stored information in response to a lawsuit or investigation. Put differently, the primary activities involved in eDiscovery fall within the core purview of the GDPR. In today's global economy, the presence of relevant data subjects within the EU in a large U.S. civil litigation or investigation is no longer an exceptional circumstance.

---

[1] Claudia Morgan and Shaun Werbelow are eDiscovery Counsel and Associate respectively in the litigation department of Wachtell, Lipton, Rosen & Katz. The views expressed herein are our own and not those of our firm or clients.

---

*Corresponding author: CTMorgan@wlrk.com

Compliance with the GDPR is no small task. Among other requirements, Article 5(1)(c) regulates "data minimization" and mandates that only the personal data that is actually needed in order to achieve the purpose requiring GDPR processing is processed.* In addition to imposing stringent recordkeeping requirements on data processors and controllers, Article 17 of the GDPR also provides data subjects with the "right to be forgotten," one of the regulation's most anticipated provisions. This right of data subjects to obtain the erasure of their personal data without undue delay has the potential to frustrate a core tenet of U.S. litigation. There is little doubt that the GDPR is likely to pose substantial challenges for, and add to the already rising cost of, U.S. eDiscovery.

In this context, various eDiscovery service providers are increasingly marketing "portable" (or "mobile") eDiscovery solutions as tools to foster GDPR compliance;[1] we discuss some of those in this chapter. While the exact design of these solutions varies from provider to provider, portable or mobile eDiscovery solutions are generally defined by their ability to take eDiscovery efforts and capabilities to the source of the data.[2]

This chapter seeks to examine whether these portable eDiscovery solutions may be able to provide needed technological innovation in the eDiscovery space in response to the GDPR. Accordingly, Part I provides an overview of certain GDPR provisions that are likely to have a significant impact on U.S. eDiscovery. This Part also notes certain assumptions made and identifies a number of issues that fall beyond the scope of this Chapter. Part II discusses the increasing prevalence of portable eDiscovery solutions. Based on a number of live demonstrations attended by the authors of this chapter, this Part also examines how these portable solutions are being marketed as potential tools to address eDiscovery issues raised by the GDPR. Lastly, Part III examines how portable eDiscovery solutions can potentially address eDiscovery issues raised by the GDPR. Importantly, however, this Part also explains how certain eDiscovery challenges under the GDPR are likely to remain outstanding given the limitations of current portable solutions.

Background

As has been well documented, the GDPR creates a comprehensive regulatory framework for how personal data of data subjects can be used and transferred.[3] To ensure the protection and privacy of their personal data, the GDPR empowers data subjects with certain rights. These rights, specified in Articles 12 to 23, include: the right of access by the data subject (Article 15); the right to rectification (Article 16); the right to erasure ('right to be forgotten') (Article 17); the right to restriction of processing

---

* To avoid potential confusion, we distinguish between GDPR processing and eDiscovery processing, which is narrower in scope (Article 4-2).

(Article 18); the right to data portability (Article 20); and the right to object (Article 21). Similarly, Articles 12, 13, and 14 mandate that data subjects are informed in a clear, concise, and transparent manner regarding the collection and GDPR processing of their personal data. A number of these important Articles are discussed in further detail below.

"Personal data" is defined broadly under the GDPR as "any information relating to an identified or identifiable natural person ('data subject'); an identifiable natural person is one who can be identified, directly or indirectly, in particular by reference to an identifier such as a name, an identification number, location data, an online identifier or to one or more factors specific to the physical, physiological, genetic, mental, economic, cultural or social identity of that natural person."[4] Given this expansive definition, a wide array of personal data will potentially be required and used in U.S. eDiscovery, ranging from email addresses and telephone numbers to communications (such as emails and other communications) sent between employees of an entity engaged in U.S. discovery. An analysis of what constitutes personal data will often be case specific, as information such as an IP address, hair color, or an employee's professed political opinions may serve to identify a data subject when viewed alongside other data.

Under the GDPR's predecessor data protection regime, the Data Protection Directive (the "Directive"),[5] two schemes were developed to provide a framework to govern the transfer of covered data to third party states. The first of those was the Safe Harbour Principles, though those were found by the European Court of Justice ("ECJ") in 2015 to be invalid.[6] In response to the ECJ ruling, the European Commission adopted the EU-US Privacy Shield framework on 12 July 2016[7] that went into effect on 1 August 2016.* Fundamental to understanding the need for these frameworks is the fact that the United States is not viewed as having adequate data protection by the European Union. It is only within the framework of the Privacy Shield that the US is recognized as providing adequate protection.[8] The Privacy Shield framework provided for "strong data protection obligations on companies receiving personal data from the EU; safeguards on US government access to data; effective protection and redress for individuals; [and] an annual joint review by the EU and US to monitor the correct application of the arrangement."[9]

With this general background, this Part highlights a small number of GDPR provisions that are likely to have an especially pronounced effect on U.S. eDiscovery. Importantly, this chapter assumes a general familiarity with the GDPR. Additionally, this chapter assumes that discovery is being

---

* Note that on 16 July 2020 the Court of Justice of the European Union declared the Privacy Shield framework invalid. Transfers of data from the EU to the U.S. now need to ensure alternate means of compliance with the GDPR

undertaken for production in the United States; the data at issue is limited to employees, not customers or other data subjects; and transfer of the data under Articles 44 through 49 has been assessed.

A. Article 5

Article 5 of the GDPR contains principles relating to the GDPR processing of personal data and is likely to impact most if not all aspects of U.S. eDiscovery.[10] On a fundamental level, Article 5(1)(c) regulates "data minimization" and states that personal data shall be "adequate, relevant and limited to what is necessary in relation to the purposes for which they are processed." In short, data minimization requires that only the personal data that is actually needed in order to achieve the purpose requiring GDPR processing is processed. This principle existed in the Data Protection Directive, but has been strengthened in the GDPR. Specifically, the prior obligation to ensure that processed personal data is not excessive has been replaced by a more restrictive obligation to ensure that personal data is "limited to what is necessary." Practitioners engaging in U.S. discovery often seek to take a "no stone left unturned" approach to collecting and reviewing information and documents. Such an approach is likely to conflict with the data minimization principle contained in Article 5(1)(c), which requires a more tailored eDiscovery strategy.

Article 5(1)(c) and the principle of data minimization can also be contrasted with Federal Rule of Civil Procedure 26(b)(1), which formally governs the scope and limits of civil discovery in United States federal courts. That provision provides that "parties may obtain discovery regarding any nonprivileged matter that is relevant to any party's claim or defense and proportional to the needs of the case, considering the importance of the issues at stake in the action, the amount in controversy, the parties' relative access to relevant information, the parties' resources, the importance of the discovery in resolving the issues, and whether the burden or expense of the proposed discovery outweighs its likely benefit." Rule 26(b)(1) was amended in 2015 (as reflected above) to explicitly constrain discovery to information and materials that are both "relevant" and "proportional to the needs of the case." Like Article 5(1)(c), this change added more restrictive language than had previously been used, which was intended to place limits on the scope of information available.[11] Nevertheless, the text of Rule 26(b)(1) remains substantially more permissive than the text of GDPR Article 5(1)(c).

In practice, Article 5(1)(c) will in all likelihood require that data processors[12] (and controllers[13]) devote increased resources towards ensuring that all personal data being processed is necessary in relation to the relevant purposes of the GDPR processing. With regards to U.S. eDiscovery, resulting data minimization efforts may decrease the amount of information available to parties involved in U.S. litigation. This may be both a benefit and a potential cost—less available data could mean that discovery efforts can be more focused and conducted more efficiently, and therefore more cost effectively. However, less data may also mean that previously available information may no longer exist to be collected, processed, and used in litigation or regulatory responses. When undertaking discovery planning this should be kept front of the mind as it may affect identification and search parameters.

In addition to data minimization, Article 5(1)(f) – 'integrity and confidentiality' – states that personal data shall be "processed in a manner that ensures appropriate security of the data, including protection against unauthorised or unlawful processing and against accidental loss, destruction or damage, using appropriate technical or organisational measures." Although this requirement remains generally unchanged from the previous Directive, it reinforces the principle that data security is a fundamental concern for all data controllers and processors. In practice, this Article requires that any tool used for eDiscovery purposes meet certain data security standards.[14] A number of EU member state supervisory authorities, including the U.K. ICO and France's CNIL, have released guidance on this topic.[15] It also has implications for the production of data and attendant protective or confidentiality orders in litigation. Portable eDiscovery tools, which by their nature handle data differently as compared to traditional solutions, might also trigger separate considerations.

Furthermore, Article 5(2) – 'accountability' – states that "the controller shall be responsible for, and be able to demonstrate compliance with, paragraph 1 ('accountability')" of the Article, which lays out the principles relating to the [GDPR] processing of personal data. eDiscovery providers, by the very nature of the work they do (collecting, receiving, and performing technical eDiscovery processing of the data that they receive) will often be classified as "processors" under the GDPR, as discussed throughout this chapter. As such, their actions must be taken into account when measuring the controller's compliance with GDPR Article 5.

This section of Article 5 could impact eDiscovery insofar as the controller may be required to demonstrate how its eDiscovery efforts comply with data protection principles. It could be relevant if any particular eDiscovery solution directly assists this process, for example, by documenting the safeguards used while data is being processed.

B. Article 17

One of the most highly anticipated (and discussed) provisions of the GDPR is Article 17 – Right to erasure ('right to be forgotten'). This Article states that "the data subject shall have the right to obtain the erasure of personal data concerning him or her from the controller without undue delay and the controller shall have the obligation to erase personal data without undue delay where one of the following grounds applies . . . ." In short, Article 17 gives affected individuals the right to erasure of their data. This right has far reaching implications.

In the discovery context, Article 17 raises a potential conflict between U.S. requirements regarding the preservation of potentially relevant evidence and the E.U. data subject's right to have data deleted. This will happen when a data subject invokes its right to erasure (right to be forgotten) under Article 17 and the personal data at issue is also subject to the legal obligation in the United States of being preserved. Under U.S. law once litigation is anticipated the person or entity that expects litigation must preserve information that is related to the expected litigation; this is referred to as a preservation obligation. Entities that do not preserve such data are subject to court sanctions for this spoliation (lack of preservation), and such sanctions can go as far as to apply an adverse ruling against such entities.[16] When faced with this situation, the controller will have to decide between two legal requirements that will be in direct conflict – the invocation of the GDPR right to be forgotten by a data subject and the U.S. legal requirement to preserve data. At that point the controller will need to assess its options under Article 17(3) and likely will invoke Article 17(3) (e) "for the establishment, exercise or defence of legal claims." While we are not aware of a case where this conflict has come to fruition, it is the authors' belief that it is only a matter of time until such a case arises. It remains to be seen what a Data Protection Authority would find in such an instance.

C. Article 20

Article 20 of the GDPR – Right to data portability – gives an individual the right to receive the personal data that they have provided to a controller in a "structured, commonly used and machine-readable format." This Article also gives such an individual the right to request that a controller transmit this data directly to another controller. These rights apply when the lawful basis for processing the information is based on consent or the performance of a contract and the processing is being carried out by automated means.

In the context of U.S. discovery, Article 20 is not likely to impose a direct obligation on an eDiscovery vendor that is acting strictly as a data processor. Nonetheless, the processing undertaken by an eDiscovery vendor will in all likelihood subject the data controller to the obligations of Article 20. Processing by an eDiscovery vendor will often involve processing of information that has been collected based on consent or the performance of a contract (for example, employee data) as well as processing by automated means (for example, automated culling and searching).

Importantly, the right to data portability under Article 20 only applies to personal data; it does not apply to genuinely anonymous data. Accordingly, anonymous data that is generated in the course of eDiscovery processing will not need to be provided under Article 20. A more difficult issue, however, involves pseudonymous data that can be clearly linked back to an individual. Such data would fall within the scope of Article 20. This provides additional incentive for an eDiscovery vendor to ensure that any pseudonymization done in the eDiscovery process cannot be linked to any individual data subject. The process of pseudonymization is discussed again at the end of this chapter, as a number of the portable eDiscovery solutions that we viewed have capabilities that touch on this issue.

D. Article 25

An overarching change introduced by the GDPR is the concept of "Data protection by design and by default" contained in Article 25.

Article 25(1) governs "data protection by design" (also often referred to as "privacy by design") and states: "Taking into account the state of the art, the cost of implementation and the nature, scope, context and purposes of processing as well as the risks of varying likelihood and severity for rights and freedoms of natural persons posed by the processing, the controller shall, both at the time of the determination of the means for processing and at the time of the processing itself, implement appropriate technical and organisational measures, such as pseudonymisation, which are designed to implement data-protection principles, such as data minimization, in an effective manner and to integrate the necessary safeguards into the processing in order to meet the requirements of this Regulation and protect the rights of data subjects."

Article 25(2) governs "data protection by default" (also often referred to as "privacy by default") and states: "The controller shall implement appropriate technical and organisational measures for ensuring that, by default, only personal data which is necessary for each specific purpose of the processing is processed. That obligation applies to the amount of personal data collected, the extent of its processing, its period of storage and its accessibility. In particular, such measures shall ensure that by default personal data is not made accessible without the individual's intervention to an indefinite number of natural persons."

In essence, Article 25 requires that organizations consider privacy even before processing begins to take place and continually through the completion of any such processing; any processing should be done in a manner that maximizes privacy. While these concepts are not new, Article 25 cements them as a legal requirement under the GDPR.

The requirement of "privacy by design and by default" should play an important role in the selection of an eDiscovery vendor and the formation of an eDiscovery plan, including the selection of an eDiscovery tool and the ways in which it will be deployed. Steps such as pseudonymisation and data minimisation – which are themselves suggested in Article 25 – should serve as critical components of any eDiscovery tool and strategy chosen. Before the need for U.S. discovery arises, a controller should consider the different portable eDiscovery tools that may be available and whether these tools can be used to maximize privacy and provide innovation not available by traditional eDiscovery tools. This is discussed in the Portable (mobile) eDiscovery Solutions section below.

E. Article 30

Article 30(2) – Records of processing activities, states that "each processor and, where applicable, the processor's representative shall maintain a record of all categories of processing activities carried out on behalf of a controller . . . ."[17]

This is a new obligation not contained in the Directive; depending on the extent of current data processing documentation, this obligation may require significant investment by processors in recordkeeping functions. As relating to eDiscovery, this Article may impose obligations on vendors to document their activities in a manner that was not previously required. While existing eDiscovery best practices call for documentation of each major step taken or decision made in an eDiscovery process (*e.g.*, documentation of the precise dates that email data was collected for each custodian as well as the specific criteria or search terms used to search such email data), one might say that this practice is more honored in the breach than in the observance. Particularly for activities that do not correspond to decision points in an eDiscovery process, oftentimes temptation exists to set aside the task of record keeping or creation of fullsome documentation until later.

Article 30(2) makes paramount proper record keeping. Article 30's requirement of maintaining a record of all GDPR processing activities, which as noted, includes the viewing of a data subject's data, increases record keeping requirements beyond those traditionally undertaken in U.S. eDiscovery efforts. This is an increased challenge both for the people and tools used in eDiscovery; however, the silver lining of such obligations is that audit trails will be simpler to pull together and defending against assertions of spoliation may also be easier with the increased record keeping.

F. Article 32

As noted above, the integrity and confidentiality principle in Article 5(1) (f) will in practice require data processors to adopt adequate security standards governing their processing activities. Similarly, Article 32, which governs "Security of processing," mandates that taking into account the state of the art, the costs of implementation and the nature, scope, context and purposes of processing as well as the risk of varying likelihood and severity of the rights and freedoms of natural persons, the controller and the processor shall implement appropriate technical and organisational measures to ensure a level of security appropriate to the risk . . . ."

The obligations imposed by Article 32 are shared by both data controllers and processors. Article 32 suggests four areas where controllers and processors should focus: (1) "the pseudonymisation and encryption of personal data"; (2) "the ability to ensure the ongoing confidentiality, integrity, availability and resilience of processing systems and services"; (3) "the ability to restore the availability and access to personal data in a timely manner in the event of a physical or technical incident"; and (4) "process for regularly testing, assessing and evaluating the effectiveness of technical and organisational measures for ensuring the security of the processing."

Under the GDPR, a large organization is likely to have security measures in place that govern varying uses of personal data. Article 32 also offers guidance on how organizations can demonstrate that they are compliant with its requirements. Organizations can demonstrate compliance by signing up for and adhering to an industry-wide data security code of conduct, or through gaining an approved certification of data security compliance. Nonetheless, eDiscovery vendors – acting as data processors – may be required to address the case-by-case demands of U.S. discovery. As we will discuss in Part III, portable eDiscovery solutions may offer certain benefits to help address these concerns.

G. Article 35

Article 35 addresses data protection impact assessment, and states: "(1) Where a type of processing is using new technologies in particular, and considering how its nature, scope, context and purpose, is likely to result in a high risk to the rights and freedoms of natural persons, the controller shall, carry out an assessment of the impact of the envisaged processing operations on the protection of personal data. A single assessment may address a set of similar processing operations that present similar high risks."

It is not clear that all eDiscovery falls within the type of processing that requires a data protection impact assessment ("DPIA"), but it appears that certain types of eDiscovery could require a DPIA. A DPIA is required when the processing involves "using new technologies." A question to be considered is whether portable eDiscovery solutions would be considered such a technology?[18]

According to Recital 75 of the GDPR, "the risk to the rights and freedoms of natural persons, of varying likelihood and severity, may result from personal data processing which could lead to physical, material or non-material damage, in particular: . . . where personal data is processed which reveals racial or ethnic origin, political opinions, religion or philosophical beliefs, trade union membership . . . or where processing involves a large amount of personal data and affects a large number of data subjects." Additionally, according to Recital 116, "when personal data moves across borders outside the Union it may put at increased risk the ability of natural persons to exercise data protection rights in particular to protect themselves from the unlawful use or disclosure of that information."

Processing through eDiscovery could thus require a DPIA when it reveals certain details listed above; involves a large amount of personal data; affects a large number of data subjects; or is conducted cross-borders.

Article 35 states that a DPIA shall contain at least: "(a) a systematic description of the envisaged processing operations and the purposes of the processing, including, where applicable, the legitimate interest pursued by the controller; (b) an assessment of the necessity and proportionality of the processing operations in relation to the purposes; (c) an assessment of the risks to the rights and freedoms of data subjects referred to in paragraph 1; and (d) the measures envisaged to address the risks, including safeguards, security measures and mechanisms to ensure the protection of personal data and to demonstrate compliance with this Regulation taking into account the rights and legitimate interests of data subjects and other persons concerned."

H. Themes

Distilling these selected Articles down, the overarching themes of the provisions that we have highlighted are:

- the importance of knowing what data exists before such data needs to be processed,
- minimizing the amount of data and impact on the data that must be processed,
- ensuring the security and protection of data that falls within eDiscovery processes,
- taking steps to protect privacy (*e.g.*, pseudonymization) particularly when data is processed or transferred, and
- keeping records of what data exists, and what processing has been done to such data.

The question facing practitioners undertaking U.S. based eDiscovery efforts then becomes what solutions are available to address these challenges?

Portable (mobile) eDiscovery Solutions

A. Marketing of eDiscovery Solutions

In this new regulatory framework and in response to the GDPR's emphasis on data protection, various eDiscovery service providers are increasingly marketing "portable" (or "mobile") eDiscovery solutions as tools to foster GDPR compliance. So what are portable eDiscovery solutions and how are they being marketed to practitioners who may need them? When one types "portable eDiscovery solutions" into a search engine the results include such statements as "fast and affordable," "best eDiscovery software," "eDiscovery simplified," and "all the eDiscovery technology you need." The results become even less concrete when "eDiscovery and the GDPR" is searched.

Portable eDiscovery solutions are eDiscovery tools, generally combining hardware and software, that are self-contained eDiscovery ecosystems, allowing for the identification, collection, and processing of data that is the subject of the inquiry. A number of eDiscovery vendors offer such solutions, as noted in the Introduction, and they have been on offer going back at least five years. As part of our research for this chapter the authors viewed demonstrations of three such tools[19] and will discuss some of the characteristics and functionality of those tools below.

These solutions were originally marketed in response to data security concerns, including both company specific concerns and a shift in the marketplace towards the view that moving data from one country to another can be problematic both practically and legally under then-existing regulations. With the advent of GDPR and similar data privacy regimes, the need and market for portable eDiscovery solutions has grown. Under the Data Protection Directive, the primary concern with European data from a U.S. eDiscovery perspective was focused on transfer of data to the United States. Under the GDPR, U.S. eDiscovery practitioners and entities subject to the regulation are now focused on data protection measures much earlier in the eDiscovery lifecycle, particularly in light of the GDPR definition of processing, and are looking for portable eDiscovery solutions to help minimize the amount of data collected in eDiscovery, well before such data may be needed to be transferred to the United States for litigation purposes.

eDiscovery vendors and articles widely available on the web tout the benefits of using eDiscovery software and tools to facilitate GDPR compliance, from reducing the need for cross-border data transfers, to identifying Personally Identifiable Information (PII), to anonymizing data, to providing security and encryption that is compliant with GDPR provisions.

B.   Features of Portable eDiscovery Solutions and GDPR Compliance

1. Bringing eDiscovery to the Data

When most practitioners think of a portable eDiscovery solution, they envision a solution that is capable of bringing traditional eDiscovery collection and processing tools to the source of data that needs to be assessed for collection, review, and potential production. This can be done in essentially in one of the two ways: (1) on-premises (eDiscovery in a box), or (2) web based/software as a service (SaaS). On-premises solutions are eDiscovery solutions that physically bring the hardware and software to the location of the data. SaaS solutions are generally solutions that are web based and accessed from the data location either through a portable device or secure portal.

The most often thought of on-premises eDiscovery solution is a mobile discovery unit. In essence, this type of eDiscovery solution is simply a computer that can be easily transported from site-to-site that contains all required eDiscovery software to identify, collect, process, review, and produce the data at issue. Portable eDiscovery solutions also come in a related method consisting of a portable device that connects the data into a web or cloud based, but geographically limited, environment to perform eDiscovery processing.

These can be custom built, portable data centers that operate behind the company's firewall without being connected to the company's network. The eDiscovery software offered by different vendors is sometimes, but not always, proprietary, and can also be customized to include additional modules such as machine translation, transcription, and automated redaction.

Both KLDiscovery's Nebula and EDT's eponymous solution bring dedicated hardware to the location of the data. Nebula is a mobile discovery unit, offering the ability to either contain the entirety of the eDiscovery process on the unit, or connecting the data to an Azure cloud based environment, which ensures that the data undergoing assessment and eDiscovery processing remains in the country in which it is located. EDT's software can be run on a dedicated laptop or tablet, the choice between the two being based on the expected volume of data to be assessed in the matter. EDT also offers its software as a service on client specific cloud instances through its partner network.

There are both benefits and disadvantages to self-contained units and web-based solutions. Self-contained portable eDiscovery solutions have the benefit of reducing the amount of data that is taken from a location or network, and disadvantages of being limited in size of data handled, and not having the scalability of processing available with web based or 'traditional' eDiscovery solutions and processes. Web based solutions have the advantage of scalability of processing capacity, and the attendant speed and processing power that comes with them, but they also have the disadvantage of removing data from its location and creating additional copies potentially subject to all the security and other obligations of eDiscovery and the GDPR.

2. Assessing Data in Place

Oftentimes, an additional feature that portable eDiscovery solutions offer is the ability to cull data after it is collected and processed, before reviewing of documents has begun. Culling is the process in eDiscovery whereby broad, usually objective criteria (*e.g.*, date ranges or the presence of certain terms) are used to identify collected documents that are highly unlikely to be relevant; those documents are then pulled out of the set that is subject to review for potential responsiveness and production.[20] Culling can be done either locally or in cloud-based workflows.

KLDiscovery's Nebula allows for such culling after eDiscovery processing and before review; similarly, EDT's tool has built in early case assessment (ECA) functionality that allows culling to take place on data before review. Related to this, ZyLAB's ONE eDiscovery software markets its ability to help identify the names of data subjects in the event that a data subject has exercised their "right to be forgotten" as discussed above.[21]

3. Minimizing Identifiable Data before Transfer

Certain tools assessed in researching this chapter can search for and automatically identify or tag certain personally identifiable information (using standard or custom rules and text mining technology), such as social security numbers. This ability is designed (and sometimes marketed)[22] to support GDPR and other data protection and privacy regulations, with the automated nature of the offering being promoted as reducing the GDPR compliance burden.

For example, ZyLAB's ONE eDiscovery software can automatically anonymize or pseudonymize personal data (such as names, places, etc.) before such information is transferred to any third-party, including attorneys or regulatory agencies. By working together with knowledgeable individuals within an organization (*i.e.*, the controller), ZyLab can create rules to identify such personal data before it is shared externally. Both ZyLAB's ONE eDiscovery software as well as KLDiscovery's Nebula offer an auto-redaction feature, which performs user defined redactions automatically.

Where these tools are able to automatically anonymize or pseudonymize personal data the cost savings are potentially enormous.

An additional feature of such automated tools is the ability to track back in an auditable (and presumably reversible) manner from the anonymized data to the source information if and as needed.

4. Additional Features and Benefits

A stated benefit of on-premises collection is that this workflow allows for more input from employee data subjects,[23] thus leading to more information and easier consent, in particular because less data ends up being transferred. Furthermore, at least one of the tools viewed in our research is developing the ability to perform social graphing and communications analysis on anonymized documents and data, in much the same way that a number of eDiscovery tools do on non-anonymized data.

Multiple vendors also appear to be increasing their focus on using Artificial Intelligence ("AI") or machine learning in conjunction with portable eDiscovery solutions, in the hope of further limiting the need for human interactions with data that is subject to GDPR protections. While AI is outside the scope of this chapter there is a lively debate[24] regarding the question of whether machine assessment of personal data is a lesser violation of the GDPR than is human processing.

Assessing Portable Discovery Solutions with Respect to GDPR Compliance

In this section, we provide our assessment of the portable eDiscovery solutions that we have viewed and examine the extent to which they address or facilitate GDPR compliance. This discussion is organized by certain eDiscovery phases (identification, collection, processing, review, and production). Figure 13.1 is an image of the electronic discovery reference model[25] and contains a visual illustration of the eDiscovery workflow and stages.

Portable eDiscovery solutions and their potential to facilitate GDPR compliance are of particular interest for the same reasons that information governance is a recurring topic of discussion among eDiscovery practitioners and the Federal Rules of Civil Procedure were amended in 2015 – namely, U.S. discovery is expensive and time consuming; anything that offers the prospect of making discovery more efficient, more in proportion to a given matter and its needs, and is less burdensome is attractive to practitioners and presents substantial market opportunities. Using portable eDiscovery solutions facilitates a shift towards localization of eDiscovery without requiring significant company or vendor investments in country specific infrastructure.

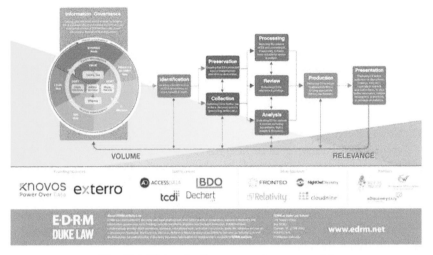

Fig. 13.1. Elctronic discovery reference model

A. Identification of data: This phase involves the identification of potentially relevant data, custodians, and sources of information in a given matter. This phase often begins with speaking to employees who are knowledgeable regarding the subject matter of inquiry.

None of the solutions viewed by the authors facilitated the identification of what data or data sources need to be part of the identification for a given matter; this is still dependent on either company or custodial interviews or searching of data sources. It is our understanding that privacy management tools exist in the information governance sphere that have the potential to assist this phase of eDiscovery; however, presently, these do not appear to be integrated into eDiscovery software.

B. Collection: In this phase, once likely relevant data sources have been identified, those sources are collected for further review and potential production.

None of the tools viewed by the authors in researching this chapter offer functionality, as of the time of the viewing, that limits the collection of data for eDiscovery purposes. Functionality that allows for assessment instead of broad collection limits GDPR processing, and therefore will assist in GDPR compliance by advancing Article 5 data minimization principles.

C. eDiscovery Processing: During this phase, collected data is ingested into eDiscovery software, whereby it is prepared for culling and loading to a review software platform. Part of eDiscovery processing includes removing certain file types (*e.g.*, de-NISTing[26]), de-duplication, and attempting to remove encryption from password protected files.

In a standard eDiscovery workflow, data is collected, removed from company systems, and then goes through processing, review, and production. Under the Directive, oftentimes these portions of the workflow would be undertaken in the European Union country where the data was located or elsewhere in the EU in order to minimize the amount of data subject to transfer outside of the EU. By using portable eDiscovery solutions, the amount of data removed from company systems is further minimized.

D. Review: This phase is where documents that have been identified (whether by agreement or not) for review are reviewed.

None of the tools viewed by the authors offered improvements to existing review options. Some offer the ability to create a mini review center on site if that is required; however it still requires human assessment of the documents and data and an investment in technology and people to perform the review for the purpose of identifying those which are subject to production.

E. Production: Lastly, in this phase documents that are determined to be responsive to the production requests in a matter and that are not protected from disclosure by attorney client privilege or similar protections are then produced.

While some of the tools viewed by the authors do provide for production of documents, with personal data in anonymized form or otherwise, they do not (and we did not in this chapter) address the topic of appropriateness and the various derogations allowing for such a transfer.

Conclusion

While portable eDiscovery solutions are being marketed as comprehensive solutions to new challenges faced in eDiscovery brought about by the GDPR, they are not yet comprehensive solutions. These tools have the potential to immensely help minimize the data subject to eDiscovery efforts, from collection through transfer to the United States – but they do not address the full set of challenges posed in eDiscovery efforts by the GDPR's provisions and requirements. The breadth of the GDPR's reach, and the definition of processing under the GDPR, pose significant challenges while conducting eDiscovery. The very act of identifying data that may be subject to U.S. litigation and discovery obligations falls under the GDPR's processing definition.

Until we have solutions that allow for a seamless integration of information governance or knowledge management efforts into eDiscovery workflows there will always be a risk that eDiscovery efforts will conflict with GDPR obligations. It is the authors' belief that while the currently available portable eDiscovery solutions certainly provide tools to minimize data subject to transfer to the United States for eDiscovery purposes, in order to maximize one's ability to remain in compliance with the GDPR such tools, and eDiscovery in general, must be used in conjunction with information governance programs, whereby entities subject to the GDPR understand the data they have and its location. By minimizing the volume and type of personal data that is subjected to GDPR processing, and subsequently to eDiscovery efforts, GDPR compliance is maximized, all the while minimizing the volume, time, and accompanying costs of undertaking U.S. eDiscovery efforts. We recommend that entities that are subject to the GDPR incorporate information governance and assessment of eDiscovery options and tools available to them into their GDPR compliance efforts.

References

1. *See, e.g.,* KLDiscovery (https://www.kldiscovery.com/solutions/nebula-private-cloud/); Zylab (https://zylab.com/applications/ediscovery-and-gdpr/); CDS (https://cdslegal.com/insights/product-spotlight-navigating-cross-border-ediscovery-with-cds-digital-customs/); EDT (https://www.discoveredt.com/blog/gdpr-meets-ediscovery-privacy).
2. The terms "portable" and "mobile" are often used interchangeably in the marketplace to refer to these solutions; they are likewise used interchangeably in this chapter.
3. The GDPR applies to EU citizens and residents, as well as to persons whose data is processed by an entity that is established within the EU.
4. Article 4(1).
5. Directive 95/46/EC on the protection of individuals with regard to the processing of personal data and on the free movement of such data ("Directive"). The Directive was adopted in 1995 and was in effect in all EU member states by the deadline of 31 December 1998. The Directive can be found at: https://eur-lex.europa.eu/legal-content/EN/TXT/?uri=CELEX:31995L0046.
6. The ruling was in the context of Maximillian Schrems' assertion that Facebook Ireland's transfer of Irish users' data to Facebook's US servers was in violation of the Directive. The Irish Data Protection Commissioner refused to investigate Mr. Schrems' claim and he subsequently filed suit. The decision can be found at: http://curia.europa.eu/juris/document/document.jsf?text=&docid=169195&pageIndex=0&doclang=EN&mode=req&dir=&occ=first&part=1&cid=162892.
7. The primary European Commission page regarding the Privacy Shield can be found at: https://ec.europa.eu/info/law/law-topic/data-protection/data-transfers-outside-eu/eu-us-privacy-shield_en. The EU fact sheet on the Privacy Shield can be found at: http://collections.internetmemory.org/haeu/20171122154227/http:/ec.europa.eu/justice/data-protection/files/factsheets/factsheet_eu-us_privacy_shield_en.pdf.

8. See the European Commission's listing of countries that have been recognized as having adequate protection at: https://ec.europa.eu/info/law/law-topic/data-protection/data-transfers-outside-eu/adequacy-protection-personal-data-non-eu-countries_en.

9. https://ec.europa.eu/info/law/law-topic/data-protection/data-transfers-outside-eu/eu-us-privacy-shield_en

10. Recall that GDPR processing (as defined in Article 4(2)) includes consultation and use of personal data. For U.S. practitioners in particular, it bears keeping in mind that the act of looking at personal data is processing under the GDPR.

11. The Civil Rules Advisory Committee noted that the change in language regarding proportionality "does not change the existing responsibilities of the court and the parties to consider proportionality." Fed. R. Civ. P. 26 advisory committee's note to 2015 amendment. Some practitioners and courts also note that proportionality has always been a requirement inherent in Federal Rule of Civil Procedure 26. *See* Michael J. Miles, *Proportionality under Amended Rule 26(b)(1): A New Mindset* (May 18, 2016), http://apps.americanbar.org/litigation/committees/pretrial/articles/spring2016-0516-proportionality-amended-rule-26b1-new-mindset.html. Nonetheless, the plain text of Rule 26(b)(1) as amended in 2015 now makes this requirement explicit.

12. A processor is defined as "a natural or legal person, public authority, agency or other body which processes personal data on behalf of the controller." Article 4(8).

13. A controller is defined as "the natural or legal person, public authority, agency or other body which, alone or jointly with others, determines the purposes and means of the processing of personal data" Article 4(7).

14. Similarly, Article 32, which governs "Security of processing," mandates that "[t]aking into account the state of the art, the costs of implementation and the nature, scope, context and purposes of processing as well as the risk of varying likelihood and severity for the rights and freedoms of natural persons, the controller and the processor shall implement appropriate technical and organisational measures to ensure a level of security appropriate to the risk . . . ." Furthermore, Article 32 suggests four areas where data controllers should focus: (1) "the pseudonymisation and encryption of personal data"; (2) "the ability to ensure the ongoing confidentiality, integrity, availability and resilience of processing systems and services"; (3) "the ability to restore the availability and access to personal data in a timely manner in the event of a physical or technical incident"; and (4) "process for regularly testing, assessing and evaluating the effectiveness of technical and organisational measures for ensuring the security of the processing."

15. *See* https://ico.org.uk/for-organisations/guide-to-the-general-data-protection-regulation-gdpr/security/; https://www.cnil.fr/en/new-guide-regarding-security-personal-data.

16. *InternMatch, Inc. v. Nxtbigthing,* (N.D. Cal. Feb 2016) (replacement of a computer without backing it up or imaging the contents of the replaced computer while a litigation hold was in place led to the loss of data, which in turn led the court to sanction the party with an adverse inference); *Roadrunner Transportation Services v. Tarwater* (9th Cir. 2016) (default judgment entered against defendant as a sanction resulting from his deletion of data from his laptops).

17. A similar obligation also applies to controllers. *See* Article 30(1).
18. *See* Article 29 Data Protection Working Party, Guidelines on Data Protection Impact Assessment (DPIA) and determining whether processing is "likely to result in a high risk" for the purposes of Regulation 2016/679, *available at*http://ec.europa.eu/newsroom/article29/item-detail.cfm?item_id=611236
19. The authors viewed demonstrations of portable eDiscovery solutions from EDT, KLDiscovery, and ZyLAB.
20. For example, all emails containing the word "news" or "alert" in the subject line may be identified and removed from the review set.
21. *See* https://zylab.com/applications/ediscovery-and-gdpr/.
22. *See* https://zylab.com/applications/ediscovery-and-gdpr/.
23. "An EDT Portable deployment enables you to 'take the tools to the data', so collection, analysis, review and production can all occur on-site, which means simplifies the consent requirements." https://www.discoveredt.com/blog/gdpr-meets-ediscovery-privacy
24. *See e.g.* Fortune "AI Has a Big Privacy Problem and Europe's New Data Protection Law Is About to Expose It", http://fortune.com/2018/05/25/ai-machine-learning-privacy-gdpr/, arguing that AI by definition goes against the GDPR's data minimization requirements; Techcrunch "GDPR panic may spur data and AI innovation", https://techcrunch.com/2018/06/07/gdpr-panic-may-spur-data-and-ai-innovation/, arguing that GDPR compliance efforts will lower barriers to AI implementation.
25. Found at https://www.edrm.net/frameworks-and-standards/edrm-model/
26. NIST is the National Institute of Standards and Technology (https://www.nist.gov/), part of the U.S. Department of Commerce. NIST publishes a listing of file types which are unlikely to contain any user generated data or be of evidentiary value, e.g. program executable or help files. DeNISTing refers to the practice of removing documents from a collection that match up to values in the NIST list.

Index

9 780367 257262